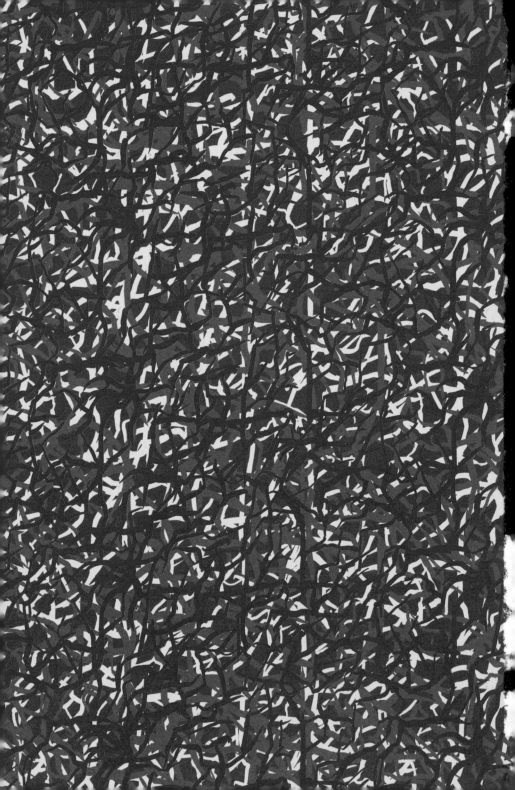

Where does **FEAR** come from?

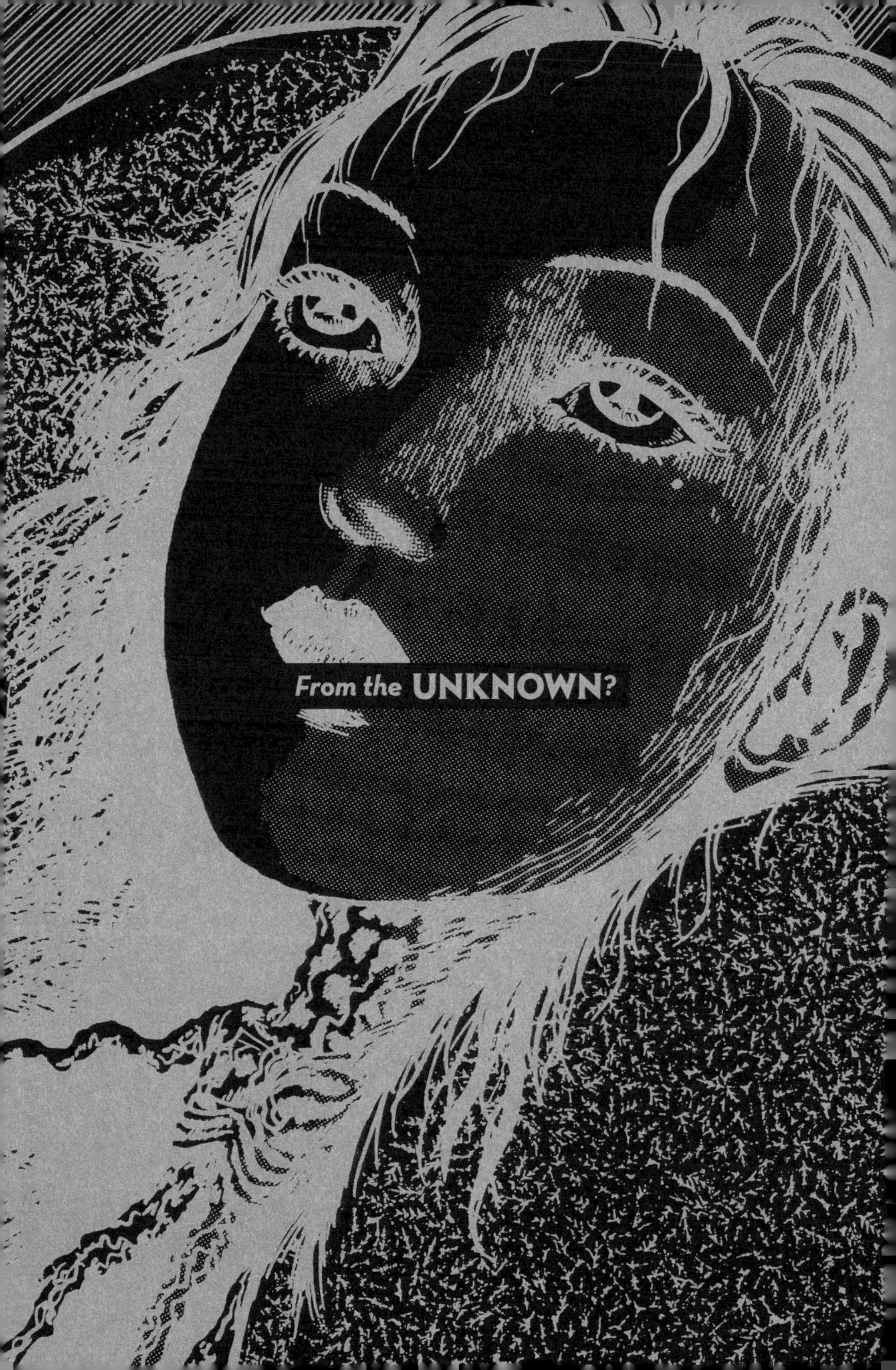
From the UNKNOWN?

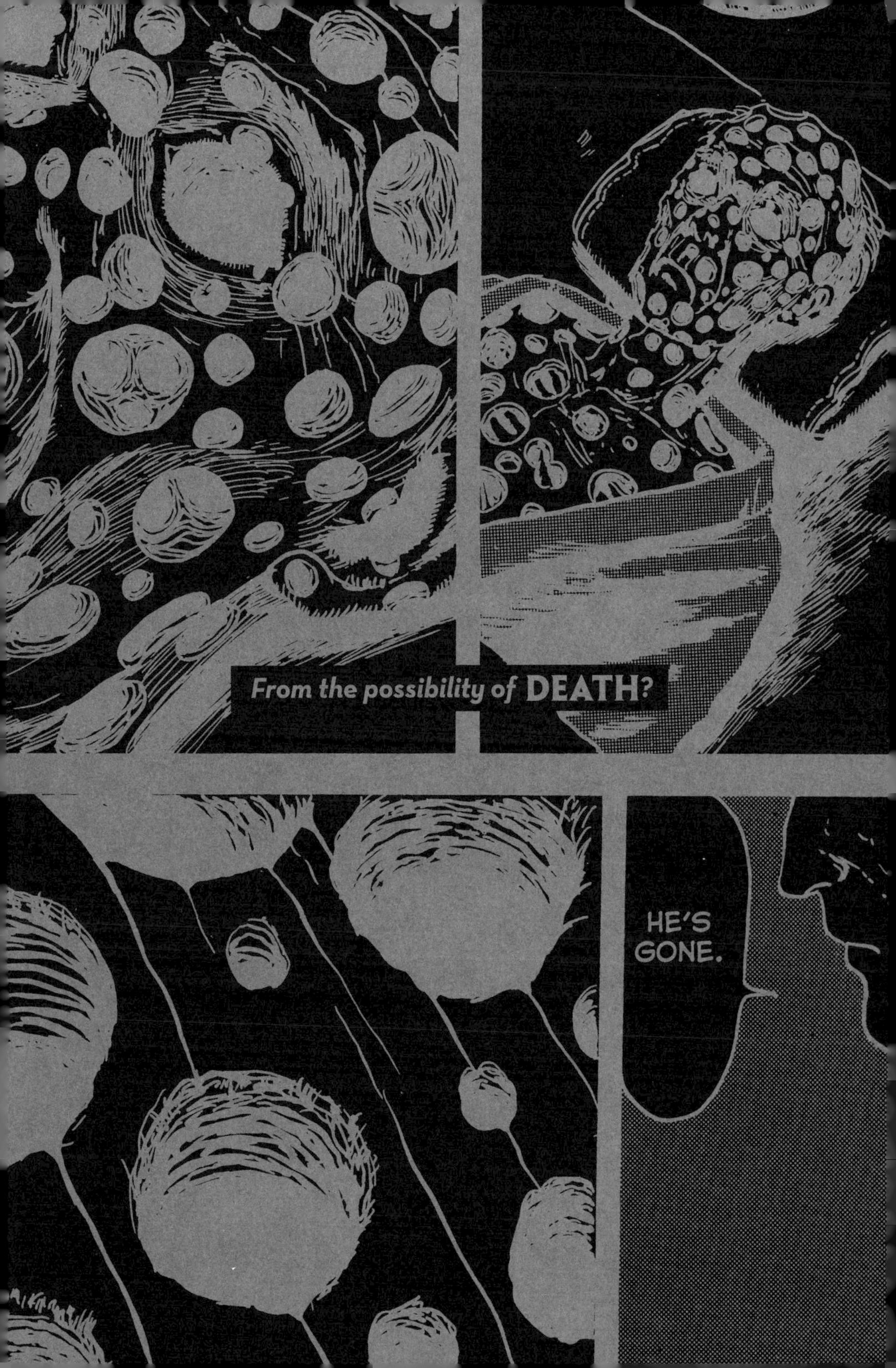
From the possibility of DEATH?
HE'S GONE.

Or from the existence of things that **DEFY IMAGINATION?**

Ghosts, black magic, unidentifiable, abnormal, atypical, drains, holes, grotesque, change, transformation, deformation, shadow, vision, mist...

...blood, corpse, void, dream, time, memory, anxiety, footsteps, isolation, solitude, ignorance, powerlessness, despair, limitation, crime and punishment, unease, maze, deadline, dead end...

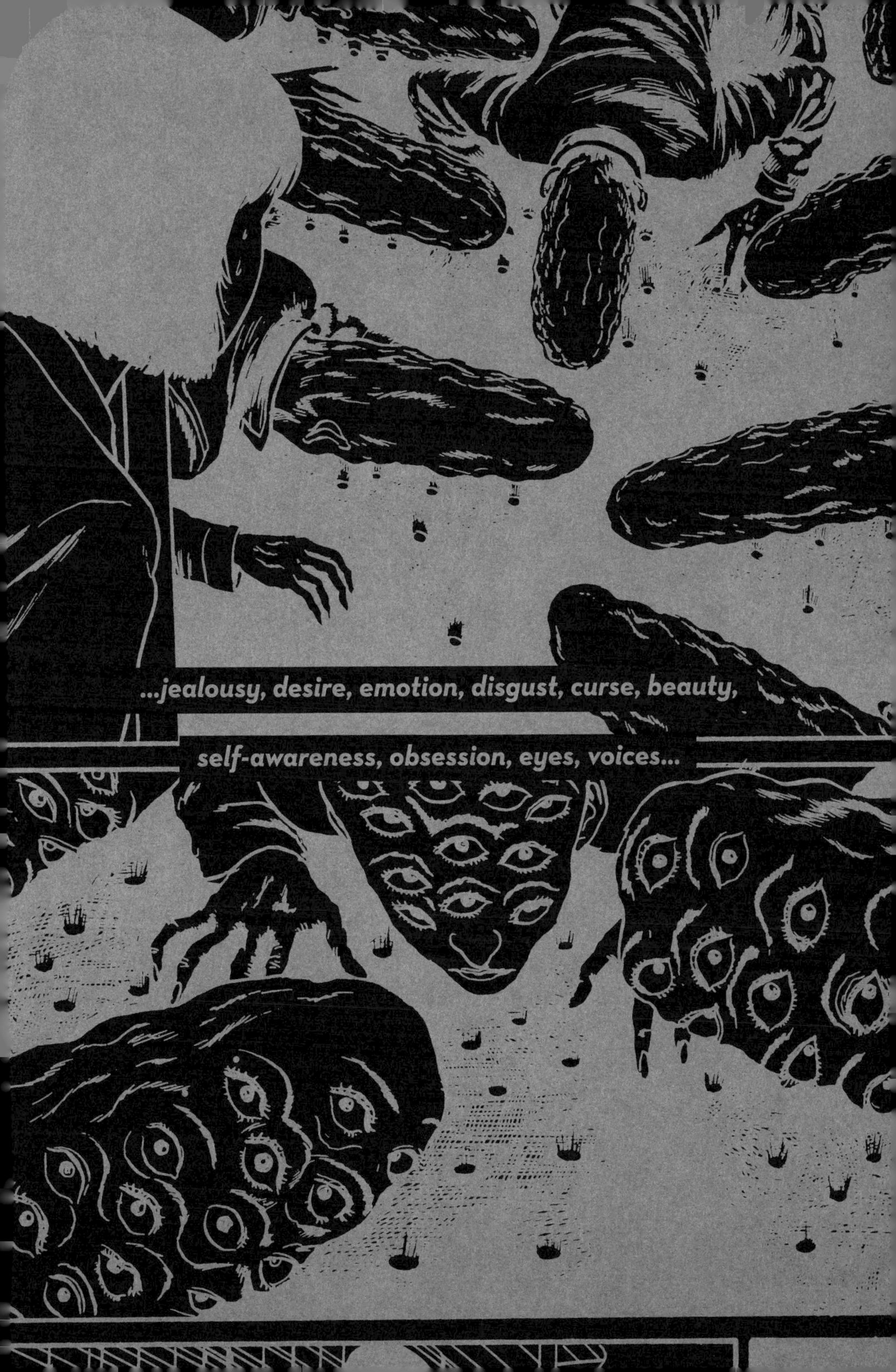
...jealousy, desire, emotion, disgust, curse, beauty,
self-awareness, obsession, eyes, voices...

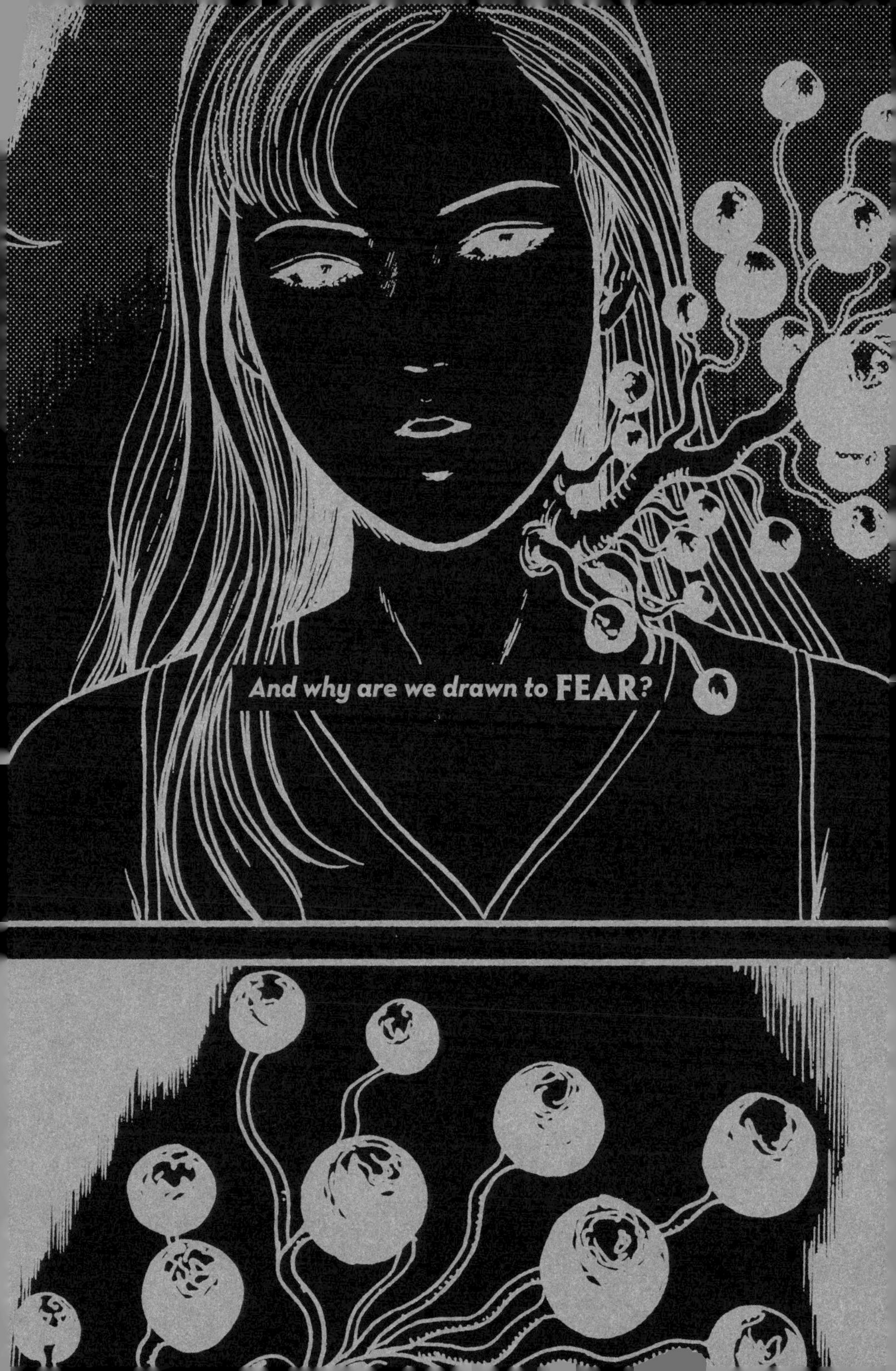
And why are we drawn to FEAR?

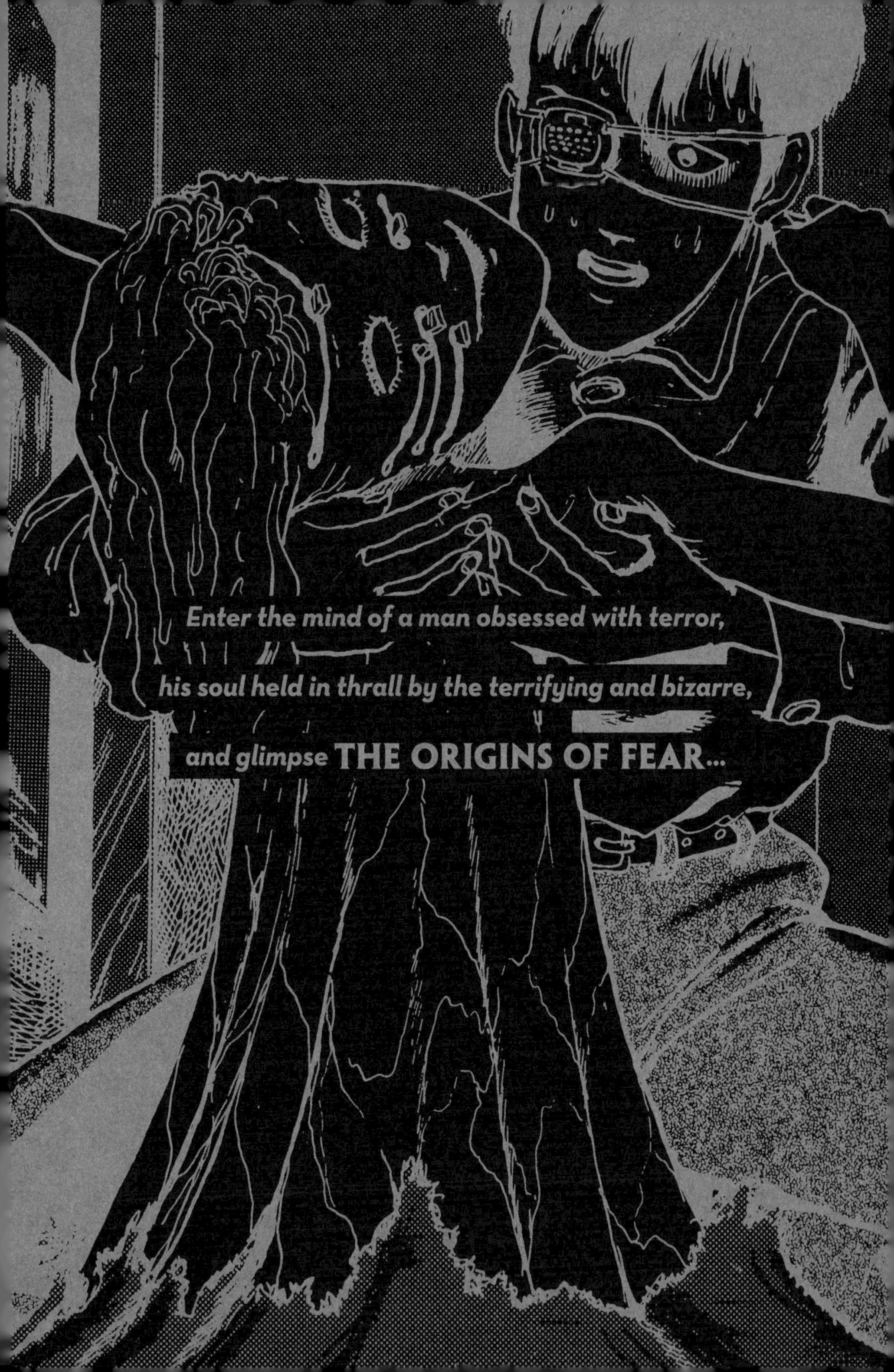
Enter the mind of a man obsessed with terror,
his soul held in thrall by the terrifying and bizarre,
and glimpse THE ORIGINS OF FEAR...

UNCANNY

CONTENTS

JUNJI ITO

UNCANNY

THE ORIGINS OF FEAR

CHAPTER

1

Who cares what other people think?

I have a somewhat peculiar job—
HORROR MANGA ARTIST.

How did I end up drawing frightening stories, bodies riddled with holes, people twisting down drains? There isn't really a simple explanation ...

My encounter with darkness

I CAME INTO THIS WORLD on a summer day in 1963. My hometown of Nakatsugawa in Gifu prefecture was then—and still is—a lush, green place. The area where I was born was actually a town called Sakashita in the Ena district, which later got incorporated into the city of Nakatsugawa in 2005.

Sakashita is at the bottom of a basin, surrounded by mountains on all sides, a little southwest of Nagiso, which thrived as a post station on the Nakasendo highway during the Edo period. At the time I was born, the silkworm industry was booming, and Sakashita was a lively little place. The Kiso-gawa River wasn't too far from where I lived, so we would go swimming there in the summer. The roads, pools, shrines, and tunnels where my friends and I played in this town all make appearances in my manga.

Surrounded by all this natural beauty, I grew up healthily, the way children do.

How did I end up drawing frightening stories, bodies riddled with holes, people twisting down drains? There isn't really a simple explanation. But by describing the world I grew up in I might be able to tell you how I became so fascinated with the bizarre and gained an interest in this thing called terror. This might seem to be the long way around, but the things we absorb from the world around us influence and affect our present selves, so I hope you won't mind joining me as I look back on my life thus far.

I was three or four years old when I first became aware of **the feeling of fear**. Going back in time through my memories, I hit upon the long, dark path leading to the bathroom in my childhood home.

We lived in a two-story wooden duplex. I'm told it was built seventy years before I arrived on the scene, so it was a relative antique. The duplex was two houses side by side when I was little, and one of these was my home. (The family next door later rebuilt, and the duplex was split up.)

At the time, there were seven of us in my family: my father, my mother, my two older sisters, me, and my two aunts (my father's younger and older sisters). After graduating from a vocational high school, my father got a job at Tokai Electrical, a company that did electrical construction work. But he had a desk job and never went out to work in the field.

My father drank, but he was shy by nature, and when he was sober, he was an extremely reserved man. On his days off, he would go fishing—his hobby—or chop wood in the backyard to heat the bath. So I have basically no memory of him playing with me. Except for one time when I was little, he drew a *kaiju*, "Guilala," for me. The drawing was quite well done, as I recall.

The fact was, he was very good at drawing. He'd actually wanted to go to an art school, but had to give up that dream because of family circumstances. He wasn't a talkative man—it was my aunts who told me this history. I didn't have too many conversations with my father himself, so I don't really know much more than this.

My mother, on the other hand, worked full-time at a factory in the area, making capacitors, an essential part in electrical appliances. She was always kind and not the sort of person to find fault with the things children did. Her personality may have been part of why I was able to immerse myself in the world of horror comics as a child.

My father's older sister was an elementary school teacher. The fingers on both of her hands were twisted up and frozen in place because of rheumatoid arthritis, and I have very clear memories of her having a lot of issues because of this. She tried all kinds of folk remedies to cure this affliction of hers.

She often bought and ate canned lamprey, which was said to be nutritious and increase stamina. I got her to let me try it once. It was indescribably bitter, and the texture was awful. It was definitely not good.

Radium hot springs are another supposedly effective treatment for rheumatoid arthritis, so we had a small plastic container of radium ore in our bathroom. Thinking about this now, I do wonder whether it was such a great idea to toss this ore into the water like bath salts, given that it does emit radiation, however minute that emission might be.

All of which is to say, my parents and my older aunt were out of the house during the day for work, meaning that it was my younger aunt alone who looked after baby me on weekdays. She managed to find fault with pretty much everything, so I often rebelled against her. You could say our family was a little unusual.

The duplex we lived in was also a bit peculiar. The town of Sakashita was one of hills, just as the Japanese characters of the name suggest—"hill" and "down." Our house was built on one of those hills, on land with a gentle slope. This gave rise to a gap between land and house, and the creation of a curious space inside that was half-underground.

At the time, we had a pit latrine type of squat toilet, and in order to get outside to the bathroom, you had to go through this underground passage. The basement never saw the light of day, so it was damp and humid, gloomy even at midday. It felt very much like something would jump out at you at any second. Obviously, this atmosphere was even creepier once night fell.

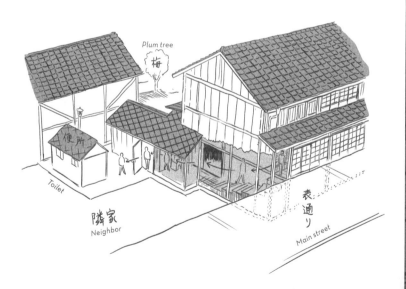

TO GO TO THE BATHROOM IN THIS HOUSE, YOU HAD TO GO THROUGH AN UNDERGROUND HALLWAY.

The floor in the basement was exposed dirt, and there were crickets bouncing around in the dark. One time, my pet hamster escaped, and we discovered him down there a week later, living free. He'd probably survived by eating the crickets.

When I think about it now, I can see how this strange underground hallway and the dubious storage room might very well have been the origin of what I feel to be terror.

There was no way a timid boy could have gone to the toilet by himself. Faced with the gaping darkness that opened up ahead of me, my young self could only race back to my room in terror and despair. That's a real pants-wetting memory!

And speaking of scary, there was also the "forbidden room" on the second floor of our house, which was full of old, dusty cabinets and folding screens. Of course, just stepping over the threshold into this room would not bring curses raining down upon your head—the room had simply been turned into a storage space where we shoved all the furniture and things we weren't currently using. We almost never went inside. So despite being in the middle of the house, this room was always eerily silent, and sneaking into it called up a strange sensation in me, a feeling that I was suddenly alone in the world, separated from the flow of time outside.

Watching *Akuma-kun* and weeping in fear

THE FIRST TIME I CAME ACROSS what could be called a work of horror was when I was **three years old**. The work? *Akuma-kun*, the TV show my sisters were watching at the time.

Based on the series by famed manga artist Shigeru Mizuki, *Akuma-kun* tells the story of Akuma, a child prodigy who comes along once every ten thousand years. Together with Dr. Faust and the demon Mephistopheles, Akuma works to destroy evil creatures and demons. The series was made into a popular anime at some point, and kids would run around chanting "Elohim, Essaim," the spell Akuma used to summon demons.

I watched the live-action TV version that was broadcast in 1966. Each episode featured all kinds of monsters—birds, mummies, wolf people, Ganma, which had eyes all over its body—and the craftsmanship of these creatures was at an impossibly high level for a TV show. (Naturally, this was not something I was aware of back then.) Because of these monsters, my curiosity would get the better of me every Thursday evening at seven, and even though I was so scared I could hardly stand it, I would sit there glued to the TV screen, crying the whole time.

I also often watched the live-action show *Kappa no Sanpei: Yokai Daisakusen*, based on another one of Shigeru Mizuki's manga. I remember one scene where a hand with eyeballs on it comes flying along—definitely my favorite.

Influenced by shows like this, I started wanting to draw monsters myself. So I cut up some drawing paper, sewed the pieces together with thread, and made my own little booklet, inside of which I drew illustrations to create something like a book of manga. The story was a bizarre one, something about a monster that had eyes on its hands, and the title was just that—"Hand Eyes." It was a clumsy work that I drew when I was five, but it was the very first manga I ever made.

From then on, I had fun plugging away at my manga and turning them into handmade books. Eventually, I had so many they filled a large plastic bag, but because my aunt kept yelling at me to get rid of them, I threw most of them out when I was in middle school. I'm sure to her, that plastic bag looked like a pile of garbage with scribbles all over it.

The god of horror manga appears

MY FIRST ENCOUNTER with the works of Kazuo Umezz, the artist I still revere as the **master of horror manga**, also came around the time I was four or five years old. It was through my sisters that I discovered him. *Weekly Shojo Friend* was serializing his horror stories at the time, and my sisters were fans of this girls' manga magazine.

Even today, shojo manga magazines have a certain number of pages dedicated to horror, thanks to the fact that stories by Umezz like *Nekome no Shojo* (Cat-Eyed Girl) and *Hebi Shojo* (Snake Girl) were big hits for *Shojo Friend*. The fact that I've been able to make a career for myself as a horror manga artist—an extremely niche occupation even in the manga world—is thanks to Kazuo Umezz clearing the way.

The Umezz manga I read back then was called *Miira-Sensei* (Mummy Teacher). The story starts with Sister Hayama, a Madonna-type teacher, patrolling a deserted school building at night. She goes down to the basement of the school chapel and offers up her daily prayers to the mummified nun enshrined there. The mummy suddenly comes back to life and takes Hayama's place.

Miira-Sensei *(Akita Shoten)*
The mystical hand of the mummy teacher sneaks closer to protagonist Emiko. The mummy came back to life thanks to the water that leaked through the ceiling and rehydrated her.

Posing as this virtuous teacher, the creature viciously terrorizes one student after another.

My four-year-old self trembled with fear at the power of Umezz's imagery and was instantly captivated. Such grotesque, disturbing drawings! And then the very next page would depict a beautiful, innocent girl. So scary, so cute, but scary, but cute—confronted with this forbidden combination, there was no way my hand could stop turning those pages.

I was a devoted fan right out of the gate, and I went on to read everything Kazuo Umezz drew as soon as I could get my hands on it. He's been a serious influence for me.

While my sisters did like horror manga, it wasn't as though they encouraged me to keep reading Umezz. The fact that I was drawn to his work all on my own no doubt means that I felt something special in it right from the start. And, considerate of my new fandom, my kind sisters gave me Umezz's *Noroi no Yakata* (The Cursed Mansion) for my sixth birthday. My sisters really are so good to their little brother.

Shivering at the words of Shinichi Koga

ANOTHER MANGA ARTIST who influenced me deeply was Shinichi Koga. I found Koga in 1966, at around the same time as Umezz. His *Shirohebi Yakata* (The White Snake Mansion) was

Mushi Shojo *(Shueisha)*
Protagonist Emi dies an untimely
death after she is locked up in the
fridge in a Western-style building.
After her death, Mari visits the
building and is transformed into
an ugly insect due to Emi's curse.

© Shinichi Koga (Akita Shoten) 1983

running in the shojo magazine *Margaret* at the time, and he was already right up there with Umezz in terms of popularity in the world of horror manga. Later, Koga would draw his classic *Eko Eko Azarak* for *Weekly Shonen Champion* and help usher in a black magic fad.

The first work of his that I read was *Mushi Shojo* (Insect Girl) published as a special booklet for the shojo manga magazine *Ribbon*. The story told of a young girl transformed into an ugly caterpillar, and Koga's drawings evoked an **eerie atmosphere** that was very appealing to me overall.

Koga's work shares elements with Umezz's, such as casting beautiful girls as the protagonists, but personally, I felt like he was much more focused on mood. He's truly a master of building the kind of atmosphere that makes the hairs on the back of your neck stand up, using techniques such as hatching and cross-hatching to effectively represent the darkness he wished to convey.

You can also see this focus in his storytelling. While Umezz crafts his stories in a way that makes sense, with a relatively clear beginning, middle, and end, Koga's come across as more like dream sequences than anything logical. His work is replete with a sense of mystery, almost like a surrealist painting, as though he's instinctively connecting to the world of the unconscious.

That said, it was only after I reached my teen years that my eyes started to notice this sort of composition and structure. At the time, I'm pretty sure my only impression of these stories was that **they made me shiver.**

Still, I'm a little surprised myself that I've been so consistently interested in horror manga since my earliest childhood. The only manga I owned besides horror was the single-volume gag manga from Fujiko F. Fujio, *Umeboshi Denka*.

Staring at the sky in elementary school

THE SCOPE OF MY INTERESTS gradually widened after I started elementary school. I was as single-minded as ever with horror when it came to manga, but a new love rose up to rival horror manga and capture my heart—flying saucers.

I became completely obsessed with Adamski-type UFOs. This was the type of flying saucer claimed to have been witnessed by the writer George Adamski, who lived and worked in the United States.

Starting in the 1950s and continuing into the early 1960s, people in the United States known as contactees came forward to speak of their experiences with aliens (or of riding in spaceships). Adamski was one of the earliest of these alleged contactees, the very person who triggered the global interest in UFO. After he released photos of the UFO he claimed to have seen, people all over the world began to report UFOs of the same shape. In Japan, TV shows would broadcast pictures and video of UFOs every so often, to enormous acclaim.

When I look at Adamski's photos now, I see the unmistakable shadow of a lampshade hanging over the silhouette of the machine. But as an innocent boy I would look up at the sky with high hopes—"Maybe I can see a UFO, too!"

I was thoroughly bored by the unchanging everyday routine of my boyhood. Naturally, I played tag and catch with my friends, and had as much fun as anyone else. But I was much more interested in the unknown, things like the Loch Ness Monster, the yeti, the *tsuchinoko* snake cryptid, and flying saucers. I was also bad at any sport involving a ball. I thought it would be vastly more interesting to chase after a UFO abducting people than a boring ball.

When I got home after school, I would sit on the veranda on the south side of the house and stare up at the sky until it got dark. Since I didn't know when a UFO would appear, I had to be vigilant. But no matter how I waited, no matter how dark the sky grew, no UFO ever appeared.

Even so, I was so desperate to see a UFO that I tried to create my own flying saucer detector, following the instructions at the end of a book called *World Flying Saucer Mysteries*. But I got frustrated with the part where you had to make a bar magnet by rubbing a needle against a magnet, and I never actually finished it.

Why wouldn't the aliens reveal their existence in Japan's Gifu prefecture when they were happy to casually show themselves in California in the United States?

Nowadays, I'm fairly skeptical about the idea that extraterrestrials would get into a flying saucer and come to Earth. But I do think it was perhaps a good thing that, when I was younger, I was able to seriously believe **so many mysteries remained in this world**.

Ultra Q and my incredible fixation on the abnormal

KAIJU ALSO HAD A FIRM HOLD on my heart, alongside flying saucers. The father of *Ultraman* and god of *tokusatsu* live-action shows, Eiji Tsuburaya launched his *Ultraman* series when I was exactly three years old. Younger readers might not know this, but the kaiju-fighting Ultraman doesn't make an appearance until the second entry of this series. Not only does the first TV show not feature Ultraman, the Science Special Search Party hadn't been formed on Earth yet. When the kaiju appeared out of nowhere to run rampant over their cities, the people were forced to stand against them on their own.

I loved the first entry in the series more than anything. *Ultra Q* is a tokusatsu science-fiction show in which Hoshikawa Airways pilot Jun Manjome, copilot Ippei Togawa, and reporter Yuriko Edogawa get caught up in some mysterious phenomenon or monster attack every episode. The reruns were essential viewing for my elementary school self.

It's actually difficult to explain the appeal of this show. The basic idea is that a different kaiju appears on the scene and causes trouble in every episode, but the show incorporated a complex mix of the occult, spiritual phenomena, science fiction, and mystery to lay the groundwork for this kaiju of the week, which made the whole enterprise seem quite chaotic. Allow me to quote a little here from the blurbs for *Technicolor Ultra Q* episodes on Tsuburaya Productions' online streaming site:

"A series of mysterious earthquakes culminates in the roots of an enormous plant reaching through the ground to attack anyone and everyone. Eventually, the massive Mammoth Flower erupts out of a building, its buds bloom, and its pollen fills the air. Trapped inside that very building, Ippei and the others are in real trouble!" (Episode 4: "Mammoth Flower")

"Young Taro ignores his lessons in favor of caring for his turtle. He's obsessed. He's sure that this turtle will take him to the legendary palace of the dragon king at the bottom of the sea once it's all grown up. But then a gang of robbers escapes with Taro's turtle after a burglary near his school!" (Episode 6: "Grow Up, Little Turtle!")

"On a passenger ship one night, Yuriko hears a doll on the floor say, 'I'm from the planet Ruparts. A kaiju has invaded the earth.' A few days later, Manjome and Ippei vanish on a flight, and only the Cessna plane returns to the airport." (Episode 21: "Space Directive M774")

Do you understand what I mean now? I think what really comes across in these blurbs is the fiery passion of the creators and their desire to make something really incredible. Back then, kaiju stories were normally big theatrical releases, such as the *Godzilla* series, and a TV series was truly unprecedented, much less one that had a budget on par with the movies. The creators' excesses and eccentric, uncompromising style gave these absurd stories a powerful persuasiveness, and no doubt succeeded in stirring the admiration of not just myself, but all the children of Japan, making us cry as one, **"I don't really get it, but wow!"**

The production on *Ultra Q* was also superb. For instance, the famous main title screen has the words "Ultra Q" twisting up from a marble-patterned vortex, an effect that was quite novel at the time. Another good example is how the introductory part of every episode would showcase an accident or incident caused by some mysterious, unexplained phenomenon, like a person buried in falling rocks or a plane crashing. As the viewer, you watch on tenterhooks, and then just as you unconsciously lean forward to warn of the lurking danger, the "dan dan dan dan dan dan dan dan daaaa" guitar of the theme song cuts in with the most exquisite timing. And then Koji Ishizaka begins his somber narration: "For the next thirty minutes, your eyes will leave your body and enter into this mysterious time..." I couldn't pull myself away from the TV.

With every episode hitting hard like this, *Ultra Q* garnered serious praise and became a massive success, capturing over 30 percent of the overall TV viewership every episode. And thanks to this show, we got *Ultraman*, *Kamen Rider*, and *Gorenger*, so it's no exaggeration to say that the tokusatsu TV show had taken root in Japan.

But not long after this, the age of color TV came along, and reruns of the black-and-white show *Ultra Q* essentially disappeared. I was very sad about this.

Horror, but striving for reality

I KEPT ON DRAWING MANGA in elementary school, except that now I was drawing even more than before. Some were science-fictiony things, but the majority were horror. Many of these stories were obviously influenced by Umezz and Koga, with titles like "Hakaba no Yurei Onna" (Ghost Woman in the Graveyard), "Doron Kaiju Doron," "Yurei to Sakkaku" (Ghost and Illusion), and "Hebime Onna"(Snake-Eyed Woman). Counting the gag manga and short pieces that I did, I'd say I probably drew around seventy manga during my six years of elementary school.

When it came to the art, however, I never once tried to copy Umezz or Koga. In the reader spotlight section of the manga magazines, I'd often see drawings that were such close copies of the original manga characters that I could almost believe they'd been done by the actual manga artist, but while I admired these as being quite well-done, I didn't think to enjoy manga in this way. If I had to say, I think I was striving for reality—I had a powerful desire to express in manga the things I'd seen on TV and in movies. (That said, however, when I look back at those manga now, there's nothing realistic about them, and the characters are

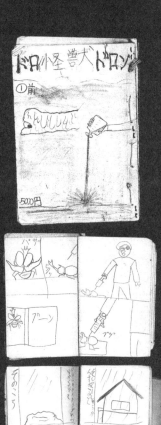

A manga I drew in third grade because I wanted to draw a kaiju story. The story, "Doron Kaiju Doron" was about a man who invents a drug that can bring anything back to life. He creates the kaiju Doron when he pours this drug on some mud. A key point was that mud comes out of the end of Doron's tail.

nothing special. They're just plain manga.)

I've been a pretty detail-oriented person ever since I was a child, and I wanted not just my art and stories to be as close as possible to those of real manga, but also the physical item itself. So I would cut up B4-size newsprint or drawing paper and bundle these pages together into handmade manga volumes, and then break the pages up into panels and draw my manga. Each volume probably had twenty or so pages in it.

This is where I'd like to sing my own praises and say I was pretty much the genuine article, but at the time I unfortunately didn't know that manga was drawn with pen and ink. I drew all of mine with the same pencil, so by the time I finished drawing the last page, the first page was black with smudges.

To be honest, I only let a few people back then know I was drawing these bizarre manga. For me, the act of drawing manga itself was the fun part, and I wasn't particularly interested in having anyone else read them. About the only people I showed my stories to were U-kun, who used to draw manga with me all the time; a couple of my good friends, and my family.

I was also embarrassed at the thought of showing people the manga I'd dreamed up. It felt like I'd be like letting them have a peek inside of my head. Plus, my drawings were bad, and my story development was all over the place, so no one ever really complimented my work. (Although I do feel like my mother alone read them with real interest.)

Now that I'm thinking about it, I did draw a gag manga once. I forget now how it started, but I came up with a character with a face like the traditional silly Hyottoko mask. I named it "Oobaka" (stupid idiot) with sunken cheeks, which was extremely well received by U-kun. when I scribbled it down in my notebook. Seeing my friend choking with laughter for a solid minute, I was certain that this was a smash hit of an idea. I immediately got to work on a manga series with this idiot as the protagonist.

One chapter in this series was "Fantastic Toilet," a parody of the American science fiction film *Fantastic Voyage*, which was popular at the time. In the movie, a medical team is shrunk down to miniature size using the latest technology, and they then enter a human body to try and save the patient's life. My "Toilet" ends with the stupid idiot eventually making his way out the other end of that body only to be crushed by a massive poop.

All young kids love poop, and I was no exception.

Daydreams produce a robot and a bird

WAY BACK WHEN, I had a tendency to tweak objects and make little improvements, or to simply make the thing out of whole cloth myself. This is a tendency that continues to this day. For instance, I've customized my work tools for my own use, adding my own personal touch to everything from G pens and keyboards to LCD tablets. As another example of my inventive nature, we once had a cat that would sit under the toilet paper and bite it into a mess, so I took the metal sheet that was on my drawing board, bent it to make a shield, and set it up under the toilet paper. (I dubbed this invention "no-bite toilet armor," but that same cat later discovered a critical vulnerability and spectacularly destroyed the shield.)

Nowadays, we put this kind of "DIY" ethos to practical use in our everyday lives, but when I was a kid, the only thought in my head was how to make my wild ideas a reality. Another hobby of mine was model building, and one day, I decided that I wanted a big robot, not merely a small model. Naturally, however, this robot only existed in the world of my daydreams. But having set my mind on acquiring such a machine, I collected a bunch of largish boxes and made an old style of wearable robot suit with a square face and body. I put the suit on and marched around the neighborhood, clanking smugly. A little kid stared at me and asked, "Who's that?" But I was quite satisfied with myself.

Another day, I decided I wanted to fly, so I built myself some wings. I often had dreams about flying freely through the sky when I was little, and many a morning I woke up disappointed to realize it had only been a dream. As with my robot project, I collected boxes to make my wings, and then I climbed up on top of our *kotatsu* table and flapped those wings over and over, practicing flying. My mother watched me with warm eyes, and even called my sisters in. "Look there. Our Jun's about to fly. Watch."

Memories of roller skating

I WAS OBSESSED with horror manga, UFOs, and kaiju, but it wasn't as though I was entirely uninterested in the real world. This was the era when I, too, would put on roller skates and race around outside with good friends.

When I was in third grade, the roller derby was a quiet hit with kids in Japan. The basic idea of the game is that players in roller skates speed around a track and compete for points. After gaining popularity in the United States in the 1960s, the TV show *Japan vs. USA Roller Derby*, which pitted a Japanese team against an American team, started broadcasting in Japan in 1972, and the sport took hold across the country.

The fun of roller derby isn't simply the speed of the competition, but also the pro-wrestling style elements the game incorporates. Two teams race around the track at the same time, and the number of points awarded is decided by how many players on the opposing team a skater passes. It resembles the short track in speed skating, except that it's full of incredibly brutal play.

Every episode of *Japan vs. USA Roller Derby* had more than its fair share of thrillingly bloodthirsty fights, with players yanking on opponents' clothes, body checking them, sliding into them, hip checking, and so on. Skaters would even lasso the neck of an opposing team's player who was surging ahead. No wonder the tagline for this show was simply, "Punch! Kick! Crush! The hottest of roller-skating games."

The Japanese team on *Japan vs. USA Roller Derby* was the Tokyo Bombers, and they quickly reached rock-star levels of popularity. We kids in Gifu would also watch them light up our TV screens and sigh excitedly about how cool they were.

I immediately pestered my parents to buy me some roller skates, and then tried to reenact the roller derby with my friends. But here, a serious problem presented itself: there was no appropriately smooth surface for roller skating anywhere to be found.

The true thrill of roller derby was rolling out the various moves while sailing around the track at top speed. But concrete and dirt tracks created too much friction, so we slowed to a stop almost instantly. It was hard to reproduce roller derby in those conditions.

"So what'll we do…" Just when we were struggling to find a way forward, some other, more experienced roller-skating friends sent a hot tip our way. There was a cemetery on a small hill on the north side of town, and that cemetery had a structure with a roof where the bodies were placed and the funerals carried out. And apparently, the floor of this structure was *very* smooth.

When we got there, we were overjoyed to find the floor of the large gazebo-type building was covered in a fine-grain concrete, a surface so smooth it practically begged you to strap on your roller skates. And so, this felicitous discovery allowed us to play roller derby to our hearts' content and grow closer as friends, the graves of the cemetery always visible out of the corners of our eyes.

The hunt for smooth ground led us to the cemetery. We shot around at incredible speed without helmets, performing all kinds of dangerous tricks. We really are lucky we didn't end up being burned in the crematorium ourselves.

Now, my heart is full of grateful apology to the adults at the time who overlooked this blasphemous behavior on our parts. We wronged all the spirits sleeping in their graves. When I think about it, though, the fact that even an innocent game of my childhood ended up being quite horroresque seems like a twist of fate.

As a sequel to this little tale, we found out not too long afterward that there was a concrete track for roller skating on the lot of a factory just outside of town. So we started to feel somewhat guilty and stopped roller skating in the cemetary.

The perfect lie

YOU COULD PERHAPS SAY that the years of my boyhood—the 1960s through to the mid 1970s—were a revolutionary period in the history of Japanese subculture. I'll note here just a few of the works released after I was born in 1963:

1963: Start of Japan's first animated TV series, *Astroboy*
1966: Start of the *Ultraman* series
1968: Launch of *Shonen Jump*
1969: Start of the TV anime series *Sazae-san*, start of the manga *Doraemon*
1971: Start of the *Kamen Rider* series, the TV anime *Tensai Bakabon*, and *Lupin the Third*

1974: Start of the TV anime series *Space Battleship Yamato*
1975: Start of the *Super Sentai* series, release of Japan's
first video game console TV Tennis

Looking at it like this, we can see that works with a fairly large influence on current anime, manga, and video games were dispatched into the world one after another through the sixties into the mid-seventies. This period also overlapped with the rapid economic growth that followed World War II. The average household was richer, resulting in both more leisure time and disposable income. This was also an era when serious interest turned toward culture, art, and entertainment. I suppose you could say that I was very fortunate to have been born in the middle of all this, which allowed me to spend my boyhood years surrounded by a thriving artistic culture.

The movies of Ray Harryhausen were one of the cultural elements that made a deep impression on me as an elementary school student. Harryhausen was a special effects creator in Hollywood from the 1950s to the 1970s, and it is a mistake to dismiss him as simply someone working behind the scenes. After studying under Willis Harold O'Brien, who was responsible for the special effects in the 1933 film *King Kong*, he became a member of the US Army's Special Services and learned the fundamentals of film technology. Once the war was over, he created any number of masterpieces as a stop-motion artist, earning a reputation as a special-effects wizard.

His film debut, *The Beast from 20,000 Fathoms*—with its story of a dinosaur coming back to life in the modern age due to nuclear bomb testing, and its special effects technology—had a significant impact on the birth of the Japanese tokusatsu special effects film *Godzilla*. Of all the films Harryhausen worked on, a particular favorite is *Jason and the Argonauts*.

Taking up a Greek myth as its subject, the film tells the story of Prince Jason as he boards the *Argo* and travels in search of a golden fleece that brings good fortune. Mythological gods and monsters such as Hera, Talos, Hekate, and Hydra make appearances over the course of his adventure. All these creatures were made to move with dolls called "models," and their modeling and movement are wonderfully captivating.

As I noted earlier, my kaiju-loving self would often watch tokusatsu monster movies and TV shows. But as I grew up, moving from elementary school to junior high, I started to be curious about the details of the images on-screen. For instance, I learned to tell if the kaiju was a person in a costume from elements such as the position of the hips and joints, and the way the creature walked. In scenes where buildings exploded or were destroyed, I would notice that the fire was too big for the size of the building or that the splash area was too large when the rocks fell into the ocean when the film was using a 1:50 scale miniature.

From an adult perspective, you might think I was a graceless child. But when it came to these artistic creations, I was unfailingly **realistic**. While I did believe in ghosts, cryptids, and flying saucers, it wasn't the case that I accepted them blindly. I was perhaps starved for an encounter with something I could lose myself to, something so real I could turn it inside out and still be able to believe that it was the genuine article.

On that point, Harryhausen was, in a word, magnificent. He used a technique called "Dynamation," which fused the actual background with monster models, instead of using miniatures, so the spectacle on-screen looked very natural. The monsters themselves were not people in costumes, but models that were moved and filmed one frame at a time, an adaptation of the trick of flip books. Rather than accepting the limitations of the structure and joints of the human body, Harryhausen successfully used this technique to produce a more realistic and nuanced range of movement for the monsters. (There was some awkwardness in the movement because of the frame-by-frame filming, but this too was fun, and added a bit of flavor.)

The climax of *Jason and the Argonauts* features a scene in which seven skeleton warriors engage in a sword fight with the hero. The sheer complexity of it meant that the crew spent four and a half months on this scene alone, unable to film more than thirteen frames a day (about half a second).

Harryhausen taught me that **if you sincerely wish from the bottom of your heart to deceive people, then you must doggedly pursue reality.**

What is cruelty?

ONE DAY WHEN I WAS IN SIXTH GRADE, I happened to stop by the only bookstore in the area, near Sakashita station, and found an unfamiliar horror manga sitting on the shelves. The title was *Dokumushi Kozo* (The Bug Boy). I was immediately drawn to the unique art style, which was unlike anything I'd ever seen before, so I snapped it up and hurried home to read it. I was astonished. **On top of being scary, the manga was mesmerizing!**

This was my first encounter with the work of Hideshi Hino.

After making his debut in 1967, Hino had a number of stories published in the legendary manga magazine *Garo*. Although this great talent had initially set out to become a gag manga artist, he received a shock reading the work of American science fiction author Ray Bradbury, and shifted his focus to horror manga.

Dokumushi Kozo was a long-form horror manga released in 1975 by Hibari Shobo. Hino took *The Metamorphosis* as his motif, the masterwork from Jewish author Franz Kafka, and his depiction of an average boy who is transformed into an ugly, poisonous bug and persecuted by others until he ends up alone is full of cruelty and pathos.

I started to pay attention to the name Hideshi Hino then, and enthusiastically followed his work. In a stroke of good fortune, he was set to publish a series of short stories in the new shonen manga magazine launched that year by Futabasha, *Weekly Shonen Action*. Every time the magazine went on sale, I would head over

Dokumushi Kozo (*Hibari Shobo*)
After Sanpei is bitten by a red caterpillar creature, his entire body begins to
break down until he eventually ends
up in the shape of a caterpillar himself.
His fearful family tries to poison him,
leading to a final great tragedy.

© Hideshi Hino

to my usual bookstore and immerse myself in the world of Hino.

His manga offered up a unique landscape of terror, with cruel portrayals like nothing I'd ever seen before—the pale skin of women, crazed facial expressions, and plots so nightmarish that the further you read, the more you wanted to run away. Hino's illustrations were truly frightening. "Scary pictures" and "pictures of a scary thing" might seem like the same thing, but they definitely are not. The cruel depictions in Hino's work contained **an energy and creepiness that stimulated the physiology and instincts in the darkest recesses of the human mind.**

In his short story "Manatsu/Genso" (Midsummer/Hallucination), there's a moment when a skull wearing a straw hat whirls around to look at the reader. That scene burned itself into my brain, and I was overcome with the desire to turn it into an anime, to the point where I made a flip-book of it when I was in grade eight or nine. (This ended in the blink of an eye, though.)

It's no exaggeration to say that my encounter with Hino heralded a new era in horror manga for me. I was particularly influenced by his cruel storytelling and depictions.

Mazo no Mura, a long-form manga three years in the making

MARCH 1976, the year *KochiKame: Tokyo Beat Cops* started serialization in *Weekly Shonen Jump*, brought with it my auspicious

Mazo no Mura

The cover shows the protagonist backed into a corner by zombies and leaping from the top of a tower, prepared to face his death. I call them "zombies" for convenience's sake now, but the word "zombie" didn't come into general usage until after the George A. Romero film *Dawn of the Dead* was released in 1979 in Japan under the title *Zombie*. I finished drawing this manga three years before that, but the monsters in it more or less resemble zombies, so that's what I call them.

Photos: Takuya Matsunaga

graduation from elementary school. And now that I was in middle school, a fiery new passion began to burn inside of me.

The object of this passion was table tennis.

I don't know how things are now, but back then, all students at the middle school I attended had to join a sports team. I doubted I'd be able to remember the rules for baseball, or any of the other more complicated sports, so by process of elimination I chose table tennis, which seemed to have the least forgettable rules. But on my first day on the team, I realized that I was bad at ball sports.

Why, of all things, had I chosen table tennis, which is 90 percent kinetic vision and instantaneous force? I should have done archery, which is quiet and moves slowly. The target wouldn't run away, either. Grumbling all the while, I wrestled with table tennis quite seriously in my own terrible way. (Table tennis has an idyllic image, but the team was surprisingly proactive, and morning practice was a constant addition to the usual weekday afternoon sessions.)

Because of this commitment, I didn't have as much free time as when I was in elementary school, but I still pushed forward with my personal creative activities on the weekends. When I was in my first year at middle school, I completed the long-form manga I'd been so diligently crafting, *Mazo no Mura* (The Village of Mazo).

Mazo no Mura tells the story of a sudden and large outbreak of zombies which attack the villagers of Mazo. A scientist on the island investigates the phenomenon and identifies an unknown bacterium as the cause of the zombification. I got the idea for the story from the horror anime *Humanoid Monster Bem*, which aired on TV when I was around five or six. The third episode was called "Town of the Dead."

When protagonist Bem and his friends visit the town, it's deserted—there's not a soul in sight. They learn that a mysterious humanoid monster threatened to slaughter the residents unless they offered a child sacrifice on the thirteenth of every month. Because of this, mothers locked their families in their houses and hid to keep the remaining children from being abducted.

Bem and his friends transform into children to pinpoint the identity of this monster. They wait hidden in a coffin at the old well where the sacrifices are left, but it is the fathers of the abducted children who come to claim them, not any monster.

The truth is that on the evening of the thirteenth of every month, the bodies of the mothers are taken over by vengeful spirits and they attack their children, a curse laid upon them by a woman the townspeople watched die. So the fathers pretend to be the humanoid monster to whisk the children away and hide them in a safehouse near the old well.

This story scared me, at any rate. The mother, charged with keeping her children safe, loses her sense of self and instead tries to kill them. I was deeply impressed by the scenes where the mothers' faces changed as the evil spirit took them over and they began to sharpen their knives with wide, red eyes. It made me want to try and draw a similarly frightening story.

But I do somewhat regret that I decided to make the zombie outbreak the work of an unknown pathogen. I feel as though I was too constrained by logic while I was drawing it. My sisters read the finished product, and they said that it would have been more interesting if it had been a supernatural curse.

This is a habit of mine. When working out the details of a story, I lean toward the scientific. My goal is to give it an air of reality, but this is a difficult balance, since the story then tends to be summed up too easily.

I started drawing *Mazo no Mura* in fifth grade, so it took about three years to finish. I had absolutely no thought of entering it in some contest—I was simply charging forward with the **single-minded desire to draw manga**. I was still drawing in pencil, and I used a mix of newsprint and drawing paper. But the fact that I'd managed to finish a story that spanned 160 pages and put it together in a book (bound by my own self) became a serious source of confidence for me.

At the same time, I had the thought that I'd done everything I could with manga. I'd burned out. I had loved manga so much, and I basically drew none for the three years that followed.

Science fiction writer Junji Ito?

DURING THE TIME that I wasn't drawing manga, I also wasn't simply playing at table tennis and working up a sweat. I had become obsessed with flash fiction.

"Flash fiction" is the term for an extremely short story filling about five to ten pages of traditional Japanese writing paper, with 400 characters per page. A classmate of mine told me about the book *SF Flash Fiction Masterpieces* that Akimoto Shobo had just released, which was the first time I came across this kind of work.

I was gobsmacked. These weren't merely short stories!

What's so revolutionary about flash fiction? American literary critic Robert Oberfirst listed the following three requirements:

+ **Novel idea**
+ **Complete plot**
+ **Unexpected conclusion**

These elements are put together with great precision, logically and without any excess in a text only a few thousand characters long.

This genre was so interesting and fresh to me that I was instantly obsessed. My hands shook with excitement when I learned about the particular technique of the unexpected twist in the conclusion. From then on, I devoted myself wholeheartedly to writing flash fiction.

Soon after I started to read this brief style of story, Kodansha launched the Shinichi Hoshi Flash Fiction Contest. There was no way that I wouldn't take on the challenge: I wanted a fiction award engraved with the name of this great science fiction author!

I burned with passion. I set pen to page—in the breaks from table tennis—to craft a story that would win the grand prize.

Looking back on it now, this was perhaps the first time I was putting my own work out in the world and seeking approval for it.

The story I entered into the contest was called "Silver Rain." A rocket on its way into space to jettison organic mercury from Earth explodes in the stratosphere, and the mercury is dispersed uniformly throughout the sky. The end result is that the sky reflects the surface of the Earth like a giant mirror. The moment I finished writing it, I thought, "Aah, that prize is mine."

But unfortunately my name was not in the newspaper article announcing the winners six months later.

I continued to compulsively write flash fiction, however. I think I probably wrote about two notebooks' full. I actually entered the Shinichi Hoshi Flash Fiction Contest three more times after that but, regrettably, all those entries also came to nothing. Thus, I quickly abandoned the road to science fiction author Junji Ito.

A fascination with the absurd gained from science fiction

MY OWN STORIES didn't really go anywhere, but nevertheless, the works I was reading at the time were, without a doubt, important fodder for my later creative efforts.

While in middle school, I often read the work of Taku Mayumura, Ryu Mitsuse, Masami Fukushima, and Chikashi Uchida. These four authors were collected in the *SF Flash Fiction Masterpieces* I mentioned earlier, and I followed them from there, reading the books they put out as part of the Akimoto Bunko SF series. Trying to push further afield, I started reading Shinichi Hoshi, and eventually, I landed on the work of Yasutaka Tsutsui.

It would be no exaggeration to say that my high school days were all about Yasutaka Tsutsui. I was utterly absorbed in the great mysteries of the world of Tsutsui. *48 Oku no Moso* (4.8 Billion Delusions), *Zokubutsu Zukan* (Picture Book of Vulgarity), *Oi Naru Joso* (The Great Approachway)—if I started to list his masterworks, there would be no end to it.

Perhaps unexpectedly, I first realized how amazing Yasutaka Tsutsui was when I read the flash fiction story "Pachinko Hissho Genri" (Fundamentals of a Certain Pachinko Win). It's about a Nobel Prize–winning physicist who waltzes into a pachinko parlor, aiming to win big using his physics calculations. The way he loses his nerve in the last scene was memorable to me.

In flash fiction and science fiction stories, I came across so many creative and extraordinary ideas—more than I saw in conventional literature. People often note that my horror manga stories are bizarre, and maybe this curious worldview was unconsciously produced by the countless sci-fi works I devoured.

Hospital of horrors

WHEN I WAS IN THIRD YEAR at middle school, I was hospitalized with appendicitis.

It started in the morning. I had this dull ache in the center of my stomach, around my solar plexus. I took an optimistic view at first. I assumed I had simply thrown off my blankets and my stomach had become chilled during the night. But the pain kept increasing with the passage of time.

When I complained to my mother of feeling poorly, she took it seriously, and I ended up taking the day off from school to go to the doctor. When I told him about my symptoms, he promptly diagnosed me with diarrhea. My mother blithely accepted this—"that's what the doctor said, so it's nothing serious"—so we got some medicine and went home.

However.

I took the medicine, but the pain did not go anywhere. In fact, by evening, I could hardly stand up, and a cold sweat was pouring down my face.

I raced to the bathroom, panting heavily, and did my business. And then I peeked into the toilet bowl and shuddered in fear. The bowl was bright red with fresh blood.

"T-there's blood in my pee!"

If this was a horror manga, this is where I would have screamed in a panicked close-up with bloodshot eyes, but I simply reported it to my mother with a straight face (I didn't have the energy for

For the surgery, they put in a catheter and extracted the pus from my body. A few days later, however, they had to remove the drain. For some reason, the removal was performed without anesthetic, and I nearly screamed in pain and terror.

anything more). We immediately raced back to the hospital we'd been to that day.

By the time we arrived, I was in so much pain, I couldn't stand up. I doubled over, fell, and tried to get to my feet again. A re-examination showed that my appendix had apparently gotten worse. Pus had built up in, causing peritonitis. But unfortunately, there was no doctor who could perform surgery at this hospital. Thus I was taken to another hospital by ambulance.

I had surgery at last the following day. Because it was done under local anesthesia, I was able to watch the whole operation. The pus—which was sucked out of my guts with a vacuum—filled several large bottles before my eyes. Watching this out of the corner of my eye, I felt keenly aware of **the mysteries of the human body**.

After the surgery, a nurse came to me lying in bed and showed me the appendix they'd cut out of my abdomen. It looked like cod roe. "Your peritonitis was fairly advanced, and we could also see some adhesion. Back in the day, before medicine was so advanced, you would've died!" she told me and left.

I ended up staying in the hospital for the next month or so to avoid bacterial infection. While I was in the hospital, some-one who came to visit my miserable self (it might have been my kind sisters) brought me volume eight of Kazuo Umezz's master-piece gag manga *Makoto-chan* to cheer me up. Delighted, I started to read it, but every time I laughed, the wound in my stomach stabbed at me painfully. But with Makoto-chan mercilessly firing off one joke after another, I was unable to put the manga down. It made me belly laugh right up until the end, and my incision screamed with pain the whole time.

In this way, my precious last summer vacation at middle school came to its end.

My anime shown at the school festival

AFTER I WAS RELEASED from the hospital of horrors, I ignored the studying I should have been doing for high school entrance exams in favor of immersing myself in the production of an anime to submit to the school festival in the fall.

It all started with an article in the culture section of the newspaper about how to make an "endless anime box." Put simply, an endless anime is like a flip-book on a loop. Get thirty to fifty pieces of paper, three by four centimeters, and draw on them the same sort of thing as you would in a flip-book. It differs from a flip-book in that you draw the character's movement and position at the end so that it connects with the first picture. Once you're done, fasten the pieces of paper together around a tube. Finally, set this tube in a box for rotation, and when you turn the handle, the flip-book can be viewed endlessly, like an animation.

When I learned about this art, I was struck by the desire to make a real animation, unlike the flip-books I drew for fun on the edges of my notebooks, and I actually made several original endless anime. Two men fighting over a roll of banknotes, a car driving on the highway as viewed through a dash cam, a boy washing his face, Black Jack taking from his pocket not a scalpel but a lollipop, Makoto-chan in her "gwash" pose—I made all of these all by myself.

On the day of the school festival, I had a classroom to myself to exhibit six works, and I think they were mostly well received.

Man of interest

HAVING GRADUATED FROM MIDDLE SCHOOL without incident, I moved on to Gifu Prefectural High School in the city of Nakatsugawa, several stations away from Sakashita. My passion for Tsutsui continued even after I started high school. At the same time, my discovery of Katsuhiro Otomo—more on that later— brought me back to drawing manga. Amidst all of this, there was a boy in my class who roused my interest. This was H-kun.

H-kun and I were in the same class from the first year of high school on. In the beginning, he seemed unapproachable, and to be honest, I didn't have a very good impression of him. Most likely, he probably also thought that I was a loathsome creature.

I found out H-kun liked manga and was good at caricatures. By some chance, I saw his drawings, and they clearly surpassed the level of an amateur. But I didn't tell him myself that I drew manga, and I wasn't interested in getting to know him any further than this. So while I was slightly curious about H-kun, I had basically nothing to do with him in our first year at high school.

When we moved on to second year, though, I found myself once more in the same class as him. I was a little annoyed with this, but I assumed that I would simply go on with him the way I had so far.

However.

One day, H-kun marched over to me and said, "Ito. You draw manga, right?"

I was completely taken by surprise. *W-what?! How does he know that?! I thought he hated me?*

I later learned that O-kun, a friend of both mine and H-kun's, told H-kun about my manga-drawing habits. O-kun was in the art club with me, and when talk turned to manga, I showed him a story I had started drawing, "Death Row Convict, Banzai" (about a scientist who uses death row prisoners in experiments to research what happens when people go without sleep) and *Mazo no Mura*, which I had made in middle school. O-kun liked it and talked about it with H-kun, who also drew manga.

When H-kun started this awkward conversation with me, I answered him curtly and brushed the whole thing off. I was on guard. But H-kun didn't give up. He came at me so often with "manga, manga" that, defeated at last by his persistence, I showed him "Death Row Convict, Banzai." He gave me his honest opinion of the story and also presented my work to another manga-loving friend, I-kun, who openly praised the work.

Suddenly, it occurred to me: *H-kun is actually a pretty good guy!* Before I knew it, H-kun and I had become good friends. From then on, H-kun, I-kun, and I would show each other the manga we'd drawn, and chat excitedly about how the initial blue jacket series for the anime *Lupin the Third* was absolutely amazing. The three of us gradually grew closer.

The influence of H-kun and I-kun

IN HIGH SCHOOL, I was more than a little influenced by H-kun and I-kun. Up until that point, I had basically only seen kaiju movies, fantastical films, and Bruce Lee pictures, but H-kun and I-kun knew all sorts of things about movies: old, new, Western, Eastern. For instance, it's thanks to these two that I know anything about spaghetti westerns (European western films that were mainly produced in Italy in the 1960s and 1970s) such as the popular film *A Fistful of Dollars*, starring Clint Eastwood as a gunman.

H-kun and I-kun were also zealous about manga. I got to learn from them about masterpieces outside of horror manga, like *Urusei Yatsura* by Rumiko Takahashi, a cutting-edge manga artist at the time; *The Poe Clan* by Moto Hagio, who overwhelmed me with her profound storytelling, and *Hi Izuru Tokoro no Tenshi* (Emperor of the Land of the Rising Sun) by Ryoko Yamagishi, who drew Prince Shotoku's life into a spectacle, and this was truly beneficial for me.

Indeed, it was also around this time that I learned about Yoshiharu Tsuge. H-kun told me he had read something really amazing, so I read it, and it turned out to be Tsuge's most famous work, "Screw Style." Tsuge's other literary manga, such as "Red Flowers," "Gensenkan Shujin," and "Realism Inn," were also deeply impactful reading experiences.

Music-wise, I started listening to the Beatles, which turned out to be a pretty big deal.

One day, we had a class where we listened to music that we liked. We ended up listening to the Beatles at the request of one of my fellow students. Because TV commercials had been using Beatles' songs to sell soft drinks and the like, I knew their name at least. But seeing those commercials, I'd basically just thought "good song." I didn't feel one way or the other about the Beatles. In fact, to be honest, the first time I listened to one of their albums in that class (it was an early album, but I can't remember which), all the songs sounded the same. It didn't really click for me.

H-kun told me any number of times that the Beatles were the best and I just needed to listen to them more, so he lent me the Red Album and the Blue Album (fans refer to the best-of album *1962–1966* as the Red Album and *1967–1970* as the Blue Album. The red and blue come from the color of the jackets of each.) Because of H's passionate proselytizing, I listened to the Beatles' songs over and over, and gradually came to understand why they were good. Thanks to him, the Beatles are special to me even now, and I often listen to them while I'm working.

H-kun and I-kun were extremely culturally sensitive boys, **wildly curious, who knew a lot about literature, art, and music.** If I hadn't gotten to know them, I think my worldview would have stayed much smaller than it is now. It was also thanks to them that I discovered H.P. Lovecraft, who would have a serious influence on me later.

Manga can be art

I WAS IN HIGH SCHOOL the first time I read the manga of Katsuhiro Otomo, the artist famous for works like *Domu: A Child's Dream* and *Akira*. I encountered his work when his short story collection *Short Peace* was covered in the book reviews of a newspaper I read at the time.

Compared with the art of manga up to that point, Otomo's illustrations were clearly of a different nature. Manga had been largely occupied with super-deformed drawings in the style of Osamu Tezuka or *gekiga* illustrations, with Takao Saito leading the pack. Otomo's drawing, however, deviates from this sort of standard manga. The eyes of his characters are narrow, and their skeletons are twisted slightly to the sides. There are no particularly hot guys or beautiful girls. He drew his characters and their lives with penetratingly observant eyes, imbuing them with such realism that it would be no exaggeration to say they were the first accurately depicted Japanese people in manga. Reading *Short*

Peace, what I felt above all else was that it was **okay to make art in manga.**

Otomo himself has said that French *bandes dessinées* had a significant influence on his work. Moebius, one of the most famed bande dessinée artists, is known for his fantastical and elaborate artwork, and inspired by his work, Japanese artists established an unprecedented new mode of expression in manga called "new wave."

Manga I drew in high school

IN MIDDLE SCHOOL, I had my sights set on science fiction for a time, but that fleeting dream was soon over, and I started drawing manga once again when I began high school. This renewed interest was thanks to my encounter with the work of Katsuhiro Otomo described above. H-kun and I-kun were also drawing their own original manga—with pen and ink.

Seeing this, I was mildly shocked. "H-kun, what the…! What are you doing?!"

H-kun might have rolled his eyes at my flabbergasted self.

Up until that point, the only tools I had used to draw manga were a pencil and eraser. Now, for the first time, I learned that even people drawing manga as a hobby used pen and ink.

Inspired by H-kun and I-kun, I went to a stationery shop in the neighborhood to buy a dip pen and immediately got to work drawing manga. I plunged the gleaming nib into ink I had borrowed

From **Short Peace** *(Futabasha)*
In Otomo's first short story collection, the drama unfolds against everyday backdrops such as school or the life of a man living alone. I was influenced by many elements in it—the beauty of the line work, the realistic characters, the unique angles.
© MASH•ROOM / KODANSHA

from my aunt. I was a little excited. The particular scent of ink filled the air, stimulating my creative urges.

This is the real thing here!

But when I actually started drawing, the line thinned and broke off before I knew it. Because the pen tip could only hold the tiniest amount of ink, I had to keep dipping it constantly. Plus, the tip of the nib was slightly curved, and depending on the direction in which I drew my line, it would catch on the drawing paper. It took a fair bit of time to get used to the nature of this pen.

And when I used my eraser to erase the rough sketch after I was done inking, the lines I had drawn with the pen also disappeared. I convinced myself with the thought that ink was actually more delicate than I had thought, but when I asked H-kun, he said, "That shouldn't happen. The ink you're using is probably just old."

Yes. When I bought a new pot and redrew those lines, they didn't disappear. They were still there on the page.

It was a constant struggle during this period as I learned bit by bit how to use the same tools as a professional manga artist. I also read instruction manuals for drawing manga for the first time, like the god of manga Osamu Tezuka's *How to Draw Manga*, and Shotaro Ishinomori's *Introduction to Manga*.

Whenever I found some free time in high school, I would get busy drawing my manga, and my friends and I would show and critique each other's work. I use the word "critique," but it wasn't real criticism. It was more on the level of "Well, I think it's maybe okay?" Harsh opinions would hurt us.

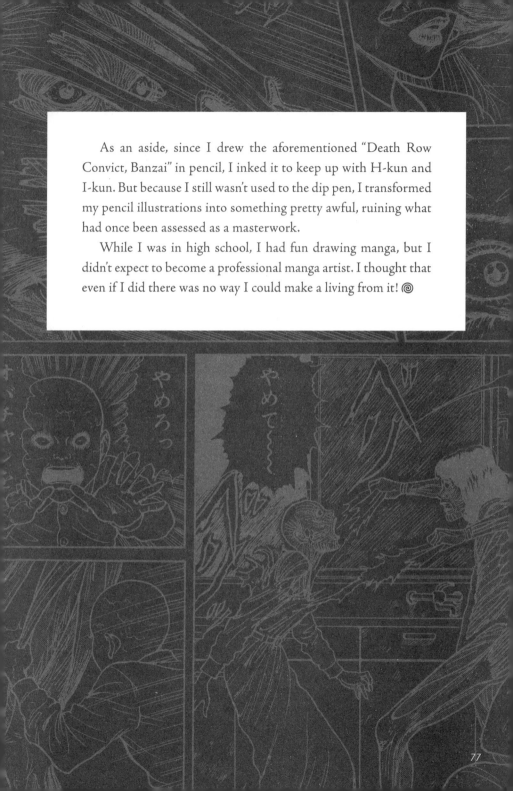

As an aside, since I drew the aforementioned "Death Row Convict, Banzai" in pencil, I inked it to keep up with H-kun and I-kun. But because I still wasn't used to the dip pen, I transformed my pencil illustrations into something pretty awful, ruining what had once been assessed as a masterwork.

While I was in high school, I had fun drawing manga, but I didn't expect to become a professional manga artist. I thought that even if I did there was no way I could make a living from it! ◉

CHAPTER

2

Indecision, anxiety, frustration:
You don't do it because it's meaningful.

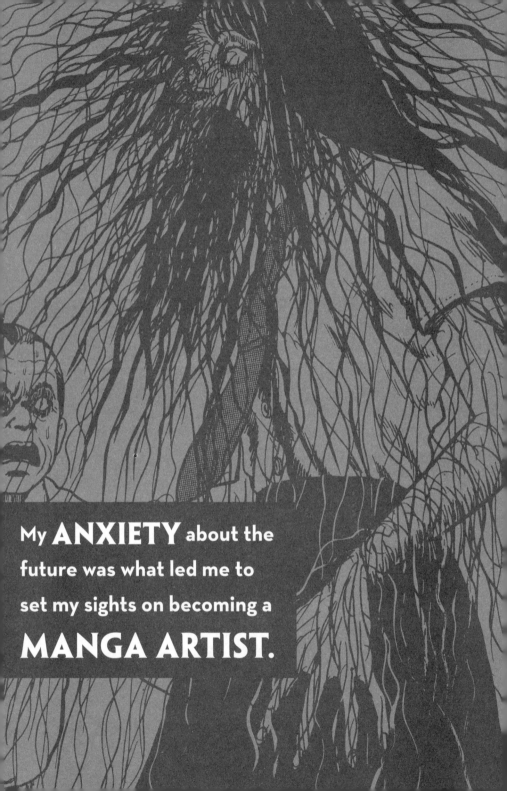

My **ANXIETY** about the future was what led me to set my sights on becoming a **MANGA ARTIST.**

I initially assumed I would be a science fiction manga artist. But then I chanced upon a contest in a manga magazine and decided to enter my work, which ended up changing my life in a big way. Given the number of coincidences involved, you might say it was fate that I stepped into my beloved world of horror manga. But I was only able to walk this dark path because my childhood obsessions—science fiction, flash fiction and tokusatsu shows—acted as lanterns to light my way forward. Sometimes, rather than doing something because it's meaningful, it becomes meaningful because you've done it. It might simply have been that once I really started thinking about how much time I had left in this life, my true ambition rose up from inside my subconscious and revealed itself.

To put it slightly dramatically, I made the choice to create horror manga because I had a premonition of my own death.

Crossroads of life

I DECIDED WHAT I WOULD DO after high school when I was in eleventh grade. Worried about my future, my teacher aunt did some research and came to me with the suggestion that I become a dental technician. According to her, this was a job where you made fake teeth, which sounded pretty interesting to me.

I could have chosen to go on to art school. But I was convinced that even if I did make it into art school, I could only become an art teacher (a job that revolved around working closely with other people, which was out of the question given my personality), so I readily accepted my aunt's proposal.

And thus, with the aim of a career as a dental technician, I followed the advice of my eleventh-grade homeroom teacher and advanced to a science stream in twelfth grade. Or I was supposed to, at least. I say "supposed to" because I ended up advancing to the arts track. I requested science, but the teacher told me that science was full—"So you're in arts, Ito"—and I was forcibly moved to the arts stream. I'm sure it must have seemed absurd to anyone watching.

But I was relieved, to be honest. Although I had steeled myself to go into the science stream, the truth is, I'm actually pretty bad at math and science. Despite this, people tended to assume that I was good at math because I have a kind of sciencey face, which was a struggle for me. (Is that the impression silver-framed glasses give?)

In particular, having to take math every day was my own **personal vision of Hell**. In a certain sense, you might say that I narrowly escaped death thanks to this tyrant teacher. Plus, my old friends H., I., and O. were also in the same arts class as me, a bit of good fortune I was grateful for.

At the time, I assumed that I needed to graduate from the science stream to study dentistry. But it turned out to be possible to get into technical school without taking a single science class, and there was absolutely no issue with me being in the arts stream. What was interesting about the entrance exam for the dental technician school was that, in addition to tests on academic subjects like Japanese and English, there was a practical test where you sculpted a tooth. I was given a square pillar of plaster called a "plaster rod" and told to carve a tooth shape out of one end of this pillar, referencing a sample tooth.

Not to toot my own horn here, but I was extremely good at sculpting teeth. Before the exam, they rounded up all the students for a practice session, and when the teacher saw the tooth I had sculpted, he was surprised that I was one of the test takers. I was embarrassed to be singled out in front of everyone, but inside, I was quite pleased.

Technical school years

IT WAS 1982. At the age of eighteen, I moved to Nagoya in Aichi prefecture to go to technical school. Because the younger of my sisters was attending an university in Aichi at that time, we got an apartment and moved in together.

Our building, Nagoyaso, was near Issha station, a metro station about twenty minutes from the central Nagoya station. The name was like something out of a Showa-era manga, and the structure itself made you feel that nostalgic romance of a bygone time: wooden, two stories, Japanese-style squat toilet, and sometimes the bathtub would leak, which got us more than a few complaints from the person living below us on the first floor. (Incidentally, this was also the year they tore down Tokiwaso, the apartment building made famous by Osamu Tezuka and the other legendary manga artists who lived there.)

I don't know if this will interest you all that much, but allow me to give you a quick overview of Tokai Dentistry Technical School. The two-year program had one class for each year, with about fifty students per class. In terms of scale, it was a pretty average school. Lessons included academic subjects, but because the end goal was to find work after graduating, the program was centered on practical training. I studied the basic techniques required for a dental technician, things like sculpting tooth models out of plaster rods (like in the entrance exam) and mixing resin to make the base used for dentures.

We also had classes where we used filling and capping materials such as gold and silver crowns. For fillings and the like, we would press a mold of the patient's teeth into a sculpted wax model, heat silver over a burner to melt it, and then pour the liquid silver into the fired mold. This was a fairly difficult task.

I produced a lot of duds in the beginning, when I still wasn't quite sure of the perfect state for the silver. If it wasn't melted enough, the silver would harden before it reached the deepest parts of the mold, and if it was too hot it would start bubbling, and the finished filling would be full of holes. (We said it was "spongy.") You had to carefully watch for a mere three-second window when it was just right and quickly pour the silver into the mold. I know I'm getting a little into the weeds here, but this is the level of fussiness and precision required in the work of a dental technician.

I was as bad as ever at studying and schoolwork, but for some reason, my classmates appeared to think I was an honors student who could answer any question. Shy and introverted as I was, I had neither the skill nor the backbone to actively disabuse them of this idea.

In Osamu Dazai's *No Longer Human*, protagonist Yozo Oba plays the fool despite the fact that he is actually quite gifted, but I was in the exact opposite situation—I had to play the honors student. I lived in trembling trepidation during that time, wondering when my performance would be found out.

What I learned from film

IT WAS THE EVE of the frenzied bubble economy period, but I did not spend my nights at discos dancing with young women after leaving my country home in Gifu for the big city of Nagoya. Instead, I went straight home the second school was over. I relaxed with movies.

The first film I went to see after moving to Nagoya was the first entry in the famed *Indiana Jones* series, *Raiders of the Lost Ark*. At the time, it was showing alongside the American film *The Blues Brothers*. (Way back then, it was normal and natural that one ticket would allow you to see two films back-to-back.)

Another back-to-back showing was the science fiction master-piece *Blade Runner* and a revival of the action magnum opus *Enter the Dragon*. Perhaps surprisingly, I'm a huge Bruce Lee fan. This was the first time I saw *Enter the Dragon* on the big screen, and I loved it so much that I ended up staying in my seat and watching it again. (This sort of thing was possible because they didn't clear the theater between shows. But this meant that I had to also re-watch the nearly two-hour-long *Blade Runner*, and after almost six hours of exposure to intense light and explosive sound, I was thoroughly broken by the time I walked out of the theater, like a spy tortured by his enemies.)

Other revival films that made an impression on me were Jean-Luc Godard's *Breathless* and *Pierrot le Fou*, and the Beatles' *A Hard Day's Night*. Needless to say, I was a regular visitor to the cinema.

When I think about it now, I feel like I was studying how to create the necessary mood for horror manga by watching movies.

For instance, the scary classic *Dracula*, featuring performances by famed actors Christopher Lee and Peter Cushing, is jam-packed with tricks from the horror playbook: run-down Gothic building, music to stir fear, lighting that creates deep shadows. These elements aren't connected directly with the story itself, but they're essential stage dressing to amplify uneasiness in the viewer and get their heart racing. Given that terror is an **unconscious defensive reaction**, I think these performance elements that can appeal to the viewer's unconscious mind and create a mood are very important.

In between school and hobbies

I CONTINUED TO DRAW MANGA while I was attending technical school. However, I was really only doing pencil drawings in a small A5-sized notebook, so it was less serious than my work up to that point.

And it seems that birds of a feather really do flock together— I had a manga-loving friend at technical school as well, and we would show each other our manga. One time, we talked about making a *doujinshi* manga together and got pretty into it. We'd decided on a title for the booklet, but we couldn't agree on what the manga inside would be about, and the whole thing fell apart while still in the earliest planning stages.

My high school friends H-kun and I-kun had also come to Nagoya for university by that point, so we used to hang out at each other's apartments and spent a lot of time together. I-kun was working very seriously toward becoming a professional manga artist. I remember him entering the newcomer contest for *Shonen Jump*. He showed me his manga once, and it was pretty interesting.

But even seeing my friend working hard on his manga, I didn't feel the urge to become a manga artist the way I had in the past. I was utterly convinced that I was going to be a dental technician. Thus, while I did draw manga, my studies always came first, and manga never moved beyond the realm of a hobby.

This was a period when shonen manga publications like *Shonen Jump* and *Shonen Magazine* were flourishing. In particular, *Jump* was a true juggernaut, simultaneously serializing manga that are still talked about to this day—works like *Ultimate Muscle*, *Fist of the North Star*, *Cobra*, *Captain Tsubasa*, *Dr. Slump*, *Cat's Eye*, and *Silver Fang: The Shooting Star Gin*. Meanwhile, I was reading *Maison Ikkoku* by Rumiko Takahashi in *Big Comic Spirits* and falling head over heels in love with the heroine Kyoko Otonashi.

Into the working world

AFTER GRADUATING, I landed my first job so easily that it almost felt anticlimactic. Essentially, I knew the right people. One of the instructors at the technical school introduced me to two dental laboratories near campus.

The first was a company with a name practically ripped from a Shotaro Ishinomori manga, Lab Kusakabe. This one came with my teacher's seal of approval—"The owner's a good guy, at any rate." The other company employed a famously quirky guy who had been a year ahead of me at the technical school. During my interview, out of nowhere, he let fly with a decidedly dodgy joke, telling me to introduce him to my sister, and I quickly decided that this was not the place for me. I politely declined the job offer.

Thus, I made my glorious entry into the working world at Lab Kusakabe, a twenty-minute drive from my apartment. It was a small workplace. When I started, there were of six of us: myself, three other dental technicians, one part-timer, and the owner. The space felt like a modified living room, slightly larger than your average apartment. Fortunately, my coworkers were all good people, and I was able to fit in rather easily. It was also nice that we were all men, and got along well.

Of all of my coworkers, I talked the most with H-san, who was two years my senior. His hobby was collecting fossils, and he was an expert at climbing mountains, swinging his hammer, and digging up all kinds of petrified remains. We both liked tokusatsu shows and movies, which gave us a shared interest to talk about and helped us to quickly open up to each other.

Decision in the face of helplessness and my own limits

DENTAL TECHNICIAN JOBS are generated by orders from the dentist. We get a set of instructions about the patient needs along with a plaster mold of the teeth, and then we produce dentures, post crowns, fillings, and the other necessary materials to the desired specifications. The industry had apparently been thriving before I got my start. (For instance, the owner of Lab Kusakabe drove a luxury Toyota Crown.) But by the time I was hired by the company, business was down across the board, and Lab Kusakabe was no exception. I think my starting salary was a paltry 110,000 yen per month. (The average starting salary at the time in 1984 for a new male graduate from a technical or vocational school was 120,000 yen, so mine was a little less than the norm.) I don't really know what caused the slump, but since we were contractors, we were forced to compete on price with larger laboratories, which no doubt caused downward pressure on rates overall.

One day, only a year or so after I started, there was an incident that illustrated how difficult business had become. The owner asked us to come over to his desk for a minute, and once we were all gathered there, he began to speak, a meek look on his face.

"I'll be honest with you," he said. "The company's in a fairly tight position right now. If I keep paying you the way I have been, I won't be able to pay myself anything at all. I'm really sorry about this, but we're going to shift to a commission system going forward. Okay?"

None of us could voice an objection, and so my salary became a commission. This was the start of life working around the clock.

I got about half of the product sale price. In order to make a living, I had to work faster and deliver a large number of products above a fixed baseline. Naturally, I wasn't credited with a sale if the client didn't get the product, so any mistakes or work that needed to be redone did not generate income for me. There was no issue with the quality of my work, but I was pretty slow. When I first started at the lab, I could barely manage to produce four or five small fillings in a day. Additionally, because these things needed to be sent out pretty much on a daily basis, I spent more and more nights working.

When the full-time employees couldn't handle the workload by ourselves, a part-timer would come into the office to help us. Incredibly, he could make, mold, and forge ten fillings all at once, when you would normally only make one at a time. I was struck by the fearsome speed of his work, but I reassured myself that he was bound to produce a few duds doing things in such a haphazard manner. But not only did all of his fillings turn out perfectly, the dentist even praised his work, saying that the precision was incredible.

I was shocked. I keenly felt my own lack of ability. I was very particular about reproducing the shape of the anatomical tooth, and sculpting products took me far too much time. And sometimes, because of factors such as the patient's bite or the dentist's skill, I couldn't make the tooth in the correct shape I'd studied at school, and I would have no choice but to sculpt an ill-formed tooth, which was frustrating. I often dealt with cases where I couldn't achieve the shape I wanted, even for front teeth, where a certain level of dental aesthetics was required. Work for a private dental clinic might have had different demands, but spending a great deal of time to produce a work of art was not particularly commendable for a general dental technician. The challenge in this line of work was producing as many items with a good fit as you could while still maintaining a certain level of quality.

My natural tendency to get chilly had an effect on my work as well. During winter, my hands were always freezing, and my fingers grew clumsier. Plus, the cold from my hands made the wax tooth sculpture cold, leading to harder wax that would break into bits at the slightest touch.

I don't know if I can keep doing this job for the rest of my life…

I started to feel my limits as a dental technician. The job of making things was very rewarding, and I got along well with everyone at the office. It was a good place to work. But in addition to the meager pay, the successive all-nighters were taking a serious toll on me both physically and mentally. I lost a lot of weight, likely because of the stress, and for a time I was so skinny I was all the way down to fifty kilos.

I'm not going to be able to live too long like this.

In the back of my head, I had the vague thought that I was probably going to die at forty. In which case, half of my life remained before me. If I was only going to be able to live another twenty years, then maybe it would be all right to devote those years to doing what I really loved, what I actually *wanted* to do.

One early morning, as I drove home after working all night,

We had a long desk and chairs in front of it in our workspace. The picture above has me in the middle of making the wax model of a crown. To do this, you have to heat up a tool called a spatula and melt the wax into shape. I was good at this, but it took me way too long.

the sky growing light in front of me, I made my decision.

I'm going to draw manga.

I was going to get serious and see how far I could go.

The eve of my manga artist debut

I BEGAN TO DRAW MANGA on the weekends and those weekday evenings when I made it home earlier. Later on, I would make my official debut as a horror manga artist, but the first thing I actually drew with the aim of becoming a professional was science fiction.

"Kaigara Senso" (The Shell War) was about a student with the ability to enter people's minds and control them. When he entered a mind, the soul of that person was chased out of their body, and this fleeing soul then entered another person. This series of collisions sets off a panic in the classroom.

I was going to enter this story in the *Shonen Sunday* newcomer contest to get started on the path to becoming a professional manga artist. The reason was simple: this magazine frequently published the work of my beloved Umezz. But embarrassingly, I didn't know that there were rules for submissions. I simply assumed that I could just take it directly to the publisher once the story was finished. Thus, I diligently scratched away at it until it had ballooned up to 60 pages. (And that was only the prologue.) There was no way it could be printed as a one-shot at that length. And so that first work of science fiction that I drew finished its life still incomplete, without ever seeing the light of day.

At the same time, I was also working to improve my drawing abilities. I wanted to draw **strange, but real worlds**. To re-create these on the page, I needed to draw well enough to naturally portray people and objects in any pose and from any angle.

At the bookstore, I picked up a collection of photographs with a variety of poses that my technical school manga friend had recommended and copied them whenever I had some free time. Drawing classes or attending prep school with the aim of getting into art school were also options to improve my skills, but because I had neither the time nor the money for those, I didn't even consider them. Thus, I mostly taught myself my drawing techniques.

However, I had taken classes with Kodansha Famous Schools in high school and continued on through my technical school years. The Famous Schools were correspondence classes for painting and illustration run by a Kodansha group company (now defunct), which often took out ads in the manga magazines I read at the time. After seeing one such ad, I took an interest in the classes and sent in an application postcard.

A few days later, someone from the school called my house. They told me that there would be an information session in the neighboring city of Enashi and invited me to attend. I asked my mother, and we decided to go to together.

When we got there, a man in a suit was sitting on a chair, all alone. Because I'd been told it was a meeting, I assumed that there would be a large number of participants, so I was a little taken aback when it turned out I was the only one. But I'd already set foot in the room, so I couldn't exactly turn around and leave. The man urged my mother and I to take a seat, so we decided to sit down and at least hear what he had to say. When I think about it now, they gave me quite the sales pitch. The man really was quite skilled in the art of conversation. The more he told me about art history and modern techniques, the more interesting the whole thing sounded, until finally, he had me in the palm of his hand.

I told my mother that I wanted to sign up for the school. Surprisingly, she readily assented, saying I should give it a go. I had done absolutely zero extracurricular classes up to that point, so she might simply have felt like this one little thing was fine. In any case, this is how I ended up studying color, sketching, and the fundamentals of composition over a period of years. (Although once I started dental technician school, I was so busy with my studies there that I tended to put my Famous Schools course on the back burner. I eventually quit halfway through the technician program.)

Kaigara Senso
Rough draft of the story starts with an unattractive boy moaning about human inequality (the absurdity of being born looking one way or another). I wanted to create the feel of the science fiction stories for boys that I had read and loved when I was in school, so I decided on a story of adolescence set in high school.

Around this time, I started drawing manga with a touch of reality to it, referencing my pose photo book. As an aside, I didn't know that each magazine had a set size for manuscripts, so I drew the story at the size I preferred. Also, my pen name was "Sebastian Zombist Ito." I wonder why? I can't remember now.

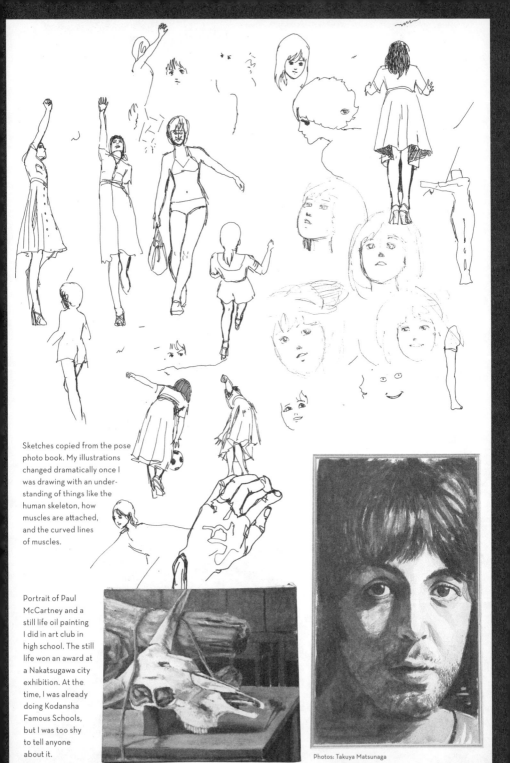

Sketches copied from the pose photo book. My illustrations changed dramatically once I was drawing with an understanding of things like the human skeleton, how muscles are attached, and the curved lines of muscles.

Portrait of Paul McCartney and a still life oil painting I did in art club in high school. The still life won an award at a Nakatsugawa city exhibition. At the time, I was already doing Kodansha Famous Schools, but I was too shy to tell anyone about it.

Photos: Takuya Matsunaga

Entering the Umezz Prize

THE YEAR 1986 saw the release of the first of the *Dragon Quest* video game series—which would later explode into unprecedented popularity—while on the flip side there was the quiet launch of Japan's first horror and occult shojo magazine, *Monthly Halloween*.

Published by Asahi Sonorama, *Halloween* was pretty ambitious for its time, with its promise to print nothing but horror and occult manga. The cover photos were intense, packed with exciting visuals that made your heart skip a beat—a butcher knife plunged into a porcelain doll, a pale-faced Santa swinging a massive axe, a beautiful girl in a swimsuit offering a mermaid some tropical juice. The pages inside were filled with authentic horror, and I was honestly delighted to see someone put out such a great magazine.

When it launched, *Halloween* was serializing *Kazuo Umezz's Curse*, but it also featured a lot of work by newcomers more or less my age, like Ochazukenori. I read every issue with deep interest, surprised to find that there were artists like these out there, and then one day I saw a notice among the announcements at the end of the magazine. My fingers froze in place on the page, and I gasped.

"Call for entries for the first Umezz Prize."

My first impulse was that I had to enter. Naturally, I was largely motivated by the fact that Master Umezz himself would be the chief judge. If I was lucky, the artist I'd adored since childhood would actually read a manga that I'd drawn. If this wasn't the opportunity of a lifetime, then what was?

Wild horses couldn't have kept me away. My entire being was focused on drawing a manga to enter into the contest. The question of whether or not I'd be able to make my debut as a manga artist was one thing, but more than anything else, I wanted Master Umezz to look at my work.

I had six months until the deadline. So, what kind of manga was I going to draw?

At the time, I'd had this vague idea kicking around in my head. A lizard's tail will regenerate if it's cut off. So what if, for instance, a human being had that ability? Wouldn't people find it scary if there was a being who kept regenerating and would not die, no matter how many little pieces you chopped them into?

This half-formed thought could hardly have been called an idea, but I sat with it and worked out the structure of my manga bit by bit while I made fillings and crowns. And this is how my debut work "Tomie" was born.

Death of a classmate and disorientation

HERE, I HAVE TO RETURN briefly to the past.

When I was in ninth grade, a fellow student lost his life suddenly over the summer holidays, in a traffic accident. I was at home studying for the high school entrance exams when I heard the news. My aunt came into my room and announced, "Your classmate K-kun was hit by a truck and killed."

At that age, you're not generally faced with the death of a peer. Naturally, K-kun's death hit me very hard, but I had trouble at first believing he really was dead. It was a fact that he was no longer a part of this world, but that fact had no *reality* to it. The fact that he was gone felt so unreal to me. Surely he would turn up at school again the next morning like nothing had happened? This idea actually felt more real to me than the truth of the situation. But he was indeed gone.

I was confused for a while, disoriented like reality and fiction had gotten twisted up and turned inside out. I didn't really know how to take the death of a classmate.

The "Tomie" story includes elements constructed from the disorientation I experienced then, and the lack of reality death held for me. (I'll note here that, of course, this experience was merely a jumping-off point, and Tomie the character is in no way, shape, or form modeled after my late classmate.)

Terror and the weight of death

THE STORY OF "TOMIE" begins with her funeral. She has been murdered, and her body is discovered in pieces. With the killer still at large, the police investigation is ongoing, and the media throngs to the high school she attended. Inside, her homeroom teacher tells her grieving classmates, "For her death to mean anything, we need to take it as a lesson. I know it's hard, but it's all we can do. The fact is, however much we miss her, she's not coming back." The instant he finishes saying this, the classroom door clatters open. It's Tomie, coming to school just like always.

The supposedly dead Tomie is alive. That's got to be a surprise. To accurately convey that surprise in the manga, I figured that I needed a setting that was no different from the real world.

In shonen manga, for example, the plot twist of "the friend you thought was dead is, in fact, alive" is not all that uncommon. And in horror manga, ghosts and supernatural phenomena are natural and obvious. In romance manga, your dead lover can never come and stand beside your bed, but this turns into an utterly commonplace development in horror manga.

In a world where people can come back to life anytime, death is not frightening. Even the introduction of an evil, brutal monster will not stir up any sense of crisis in the reader, but only leave them feeling somewhat blasé.

In order to craft real fear in a situation where a person keeps coming back to life every time they're killed, death has to be something that cannot be undone, just like in the real world. For me, the fact that this was horror manga was exactly why it demanded a stage that made the reader seriously feel the **weight of death**.

You can kill her, but she won't die

SO THERE I WAS, thinking about how to express death's true weightiness, and I came up with the device of making the killer the victim.

"How can she be alive?! It's totally impossible! There has to be some mistake!"

If anyone felt this sort of fear and panic at the fact that Tomie was alive, it would be the person who knew for a fact that she was dead. In other words, it would be the person who had killed her.

I settled on a setup in which all of Tomie's classmates worked together to kill her. Multiple assailants would make it easier for me to create a panic situation when Tomie returned. Not to mention that storywise, the murderer hiding in a group of people is pretty standard, so I thought that by inverting that schema, I might be able to depict a type of abnormality and the terror of mob mentality.

I was also very focused on drawing the murder victim Tomie in an extremely human way. She's different from ghosts and monsters. She can't walk through walls, she can't use any shady telekinetic abilities. She lives in the real world, she has a body that can be touched, and she can even be killed like a regular person. She's an average or perhaps weak girl.

Thus, the only unknown is why she won't die. There's something disturbing about this single point being incomprehensible, and it makes Tomie forever the object of people's fear. (Or that's the story I told myself, but the fact is, I'd exhausted typical ghosts and characters and techniques, and unless I took a slightly different tack, I'd never stand out from the crowd. This kind of cynical thinking might have been part of it.)

I had a good reason for making Tomie excessively proud of her looks, deeply jealous, and quick to make a fool of others. It was simple, actually—I thought that if she was so unpleasant a person, it would be no wonder that her whole class hated her enough to kill her. In other words, I came up with Tomie's queenly disposition to create the sort of situation where it would seem like it was only natural for her classmates to murder her.

I discussed this with my coworker H-san at the lab a little later, and he immediately reacted with, "No way. Not a chance." He argued, quite reasonably, that the average person would never think of killing a girl, no matter how awful her personality was. I groaned at this and struggled to find a response. So, to weave a bit more logic into the story, I added the fetishistic element that Tomie is so beautiful that anyone who looks at her wants to make her theirs, even if the only way they can do that is to chop her to pieces.

Drawing the greatest beauty in all of history

THE OTHER THING I wanted to tackle in "Tomie" was drawing the most beautiful girl in this world. I touch on this a little later, but for a horror manga, the pretty girl is the butter on the bread, the ketchup on the hot dog, the icing on the… Well, anyway, she's an essential element to ramp up the fear factor. Put another way, she's a **device to highlight and amplify the scariness.**

I didn't come up with this idea myself. You can see it at work in Kazuo Umezz's *Miira-Sensei*, which I discussed on page thirty-three, and artists since the early days of horror manga have often positioned the monster next to a pretty girl to make the monster look even more horrific. Plus, a neatly proportioned face can communicate terror through her facial expressions to the reader in an easy-to-understand way.

In the case of Tomie, however, you could say that she's a little removed from this tradition of horror, given that the monster *is* the beautiful girl. And maybe this is a bit of an exaggeration, but because she's supposed to be so gorgeous that the men who meet her lose their minds, she had to be the most beautiful girl to ever exist in all of history. To create her face and general style, I copied faces and other elements from my pose photo book and models in fashion magazines.

Another important set of references for me was the illustrations of girls in juvenile science fiction works by artists like Takashi Yorimitsu and Toshihiko Tani. I'd always been more

captivated by drawings of beautiful girls with a realistic touch over the cute style of manga. (Kyoko Otonashi, however, is the exception to this rule.) The Alice band that Tomie wears was inspired by an illustration of a girl in Taku Mayumura's science fiction novel *Nazo no Tenkosei* (Mysterious Transfer Student). In this way, Tomie was born not from any one specific model, but rather as an aggregate of a variety of beautiful looks.

Incidentally, I got the name "Tomie" from the lyrics of the popular song "Otomi-san" by Hachiro Kasuga, a singer of popular Japanese traditional music known as *enka*. It includes the lyrics, "You were supposed to be dead, Otomi-san/You lived unknown even to the Great Buddha, lost Otomi-san," and even if it was a coincidence, I was astounded at how much it sounded like the manga I was working on, so I gave her the name as a joke. "Tomie" also had an old-fashioned ring to it somehow, and I figured I could change it later if I wanted to. As time passed I began to feel fond of it, until finally I gave in to the appeal of the joke and made that her official name.

Mixing the everyday with the exceptional

SPEAKING OF JOKES, my manga sometimes gets comments like "I can't tell if this is serious or if it's a joke" and "Is this supposed to make me laugh?" I can only say that the answer is yes, and also no.

There's a scene in "Tomie" where, after they finish dissecting Tomie's body with coping saws, the teacher tells the male students that they did a good job, and I did intend for this to be a joke. It might seem like I tossed in a gag off the cuff, but I actually had a stock of gags in my notebook, and I tried to include one wherever there was an opening (as long as it wouldn't ruin the horror mood of the moment).

Also, in the middle of dismembering Tomie, the boys have a slightly absurd conversation—"Her...large intestine is...big" followed by "She must've had a sandwich for lunch... Lots of carrots..."—and depending on how you look at it, you could say that this was just the logical extension of the gag.

I feel like Yasutaka Tsutsui's and Katsuhiro Otomo's early works were a strong influence on why I find this sort of black humor fun. There's just something funny about the juxtaposition of surreal situations and mundane exchanges of dialogue.

On the other hand, more than a few times, I was deadly serious when drawing the scene, but readers later told me that they couldn't stop laughing. It's quite alarming as a horror manga artist to learn that something you intended to be scary ended up being inadvertently funny. But maybe there's some truth to what experts say, that while fear and humor are at first glance totally different, the roots of these emotions are actually extremely close to each other in our psyches.

The poses and viewpoint angles incorporated into "Tomie" were also likely influenced by the work of Otomo. When I was younger, I had a serious desire to draw novel perspectives that had never been seen before, like someone running from directly above or two people talking with the "camera" looking up from below. Because of this, I actively used cinematic compositions in my manga, things like shots from directly above people walking with umbrellas open, like in old Daiei films.

The last scene of "Tomie" happens to be a perfect example of my using influences from film. On the last page, a student is shocked when she discovers that Tomie is regenerating from her heart, and while I was creating this, I had in the back of my mind the last scene in *Planet of the Apes*.

In this way, I mixed together a variety of goals, hopes, and coincidences, and the character and story of "Tomie" coalesced bit by bit. Perhaps not all of those ideas succeeded, but I think I was very fortunate to manage to create, however imperfectly, this unfathomable being—not human, nor ghost, nor monster, but a creature who can only be said to be Tomie.

Professional manga artist debut

THE TRUTH IS, "Tomie" was the first manga I ever completed using pen and ink. I was drawing with a Rotring pen on regular drawing paper, the kind you could get at any stationery store, so when you look at the manuscript, the lines are bleeding all over the place. Because I also made the wrong choice for screentone, there are places in the printed manga where the eyes are too narrow and just crumple into blackness.

Despite how utterly at sea I was with these unfamiliar tools, I nevertheless spent my weekends and days off drawing with single-minded focus. After about three months, I finally finished "Tomie" and sent the manuscript to the *Halloween* editorial division.

One day a few months later, when I staggered home exhausted after finishing work in the middle of the night, the glass door of the room next to mine clattered open, and my sister came in, rubbing sleepy eyes.

"Jun," she said. "Someone from this Asahi Sonorama place called for you today."

This is it!

My heart started racing immediately. It had to have been the announcement of the winner of the Umezz Prize.

"Huh. And?" I replied, working hard to keep my calm. In my heart, I was already congratulating myself—"You magnificent king, you!" But it was too soon to get excited just yet.

Tomie

• Concept for Tomie

1. Personality:
   1) First and foremost, craves the limelight
   2) Egotistical, self-centered
   3) Crazed, kind of a pathological liar
   4) Narcissist
   5) Short temper

2. Tomie's physical makeup:
   1) Infertile (or rather she doesn't have reproductive function) → She can't have kids. She also has no period. What else instead of a period?
   2) Instead, she can make copies of herself. Basically, like a lizard's tail. If her body is chopped to pieces, all of those parts can regenerate Tomie. This phenomenon could be said to be the embodiment of her narcissism, and instead of being able to produce children with members of the opposite sex, she produces herself. Something like self-fertilization?

Revision Sept. 5, 1995: Normal people can produce a younger offshoot by having children, but Tomie can only produce an offshoot the same age as she is at the time. This is fine when she's younger, but once she gets older, she makes older offshoots. Tomie's beauty is only for a single generation. Thus, she is fixated on leaving something behind to make her beauty last for the ages. But she appears grotesque in photographs, as she does in paintings.

3) In short, Tomie is a clone. *At the time it's generated, the age of the clone is the age when she was hacked to pieces.

3. Meaning of her existence
Those who love Tomie (but not limited to those who love her) develop the urge to hack her to pieces while they interact with and look at her. This makes the whole class taking part in "Tomie" make sense. Essentially, even as she's tragically slaughtered due to this human impulse, new individual Tomies go out into the world one after another. This is how she secretly increases her numbers.

(Tomie)

A guy hits on a girl sitting on a bench in the park. She goes with him without a word. When he asks her name, she replies, "Tomie."
4. When any Tomies run into each other, they fight.
They can't stand that there could be more than one. "Don't you dare show your face to me again, It won't be pleasant." Or she kills her and chops her to pieces.

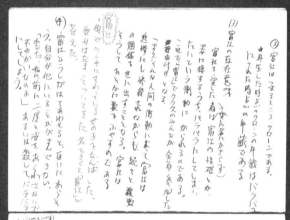

Revision Apr. 30, 2000:
5. When her bodily fluid enters a child, that child grows up into Tomie. They don't usually get chopped up until they're grown.

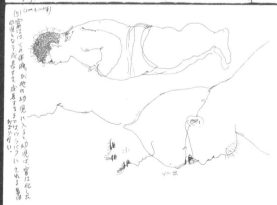

Tomie 4: Photo

- Tsuki Izumisawa is in the photo club.
- She's making money. At the request of her fellow students, she secretly takes snapshots of whoever they're attracted to and sells them for a high price.
- She tells Yamazaki that a friend asked her to do it, and sometimes gets him to let her take his photo. Tsuki has something like a sixth sense.
- One day, Tomie of the ethics committee comes along, discovers Tsuki's business, takes the photos, and tells the teacher (all the while saying that she will keep it quiet this time).
- Tomie searches Tsuki's bag, saying she probably has other photos, and pictures of a certain boy student come out.
- They're photos of Tetsuya Yamazaki, the boy Tsuki secretly likes (one-sided), but Tomie confiscates all of them.
- Yamazaki comes to Tsuki and asks her for a photo. Surprise! When she learns he wants it of Tomie, she's double surprised.
- Yamazaki: "Thanks. I have a favor to ask."

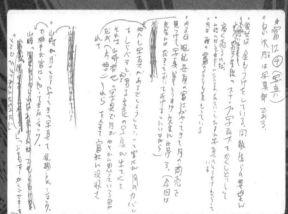

- So, with no other choice, she secretly snaps Tomie, but Tomie notices and tells her, "This is my best side." Tsuki's about to run away. "If it's me you want, by all means fire away. Why don't you take a thousand? Then you can scatter them all across the school."
- (Scene in here being raked over the coals by the teacher)
- Tsuki is shocked when she develops them. The photos of Tomie are all disturbing, things like multiple torsos growing out of her body.
- Tsuki scatters these across the school. Once Tomie learns of this, she's furious. The boys who are her henchmen (Taichi and Kimata) try to capture Tsuki. → Next, boys looking for Tsuki.
- Tsuki runs away. Tomie tells the boys to kill her, and they go after her with knives or something.
- Shows her friend the next day. "Hey, Michiko, what is this all about?" "What the..." Before they know it, Yamazaki's behind them. "What exactly were you planning with these faked photos?!" "They're not faked."

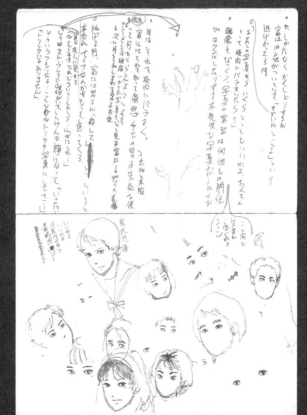

Fine, it's fine. Today's the last entry in your diary.

Tsukiko Izumisawa

▲ "Tomie" (1987)

I continued to draw the Tomie that I completed in 1987 as a series over the following thirteen years. I changed her age and hairstyle with each story.

▲ "Tomie Part 2: Morita Hospital" (1988)

▲ "Basement" (1989)

▲ "Photo" (1989)

▲ "Painter" (1995)

◄ "Gathering" (2000)

◄ "Passing Demon" (2000)

▼ "Moromi" (2000)

TOMIE
...

TOMIE,
I LOVE
YOU...

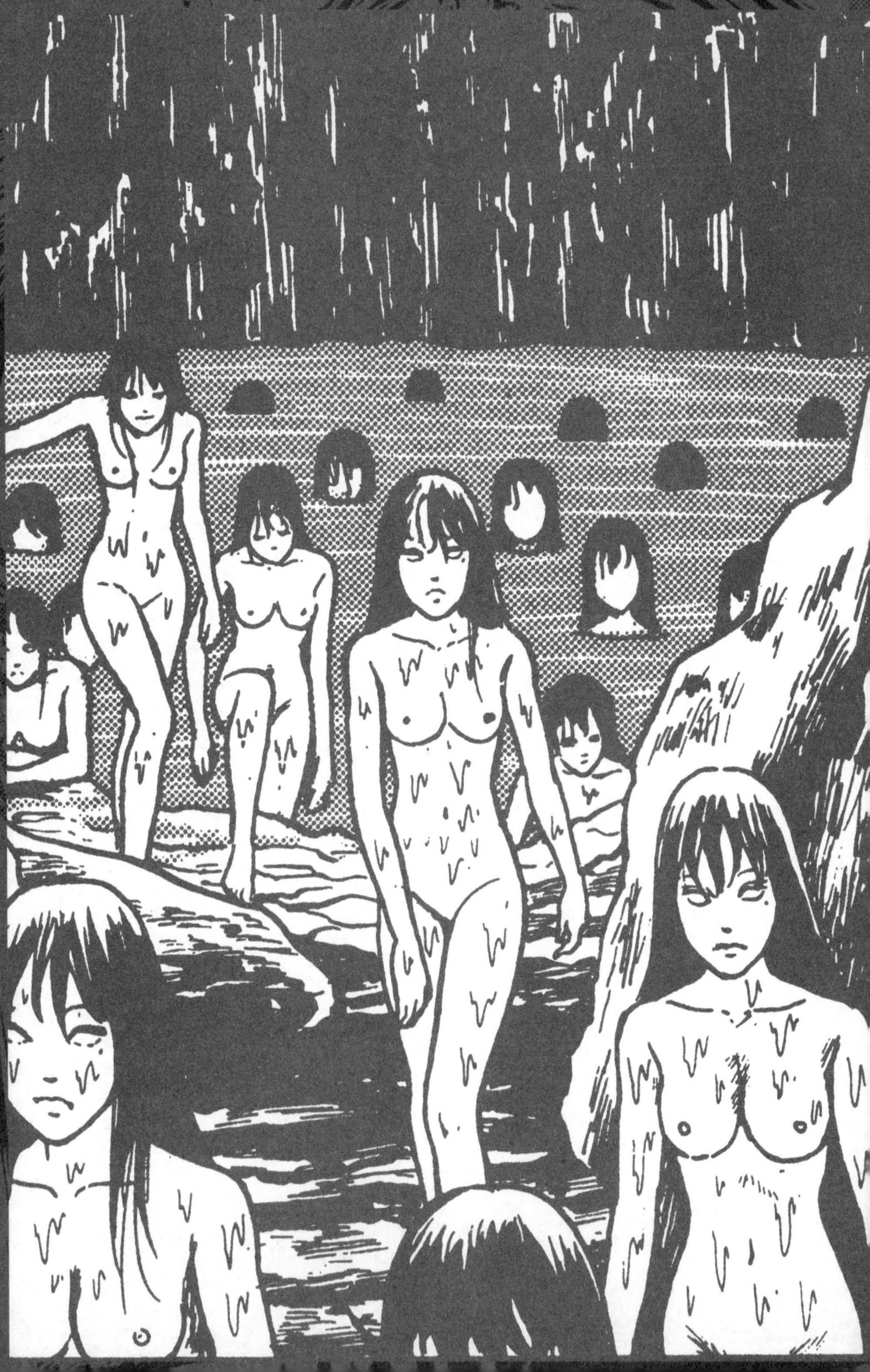

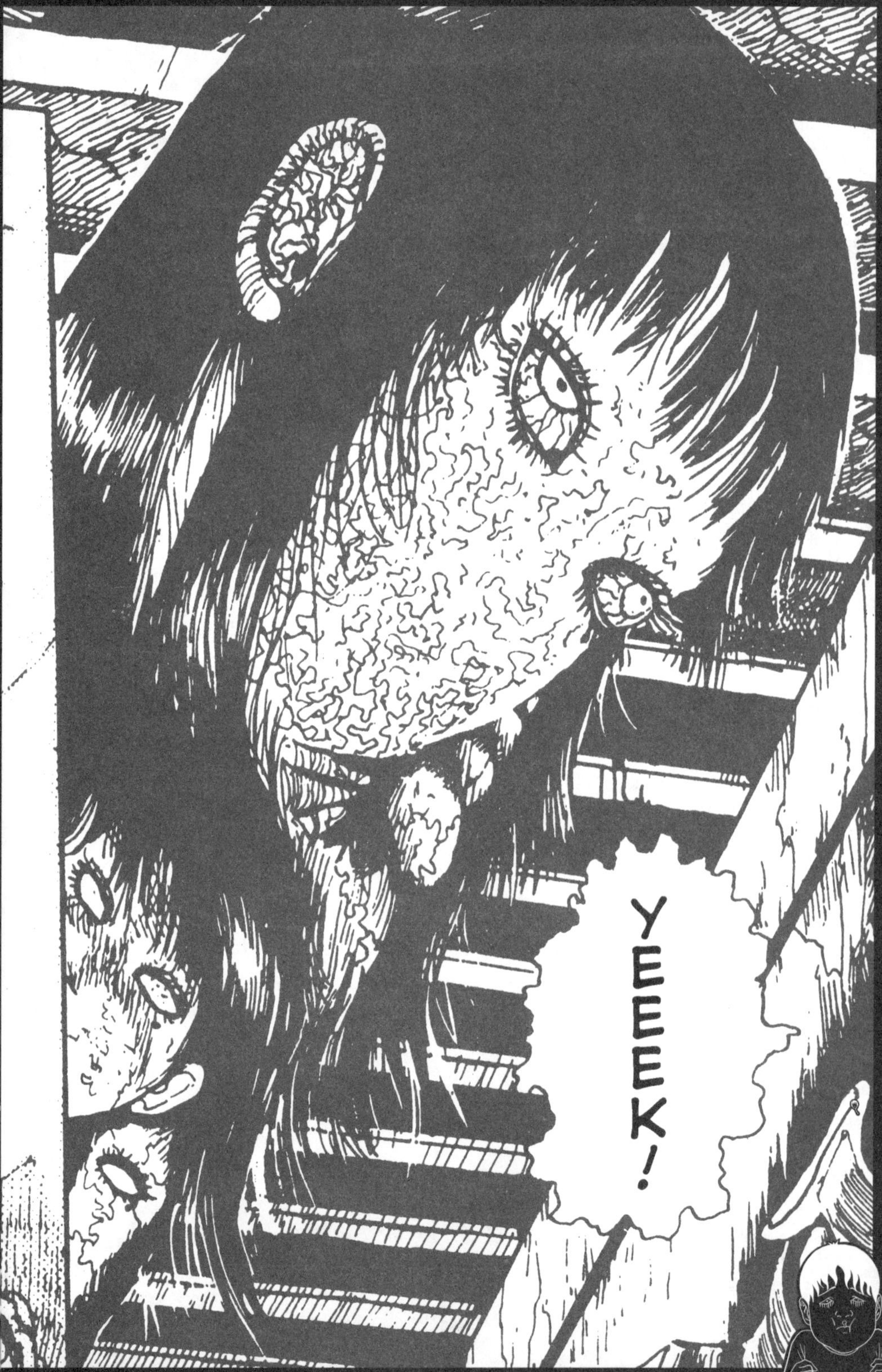
YEEEK!

It was true that I felt like this story was something special. I'd already dreamed twice, incredibly, of winning. But I'd also had plenty of confidence with my entry to the Shinichi Hoshi Flash Fiction contest. And the time I sent a caricature of Orson Welles to the readers' letters page of *Roadshow*, I'd been smugly smiling, convinced that it would make it into the film magazine. But had these expectations of mine ever once been rewarded? I couldn't get ahead of myself.

"So, what did they say?" I asked.

"They said your story got an honorable mention," my sister told me.

"Oh. Yeah?" I answered, and my sister went back into her room, sleepily.

After she'd gone, I sat down at the low table in my room. My legs were shaking, and I was totally excited.

I did it… I won the Umezz Prize (honorable mention)!!

I had wanted Master Umezz to see my manga, just once. This was the moment when my wish reached him and was granted.

A few days later, Asahi Sonorama editor Toshiyasu Harada called me, and I was officially informed that I had been awarded an honorable mention. From what he told me, the jury hadn't selected anyone for the grand prize in that first contest. Four entries made it to the final judging, including "Tomie," and of those, only mine had been selected for an honorable mention.

But at the time I won the prize, I still didn't know whether or not I'd be able to make a living as a professional manga artist.

"Tomie" was going to be published in the magazine, but because it had only gotten an honorable mention, I wasn't given any definite promises of future publication.

Nonetheless, I was on cloud nine, and rather than worrying about my future in publishing, I was filled with expectation for the nonexistent award ceremony—"Maybe I'll get to meet Master Umezz!" (Naturally, since there was only the honorable mention, there was no award ceremony. As an extra prize, I received fifty pages of special manuscript paper.)

Commotion over "Bio House"

AFTER SOMEHOW making my manga debut with "Tomie," my next opportunity came unexpectedly soon. Harada called to tell me that readers liked "Tomie" and asked me to put together another story. I immediately drew the 24-page "Bio House" and sent it to him.

"Bio House" is the story of a company president who loves to eat weird things like bugs and reptiles. After eating so many of these meals, his blood runs far too hot, so he cuts his own throat and lets his secretaries drink the blood—a grade-A pervert.

More than a few people have drawn stories about the desire to drink other people's blood like a vampire over the years. And while this wasn't quite its opposite, I'd never come across the idea of wanting to make other people drink *your* blood. I thought it

入選のことば———伊藤潤二

　漫画は小学校1年の時から描いていますが、ペン入れなんて知らず、全くの遊びのデタラメな漫画でした。実は単行本漫画の頃から母親がずっと先生のファンで、最初に読んだのが「うぐう先生」です。以後、「のろいの館」とか「恐怖」とか愛読してきました。今度、「漂流教室」が映画化されるとか、狂喜しております。先生の作品の中では「おろち」が特に好きです。僕の漫画も描きだしたのは、まわりから保因生主の影響なので。

　高校時代以後は、がに退いていましたが、今度「即図賞」を知り、遊半最高のカキみたいな魅力だったので「富江」を描きました。恥ずかしながらペン入れもして作品として仕上げたのはこれが初めてです。こんな衝動的なものに「佳作」をいただき、夢ではないかと思っております。投稿者、応募も更に見えるためので……。

　主人公（?）の「富江」という名前は僕が入部さんの「お客さん」から頂戴しました。生きているとはカシュカ様でも知らなかった訳です。

　ところで、怪奇とか謎が的な事件は僕らな現実にはほとんど体験できません。だからこその他に連載にする価値がある、となまいきながら思います。本当は自分で体験したいといつも思っているので、それができたら漫画を描く必要もなくなるでしょうが……。

　「月刊ハロウィン」は創刊号から買っていますっと。

伊藤潤二———漫画
昭和38年7月31日、岐阜県に生まれ。中津高校85年卒業。歯科技工士学校卒業後に歯科、歯科技工士。

"Tomie" was published in the February 1987 edition of *Halloween*. Two pages of the manuscript were published horizontally on each page, so readers had to keep flipping it around to read it. This was inconvenient, but the roughness of the manga didn't stand out, and personally, I think that was a point in my favor.

could be an interesting manga if I did it right. (A friend later pointed out to me that there is a Stephen King story that covers this same topic.)

But this manga ended up causing a bit of a commotion. When "Bio House" was published in a special edition of *Halloween*, I was still working as a dental technician at Lab Kusakabe. My colleague H-san read the story and came to me with a question—"This looks a lot like our boss?"

Of course, I rejected the idea, but H-san wouldn't back down. "No, but it looks *exactly* like him. This is definitely our boss!" And then, of all things, the owner's wife heard about this from H-san, and I ended up in the impossible position of explaining to her that, no, this pervert was absolutely not modeled after her husband.

At any rate, I will say here and now for the sake of the owner's reputation: I did not draw the president in "Bio House" based on the owner of Lab Kusakabe. It really does look a lot like him, though. But that's almost certainly because the only picture of "company president" that I had in my head was the owner of Lab Kusakabe, who I saw on a daily basis. The end result was that his wife laughed the whole thing off, and all was forgiven. But it was disrespectful to the owner, and I made a firm vow to be careful to make sure that nothing like that ever happened again.

Anyway, unrelated to this little kerfuffle, "Bio House" led to a situation that I wasn't particularly happy with. After the story was published, I heard nothing from Harada. I assumed it was because the readers hadn't liked "Bio House."

Panicking, I drafted a new story that he hadn't commissioned and sent it to him, pleading for him to take a look. I promised I would work hard on it. Before too long, he called me and requested it for publication. "This is pretty good," he said. "Please draw it for the December issue." And that's how I came to draw a story called "Face Thief." I managed to keep hanging on as a horror manga artist by the skin of my teeth.

Editor Harada's patient guidance

SINCE I WAS IN NAGOYA, I would meet with Harada over the phone to discuss the details of my manga. Not only did none of us have smartphones in the late 1980s, computers and cell phones were also not widespread. Nowadays, I can just send the file via email for any manuscript checks, but back then, we did it through the post. I would mail the storyboards (rough sketches), get Harada's opinion on them over the phone, revise the thumbnails after he sent them back to me, and then go ahead with the first draft of the story. Sometimes, I would also have to send him the revised thumbnails. I didn't know to send a copy of the thumbnails, so I sent the actual pages, meaning the whole process took a lot longer.

Because I drew my manga far from the editorial division in Tokyo, I still hadn't met Harada in person a year after I made my debut. I finally got to meet him when I was twenty-four. He happened to be coming to Nagoya on some other business, so it was the perfect chance. We decided to meet in the lounge of a hotel in the Marunouchi area.

My first impression of him was a relaxed middle-aged man. I suppose Harada would've been just under fifty at the time. I was so nervous that I couldn't speak, so he told me about his work editing Kazuo Umezz and Yosuke Takahashi's *Mugen Shinshi* series. He also shared some valuable industry stories, like how he'd rejected the manga of one artist he'd edited in the past because it was too brutal.

Harada hated cruel depictions and plot developments that left a poor aftertaste, anything that would make readers uncomfortable in a bad way. When I drew something that was too grotesque or suggested subjects like deformities or mental illness for stories, he would tell me until he was blue in the face that I couldn't draw such things.

At Harada's request I significantly rewrote "Neck Specter," a manga I drew not long after I made my debut. Initially, the story was of a girl who went to school like always, without realizing that her neck had grown abnormally. Her classmates were afraid of her and yelled about her long neck. When he saw it, Harada told me not to draw it in a way that punched down. He wanted to convey to me that it didn't matter if the characters and story were fiction, it wasn't right to include discrimination and abuse without justification. I hurried to change my original story, and it took shape as the published "Neck Specter."

Harada was my editor for twenty-four years after that. I had never worked as a manga assistant, so I was basically a total layperson when I made my debut. The reason I've been able to keep drawing manga right up to the present day is primarily due to Harada's patient guidance. I'm eternally grateful to him.

If I'm going to die at forty, anyway...

AFTER THE PUBLICATION of "Face Thief," I had a new story in the magazine roughly once every two or three months. I wasn't in it every month because I was still working as a dental technician and couldn't take more time for drawing. Even after my first book was released, I still didn't feel like I could make a living from manga alone.

Fortunately, my boss and colleagues at Lab Kusakabe were very understanding of the fact that I was moonlighting as a manga artist. As I mentioned earlier, this was an era without cell phones, so Harada would call the landline at the lab. Most employers would have scolded me for wasting time and demanded that I do the job I was hired to do, but the owner of Lab Kusakabe was actually intrigued that I'd become a manga artist and even scheduled me so that I would have a little more time for writing.

The other employees (although there were only the three of us by then—myself, H-san, and a new person who'd previously been in the Self-Defense Forces) would read my manga and tell me their opinion. H-san in particular got all worked up idly chatting about "Tomie" being made into a movie. He joked that if a swimsuit competition were part of the audition for the role of Tomie, I'd have to be a judge as the creator of the original work, which we laughed about. (Twelve years later, *Tomie* really did end up being made into a movie, but naturally, there was no swimsuit competition.)

I feel like it was precisely because the company was small and like a family that I was able to hold down both jobs for a while there. I know it's a bit belated at this point, but I have to say that I'm deeply grateful to everyone at Lab Kusakabe. Thanks to them, I managed to wear the two hats of dental technician and manga artist for about three years.

Meanwhile, my family was fairly concerned about my future. They had fun with my manga career when I first made my debut, going around to all the relatives to show them the magazine with "Tomie" in it and things like that. But once they understood that I intended to continue wearing the two hats—and that not only was I not going to give up on manga, but my end goal was to pursue manga alone as a career—they did a complete one-eighty in terms of attitude. They were convinced it was impossible. Even my mother, who never found fault with anything I did, would frown at me, troubled. My teacher aunt held the belief that manga was a waste of time and showed zero interest in anything I drew. She would often tell me, "It's about time you came home and got a job with a dentist here!"

My father had already passed away by this time. He suffered a brain hemorrhage when I was eighteen and attending technical school, and never came home again. (Incidentally, my oldest sister got married two years after our father's death, and a few years after that, my aunts moved to a house next door to her home in Nakatsugawa.)

I did feel bad about making my family worry, but even so, I remained firm in my desire to make manga my main job. Plus, now that I had several publications under my belt, I was getting the hang of it and building a readership. But more than anything else, I strongly felt that **if I was going to die at forty anyway, I wanted to do what I enjoyed until that time came.**

In the end, my family came around in the face of my determination to go all the way, and quietly accepted my life as a professional manga artist. Apparently, one reason they decided to stop fighting me was because they knew how low my commission salary as a dental technician was. When my brother-in-law later saw my pay slip, the small figure on it stunned him into silence.

The courage to reach for my dreams

IN GENERAL, rates for manga are calculated per page, and the page rate naturally differs from person to person. In my case, it was about four thousand yen when I was a newcomer. Perhaps you're shocked at how low this rate is. But most manga artists make their real income off the royalties from their book sales, so you can make a more-or-less decent living even with a low page rate. (Which is why it's really rough when your books don't sell…)

But my salary as a technician was so low that I was delighted with my page rate when I was a newcomer—"This is amazing. I can't believe I can make this much money drawing manga!" (Around the time of my manga debut, a punk-type guy living in the same apartment building as me crashed into my beloved Toyota Starlet and sent it to the great beyond. But thanks to my manga money, I was able to buy a Toyota Corolla FX.) That said, however, paring it back to manga alone would indeed still have been hard financially. I continued in my technician role while on the road to becoming a professional manga artist because I never knew when I would be cut loose.

Eventually, I decided to go all in on manga simply because I had reached my physical limit. By my fifth year at Lab Kusakabe, H-san and the former SDF member had both quit, and the company was down to just me and the owner. Naturally, the amount of work I had to do increased, and balancing the job with manga was becoming increasingly difficult.

Thoroughly exhausted by the double life, I told Harada over the phone, "I'm maybe at my limit here. I want to quit working full-time as a technician and focus on manga. I can pick up the slack at some other part-time job." And here, Harada offered me a lifeline. "How about we have you do more stories, then?" he proposed, and set aside thirty pages for me to do a one-shot in the magazine every month. I was over the moon. Now, by drawing just one story, my income would be a little more than my monthly salary as a dental technician. I could get by without taking on a part-time job.

The day had finally come, and I was now a fully-fledged manga artist!

But to do this, I had to tell the owner of Lab Kusakabe that I wanted to quit. This took a lot of courage. I felt deeply indebted to him, and thought my resignation might be the thing that finally pushed the teetering company over the edge. I was overwhelmed by the notion, and I couldn't quite manage to bring the subject up with him.

But I also couldn't give up on my own dreams for the sake of the lab. So, I steeled myself and told him I was quitting to devote myself to manga. He didn't try to stop me. Perhaps he'd been expecting me to quit someday. He readily accepted my notice, with a resigned air.

After I quit, the owner took over all of the work in the lab instead of hiring anyone to replace me. He sent me a New Year's card a few years ago saying that he had quit at last because he was at that age.

Living as a horror manga artist

THUS, THREE YEARS AFTER MY DEBUT, at the age of twenty-six, I became a full-time manga artist.

Soon after I left the lab, I decided to move back to my Gifu family home with my older sister. She was going to be living there for a bit because of her upcoming wedding, so I decided to move out of Shibata Mansion with her. (We'd moved there from Nagoyaso a few years earlier.)

The years after that were a blur of action—we built a new house in Gifu, I got married, had kids, moved with my family to Chiba—but the constant in my life was devoting the majority of my week to drawing. It's not just me; most manga artists live an extremely unglamorous life in fear of our looming deadlines as we spend nearly twelve hours a day chained to our desks, scraping together our stories at the cost of our health. And since I lived for a long time in the countryside of Gifu and drew my manga alone, it wasn't unusual for me to go without speaking more than a word or two from morning to night.

To give an example of my monthly schedule, I usually took ten days to think up the story and write the script, another five days for the storyboards, and then the remaining fifteen days were spent drawing the manga. If I still hadn't finished the story by the middle of the month, I'd start to feel shivers of panic and anxiety shoot up my spine. And given that I was writing a one-shot every month—and in the horror genre to boot—I couldn't stretch out the story or recycle characters. (After all, the protagonist would generally die in twenty or thirty pages.) Not to mention the fact that because I was doing all of the work by myself, I had no way to shorten the actual drawing time.

You might think that I should have just hired an assistant, but I'm extremely bad at giving people instructions and having them do things for me. Whenever I think about the effort involved, I always end up feeling like it would be faster to do it myself, and I give up on the whole idea. When I was in Gifu, I would get my mother and my sisters to help me with inking backgrounds and applying screentone—the price of being related to me. Most of my manga from my debut into the middle of my career were produced by the Ito Family Workshop.

In the blink of an eye, the end of the eighties arrived. While young people all over the country danced at discos, housewives got excited about trendy TV dramas, and children desperately searched for Waldo at the end of the bubble era, I was at home each and every day, letting my imagination roam free in strange worlds.

A village with an ominous siren blaring, an old record that plays the voice of a dead person, an alley in one corner of town that no one knows about… What if such worlds existed?

This is how I ended up spending the rest of my life as a horror manga artist. ◎

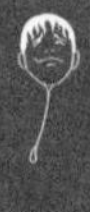
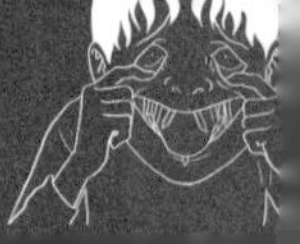

CHAPTER

3

Ideas: When fantastical stories come into being

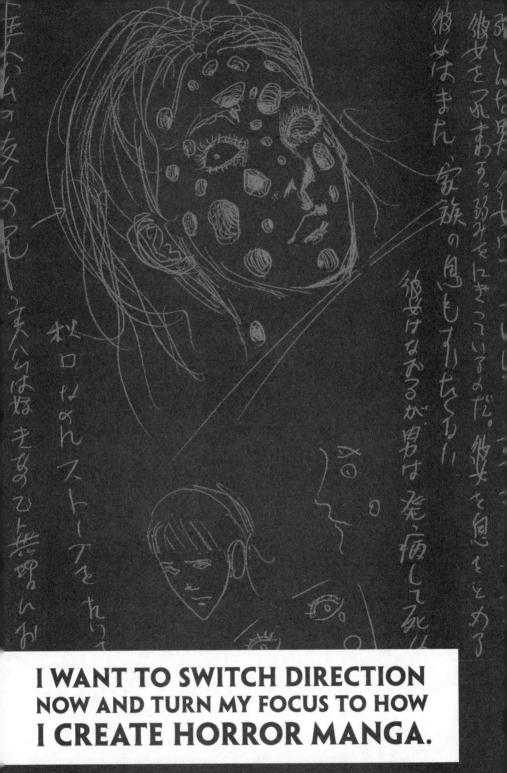

I WANT TO SWITCH DIRECTION NOW AND TURN MY FOCUS TO HOW I CREATE HORROR MANGA.

I'll discuss a number of specific examples in the first part of this chapter, and then offer up some general remarks to summarize ideas common to my entire body of work. (Chapters four and five will be in a similar vein.)

About story

IN THIS CHAPTER, I would particularly like to go over my own thinking on **how to generate ideas** and how to develop those ideas and **create stories**. But before we get to that, let's start with the question of what elements need to come together for something to be called "horror."

It may sound like I have all the answers, but I'm sorry to say that I've never actually thought about the requirements for horror before now. The fact is, I read the manga of masters like Kazuo Umezz, Shinichi Koga, and Hideshi Hino, which made me want to draw manga myself. Then I got lucky and was published in a horror manga magazine, and I just kept on drawing until, at some point, people started calling me a horror manga artist.

I remember Master Umezz once said, **"If something strange happens inside the house, that's horror; if it happens outside, it's science fiction."** And it's true that when you look at the majority of horror stories, the spirits and monsters do often appear in the home. And they like small spaces—the bathroom, the shower, under the bed, the basement. We could say, in other words, that horror is the **bizarre occurring in an enclosed place**.

The small space is important because it removes any possible escape for the protagonist (victim). Imagine if a lone zombie broke into your house right now. You would fight it off with everything you had. But if this zombie made its appearance in some distant country, you would wait for the miliary to mobilize while you went about your business online with a coffee in one hand. In other words, the specter in horror stories has to be **personal.** People are most afraid when the mysterious intrudes on their own safe places.

The mystery happening in a closed space also provokes the terror of not being able to share the terror with anyone else. Curses like **"You're next"** and the hero being the only one who can see the ghost are classic techniques for making the reader feel fear. Having a lone victim in a work of horror is an important device to amplify the panic and isolation of the protagonist and thus of the reader.

If we look at my work with these conditions in mind, I doubt if it could be called traditional horror at the end of the day. But I do hope that in re-examining it in this light, you come away with a new understanding of the work, and see that this is another way of viewing my stories.

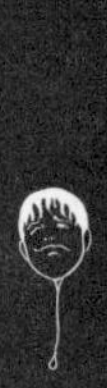

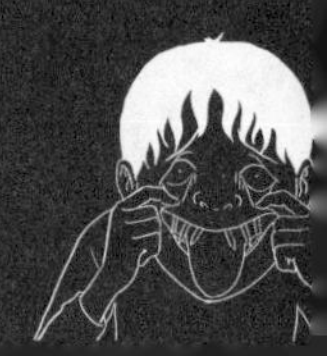

THE CORE OF THIS STORY is the fact that the student Kamei can change her own face into a perfect copy of anyone else's, a characteristic inspired by a chameleon's ability to camouflage itself. When you apply the surprising abilities of reptiles, insects, and animals to human beings—like how I used the idea of a lizard's tail for "Tomie"—you can sometimes get surprisingly interesting results.

Adolescence is a time when you're particularly concerned about how other people see you. I was no exception, and I would occasionally get jealous of my better-looking classmates. I would wonder longingly how much easier life would be if we could trade faces, and Kamei's ability is in part linked to this sort of desire.

Because Kamei has always stolen other people's faces, there is no "real" Kamei. This, too, is an allusion to young people not being confident in their own selves.

In depicting this shape-shifter, I really struggled with how to draw her face changing in a way that would be easy to follow. The final punch line came to me relatively easily, but I was extremely ignorant at the time of copyright and licensing, and caught up in the momentum of the story, I ended up drawing the faces of a number of famous characters. No one came after me for it, so I'm probably all right, but I'm still a bit nervous about it even now.

Sketches of Machida being followed by Kamei and having her face copied. I made Machida a delinquent because I thought I could use that to show how weird and creepy Kamei is when Machida beats her to a pulp and she still sticks to her like glue, as if nothing had happened.

2. Born from a memory of the past: "Bullied"

(First published: *Halloween*, Aug. 1990. Included in *Deserter: Junji Ito Story Collection*)

"BULLIED" IS ABOUT a little girl who becomes aware of sadistic feelings while she's watching a neighborhood boy, and the gradual escalation of her abuse toward him. You could say this story is unique in that nothing mysterious happens despite it being horror. It came about when I decided to expand on a memory that has long weighed on my conscience, and turn it into a manga.

When I was a kid, there was a small park in the neighborhood where I often used to play. I arrived one day to find a little boy I didn't know staring at all the other kids, looking like he wanted to play too. He lived in the old rental house beside the park, and I think his family moved a lot for work.

On another day the boy climbed up to the top of the slide, and the other kids on the ground got all excited, yelling for him to jump down instead of slide. He eventually burst into tears, too scared to jump. His mother came out of their rental house, grabbed the boy, lifted him down from the slide, and then went back to the house with him. She didn't yell at us kids, but rather left the park with a smile on her face. I never saw the boy again, so maybe they moved away soon after.

I don't recall taking part in the bullying myself, so perhaps I merely watched from the sidelines. But the small guilt at not being able to stand up for the boy lingers in my heart to this day.

- *Ordered to jump from the slide, OO [Naoya] is crying, "I'm gonna jump," when his mother comes along. "OO, honey, what are you doing?" Kuriko says, "Ma'am, OO says he's gonna jump."*
- *When he's totally worn out after being bullied too much, she says, "Well, poor you. You're so sad I could almost eat you up." And she bites him.*
- *Even still, OO doesn't stop hanging out with Kuriko. "Why do you keep following me?! It's super annoying!"*
- *And then, when she throws the ball into the yard of a vicious dog and orders him to go get it, he does just that, gets bitten by the dog and is seriously hurt, and moves away.*
- *Place is the park again, now. "The park hasn't changed at all, huh? But I never dreamed I'd run into you. I've never forgotten about you. You were the only one who'd play with me. I really looked up to you. You were always so beautiful."*

"I'm sorry. I was so mean to you... I kept hurting you. When I think about it now, I want to tear out my own heart..."

"You forgive me then..."

Since *Halloween* is a shojo manga magazine, I added elements of romance in consideration of the readership. Kuriko grows up from a little girl into a beautiful woman, and I wanted to draw the intriguing dissonance of her reverting back to a cruel child in the end.

3. Taking a hint from biography: "Deserter"

(First published: *Halloween*, Sept. 1990. Included in *Deserter: Junji Ito Story Collection*)

FOR THIS STORY, I took up the motif of *The Diary of a Young Girl* and the famous Anne Frank story. I'd seen a show on TV talking about how Anne had fallen in love with Peter, a boy whose family was also in hiding with hers in the secret annex. It made a real impression on me, and I wondered if I couldn't rework the idea a bit and turn it into a manga.

I wasn't confident enough to do a story set in another country, though, so I decided to make the setting Japan during the Pacific War. When I considered who would need to live in hiding in Japan at that time, the first thing that came to mind was a man trying to escape conscription. But I later changed this to a deserter for more of an impact, and I had a romantic relationship develop between him and a woman in the family hiding him. Finally, to incorporate some elements of horror, I decided to make the ending an unexpected twist—the deserter had long since died and become a ghost.

When I first got the idea, I intended to draw the period from the Pacific War to the present day (the late eighties). But when I talked with my editor Harada, he pointed out that it might be a bit of a stretch to have the family hide him for forty years without realizing he's a ghost. So at Harada's suggestion, I decided to focus on the Korean War era, five years after the Pacific War. At the time, postwar Japan was booming because of the Korean special procurements, and so I could still depict the contrast between re-ality and the world of the deserter who was convinced it was still wartime, which made it the perfect period for the story.

To learn more about how things were during the war and work out the details of the story and the drawings, I interviewed an older man by the name of Yoshimura who lived next door to my childhood home. I was born eighteen years after the war, so when I was a child, there were still people in my neighborhood who had lived through the war, and traces of conflict remained in buildings here and there.

In the story, the deserter hides in a storehouse next door to the family's residence. I often used to see such storehouses near my parents' house, sometimes even attached to residential homes. The walls of most of them were painted with spiral shapes in black ink. Painting the white plaster walls black would have made them less conspicuous and kept them from being bombed during nighttime air raids. But I think that, because of material shortages, people couldn't paint the entire wall black, so they painted the spirals instead and tried in this way to reduce the brightness of the white walls.

They also used firewood in the kitchen back in the day, with cooking taking place over an open fire. The water for the bath was heated with firewood, too, and because of this, the walls through-out the house would be filthy with black soot. I worked with the drawings in "Deserter" to re-create that dark air of a house during wartime.

★ *Deserter*
1924/Taisho 14
Plan No. 1
· *Deserter lives in attic.*
· *He deserted from XX regiment. He was tortured or something and escaped. He tells someone in the family the detailed story. (He comes out of the attic at night.)*
· *Only gets the evening meal. He's skinny.*
· *Gets his friend to hide him at his house. This friend is the head of his household. (Obviously.)*
· *Is conscripted when he's 18 or 19 in 1942-3.*
· *Thinks the war's still happening. Because the people in the family keep lying to him. Why do they keep lying to him?*
· *Time period is around 1954.*
· *Family makeup*
· *The people in the family have to hate him. And it's not enough for them to just hate him. Reason they need to keep him locked up in the attic → Bad for them if he could leave. In other words, the outside world.*

"Please... don't give me over..."

• Two people deserted. A and F. (Friends)
• One of them (F) twists his ankle and is caught by guards. But the other (A) gets away. After being caught, F is put into confinement, and then sent to the front lines. (After demobilizing, he pretends to be military police and tricks A.)
• Having escaped, A runs to his friend's house in the country. Friend B hides A. Friend's parents are dead, and in addition to A, there's the oldest son, the oldest daughter C, middle daughter D, and youngest daughter E.
• Eventually, C starts to have feelings for A, as does D, but A appears to love C. D despises A. Brother B would have accepted the relationship with C as a friend, but whatever else, A is a deserter. The situation being what it is, brother tells A to be careful. Even still, A and C meet in the attic.
• One day, C says she's going to get food for A, goes out into the field to pull up some potatoes, is caught in machine-gun fire from an American military plane, and dies.
• And then the end of the war comes, but the family continues to keep A locked up in the attic, although they have mixed feelings about it. Thinking of his dead sister, brother couldn't stand it if A were to get out of there and marry some other girl, and he also feels a little bit like C's death was A's fault. He doesn't tell him that the war is over.

・脱走したのは2人　AとF（友人同志）
・途中一人が足をくじいて衛兵につかまる。しかしもう一人（A）は逃げきる。「つかまったFは重営倉に入れられ、後、前線へとばされる。（除隊後、けんぺいをよそおってAをだます）
・逃げきったAはいなかの友人の家へにげこむ。友人Bがかくまう。友人の家族は、両親は死んで兄以下長女C子、次女D子、三女E子の4人家族。
・やがてC子もAに思いをよせるが、AはむしろC子を愛したようだ。D子はAをうらむ。兄BはAとC子との仲をゆるす気でいたが、なにしろA脱走兵、時局も時局だけに、いいろ…でもAとC子は屋根裏であっていた。
・ある日C子はAにたべさせるといってイモを畑からとりにいって米軍の小さな機銃掃射をうけて死亡。
・そして終戦をむかえたが、兄たちは複雑な心境でAを屋根裏にとじこめつづける。それは、死んだC子のことを思うとAがそこから出て他の女と…それがゆるせないのとC子が死んだのはAのせいでもあるような気がすると思っていたので、戦争が終わったことは知らせなかった。

屋根うらべへのかいだん

Stair to attic.
Door →

I drew blueprints for the exterior and interior construction to figure out the layout and shape of the house where the deserter hides. I reflected everything I'd learned in my research in the characters' hairstyles and clothing.

4. Connecting reality and fantasy: "Alley"

(First published: *Halloween*, Mar. 1992. Included in *Alley: Junji Ito Story Collection*)

IN MY HOMETOWN, there are lots of narrow alleys between the houses. We often used to play tag and other games in them as kids, and I thought that maybe I could turn the creepy gloom and almost claustrophobia I felt back then into a manga, which led to me drawing this story. I had the idea that it might be fun if some part of the maze of alleys was connected to another world or if there was a secret road in among them that no one had ever set foot on, and I got to work figuring out the structure of the story.

I was drawing this manga at the same time as "Town of No Roads," which was published in a special issue, so my schedule was grueling. I had actually wanted to make the pages themselves dark in order to highlight the spooky alley atmosphere, but I didn't have the time to draw all that detail, so I submitted it with the white spaces still on the page. I was a bit upset about this. I felt like I'd really messed the story up, and then to my great surprise, it was number one in the reader survey that issue. I've never really gone back and reread this piece, so I still don't know why it landed so well with readers.

I learned from this that I don't need to fill in the space, which was a good lesson to be sure. But even so, if the page is too white, I get anxious, and I end up diligently filling it in later.

Alley

- People endlessly attached to the alley where they used to play, go there all the time. They come even when they get older. (Which is no big deal?) It's nothing but a lane, but it's a somehow memorable alley that captivates people.
- The protagonist has a tendency to put on weight, but still brings home sweet treats (fruit and things). Throws these out the window into the alley. → Tosses them toward drawings of faces.
- There's a secret window in the protagonist's room, and when you open it, the alley is outside. But for some reason, the alley's an empty space, blocked by buildings and locked up by some official. The only passage to it is the window in her room. The space is forgotten by everyone but her. (Her room is on the second floor.)
- She decides that it's for her alone. She can bring her secrets here. She draws a classmate she hates on the opposite wall, harasses it → how to harass it → drawing the face uglier, etc.
- They moved here when she was little, and she found the hidden window in her room. Her parents don't know about the space, either. She hangs a rope ladder and climbs down. There are lots of drawings of hated friends she's scribbled (she's been drawing since she was a child).
- Someone (with several others in tow) comes to visit, nostalgic for the place they used to play when they were little. But it's closed off, so they come to ask if there's a way in. They share fond memories of playing there. Because it was an interesting place in terms of terrain. The protagonist chases them away.

The drawings come off the wall. They play in the alley. They talk about killing the protagonist. They draw weapons on the walls, pull them off, and try to attack the protagonist. Or they draw a rope and try to climb up. They draw a picture of the protagonist, lure her out, and slaughter her. Tear her limb from limb. (No blood and guts, almost like she's cut with an eraser.)

They all used to play together in this alley when they were kids. But the protagonist was left out.

Why was the alley closed off in the first place? Because it's dangerous. Why is it dangerous? There's a hole that leads underground, and a couple people wandered into it and disappeared. (Story from the protagonist's childhood. They were the protagonist's childhood friends. After that, this alley was blocked off with a wall. They could just fill in the hole, so why the wall?)

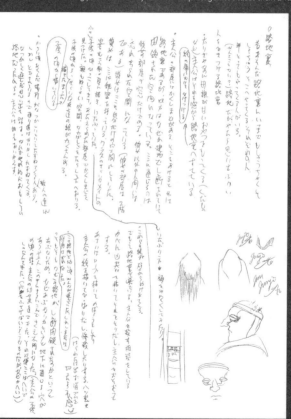

At first, the story was that a baseball falls into a sewer in the alley, and the boys who go looking for it disappear. The last scene with the stains coming off the wall was something I came up with and added later.

5. Destroying real-world balance: "Town of No Roads"

(First published: *Nemurenu Yoru no Kimyona Hanashi* [Strange Stories in the Sleepless Night], vol. 6, 1992. Included in *Alley: Junji Ito Story Collection*)

FOR THE MOST PART, towns are made up of buildings and roads. What would happen if the roads disappeared and houses reigned supreme? This question became the basis for a story idea.

Without roads, people would have to travel through other people's homes. Private space would be effectively eliminated. This chain of thought was what led me to the theme of losing all privacy. It's often the case with me that the theme of the work comes later like this.

Because I'd been commissioned for a large number of pages with this story, the idea of houses taking over the town wouldn't have been enough in and of itself. So I pulled together some additional plot points and parked them in this one story.

The Aristotle incident at the beginning originally came from something about experiments with dreams in a book I read once. While a person slept, another person provided some stimulus to the sleeper, which apparently led to the sleeper having a dream related to the stimulus. To take up one example, after stroking the cheek of a sleeping person with a feather several times, they woke the person up and asked what they were dreaming about, and the sleeper answered that they dreamed of being attacked by a bird.

This intrigued me, and I wondered if you could get someone to have feelings for you by whispering, "I love you" over and over in their ear while they were sleeping. I named this game "Aristotle" in the manga because I'd read that the philosopher Aristotle had also studied dreams.

By having characters sneak into bedrooms without permission and manipulate other people's dreams, I managed to connect several episodes in the story to my original theme of privacy. In that sense, everything up to the protagonist Saiko arriving in the town overwhelmed by houses could be said to be one coherent, consistent story, but it does develop rather quickly, so that might not be clear every step of the way.

Yoshiharu Tsuge's "Screw Style" was also a bit of an influence on the mood of the town with no roads in this story. Tsuge depicts people calmly going about their business in what seems like a dream world where the logic of the real world doesn't apply. A bit of this surreality also hangs in the air in "Town of No Roads."

Town of No Roads
- Go into this town for some reason. Families peer at Saiko. 1–20. 20 pages.
- She follows someone. Or someone shows her the way. (XX halfway) 21–26. 6 pages.
Runs away from home, goes to aunt's house.
- Residents stop her. Rumors of Eyeball Jack. 27–40, 14 pages.
- As she goes forward, strange residents, monsters, plants, lawless areas, cars (pinned in cars).
- Encounter (showdown?) with Eyeball Jack. Eyeball Jack death. 41–60. 20 pages.
- (Goes out onto roof or) river. Plots escape via river. Monster attacks.
- (Split into two)
  ↕
- Witness house being built. Mysterious shadow is building a house. 61–70. 10 pages.

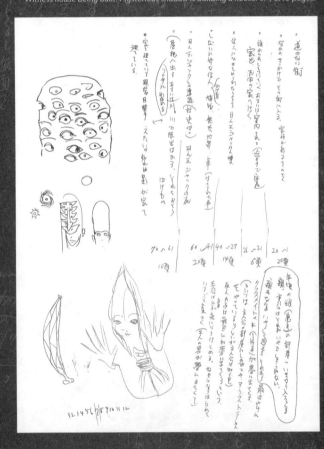

Parent suddenly coming into the room of a girl (boy) of a certain age. The protagonist can't stand this. Feels like they don't need parents and all this garbage. And lately, classmate K (K-ko) has been showing up in their dreams a lot. (He's sneaking into the protagonist's room and doing the Aristotle thing, but the protagonist doesn't know this.) Friend A-ko mentions how L is showing up in her dreams lately. Protagonist starts to take notice of K (Kishimoto). Realizes she's starting to like him. (Two boys show up in her dream.)

Meets a family not wearing masks. They look haggard. She visits her aunt's house. She asks why she's not wearing a mask, and her aunt says it's too annoying. Instead, she's forced to feel the loss of her privacy. People come in nonstop in their outdoor footwear. She thought she could just stay on the second floor, but people come through the windows upstairs, too. And then they move in. Random people come to the houses that make up the roads and settle in. She doesn't know where these mysterious groups come from. (Or people are already living in the houses that are built.) She can't go shutting the door to protect her privacy. A house like that would block traffic. (They poke holes and peer in.)

"Why would you stay in a place like this?" "Losing my privacy gave me an even greater humanity. We should get rid of privacy. We get depressed because we carry around secrets we can't tell anyone. We should open up our hearts. Take a look. We're all extremely healthy now. This town is an amazing environment for us."

But no matter how you look at them, these people all look unhealthy. They seem worn out. And they pepper Saiko with questions. They tell her they put everything out on display, so she should reveal all, too. (And in exchange, they entertain themselves peeping and get their fill of other people's privacy.) 45 pages.

• Somehow manages to run away.
• Saiko is worried about her beloved aunt and searches for her desperately.
• She encounters people who have wandered into this town. They say the deeper you go, the stranger it is, and they saw some weird people. She asks what kind of people, and they say, weird at any rate. Mysterious people come from who knows where and move into the houses built on the roads in this town. Or that the faces of the people who have lost their privacy change into something like masks. 50 pages.
• What exactly has happened to her aunt and uncle? "I think it's around here." Aunt's house is in this area. Because a familiar tree is inside a house, and part of a door is a familiar wall.

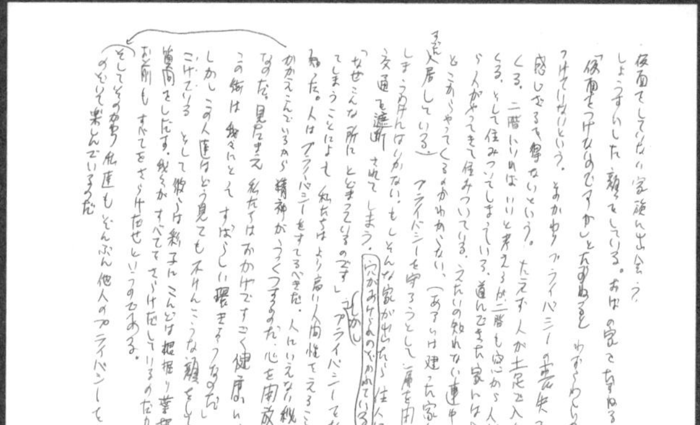

仮面をしていない家族に出会う。ようすいした顔をしている。おばの家でたずねると「仮面をつけないのですか」とたずねるとわずらわしいからつけていないという。そのかわりプライバシーの喪失を感じざるを得ないという。たえず人が土足で入りこんでくる。二階にいればいいと考えるが二階も窓から人が入ってくる。そして住みついてしまっている。道んできた家にはどこからか人がやってきて住みついている。えたいの知れない連中でどこからやってくるのかわからない。(あるいは建った家に人がすでに入居している。)プライバシーを守ろうとして扉を閉してしまうわけにはいかない。もしそんな家が出来たら住人は交通を遮断されてしまう。(穴をあけてのぞいている)

「なぜこんな所にとどまっているのです」「プライバシーをなくしてしまうことによって私たちはより高い人間性をえることを知った。人はプライバシーをすてるべきだ。人にいえない秘密をかかえこんでいるから精神がうっくつするのだ。心を開放すべきなのだ。見たまえ、私たちはおかげですごく健康になっている。この街は我々にとってすばらしい環境なのだ」

しかしこの人達はどう見ても不けんこうな顔をしている。つかれている。そして彼らは彩子にこんどは根掘り葉掘り質問をしだす。我々がすべてをさらけだしているのだからお前もすべてをさらけだせというのである。

(そしてそのかわり私達もぞんぶん他人のプライバシーをのぞいて楽しんでいるのだ) 45頁

○なんとかその場は逃げだす
○彩子は大好きなおばの事が心配になってさがす。
○途中この街にまよいこんでしまった人達と出会う。彼らはこの街の奥に異常で異様な人間を見たという。どんな人間かときくと、とにかく異様なものだという。
この町には道路の上に建った家にどこからかやってきて住みついているという。えたいのしれない者が、あるいはプライバシーを失った人間が仮面のような顔にかわっている者もあるという。 50頁
○おばさん夫婦は一体どうしてしまったのだろう
「このあたりだと思う」おばの家はこのあたりだ。なぜなら見覚えのある木が家の中にあって片方の壁は見覚えのあるへいだ

The strange residents that appear in "Town of No Roads." The multiple eyes are a metaphor for an even greater infringement of privacy. I also used these monsters to fill out the long 70 pages.

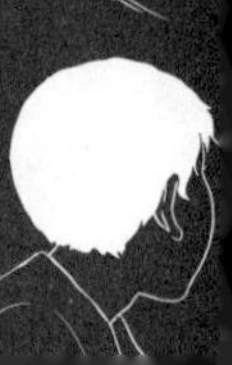

6. Conceived in a dream: "Hanging Blimp"

(First published: *Halloween*, Jan. 1994. Included in *Shiver: Junji Ito Selected Stories*)

I WAS STANDING ALL BY MYSELF in an unusually large airport. Suddenly, I looked out at the sky, and I saw something in the distance flying toward me. When it got closer, I saw that it was a doll with long, yellow hair with a rope in a U shape hanging down from it. The doll was charging me with ferocious speed to try and snag my neck in its rope. In fear for my life, I ran, trying desperately to escape, but the doll finally caught up with me, and... This dream I had as a boy was the start for the story "Hanging Blimp."

At first, I had the picture of a corpse with a rope around its neck hanging from a regular black rubber balloon. It drifted through the sky like a UFO, and some unfathomable incident happened when it appeared over town. I wanted to draw it as some sort of ominous portent.

However, absolutely nothing came to mind for the incomprehensible event at the heart of it all. I wrestled with a bunch of ideas until I had the thought that it could be interesting if the blimp itself tried to hang people. And rather than a single black balloon, a group of them would attack in formation.

Even so, the story was weak. It didn't jump off the page when I tried illustrating it, and I was having trouble thinking of other elements to build it up. So I grappled with the whole thing some more, and just when I was sick of thinking about it and went to take a bath, I suddenly had the idea of giving the balloons human faces. These blimps would be like dopplegängers, and they would attack and hang the person with the same face. This would be more visually interesting than a plain round balloon, and it would also make the balloon attack inevitable and inescapable.

Yes, this! I left the bathroom, buoyed with delight, and started in on the script at once, while I was still excited about it.

I devoted a fair bit of attention to even the most trivial details to set the stage for this story. For instance, I chose to link the blimp face and the person's own face to force the protagonist into a corner and remove ways to resolve the issue. If the balloon got shot and deflated, the person would also die. For the same reason, I decided the line attached to the blimp was made of steel so that it couldn't be cut with scissors.

In my personal opinion, you can't neglect these kinds of little things if you want to create an aura of urgency and fear. If I hadn't given these details the thought that I did, readers would have found any number of ways to escape the horror—"They could just shoot the balloon," "They could just cut the rope"—and the panicking protagonist would end up looking foolish. One important point in creating a story is to build limits into it that force the protagonist to do what you want them to do.

Hanging Blimp

• Shared anxiety among group members. Anyone who does something wrong turns into a hanging blimp and flies off.
Or there is a person who's sending out the hanging blimps.
• Several hanging blimps float up into the sky.
★ It's like the blimp is alive. A rope for hanging people dangles from it, and it floats in the sky like it's alive. (Several) When they find people, they swoop in to loop the rope around the person's neck, yanking them up and hanging them.
★ Try to pop them with a rifle.
★ Anxious group and the hanging blimps.
• Best friend goes missing and then appears as a hanging blimp. (Friend left a note behind and apparently went off somewhere to kill themself.) Why did the friend decide to commit suicide? But there's a rumor that it was murder. And the blimp is small, and after it's popped, can't tell what kind of gas was in it.
• Is someone maybe controlling them from somewhere?

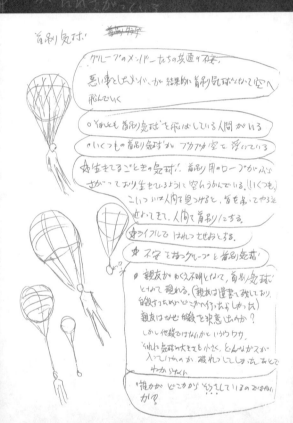

• When the police fire a pistol at a balloon chasing the person, the balloon deflates and drops to the ground, but scarily, the person also deflates just like the balloon, right down to their face. After that, they can't shoot the balloons down anymore. Because the person will also die. What's even scarier is that if you shoot a blimp with the person hanging from it, instead of deflating, it gushes blood from the spot where it was hit.
• Incident where someone takes advantage of this and pops the balloon of someone they hate.
• Some blimps also pop on their own.
• Crazed hunter shoots down balloons indiscriminately. This causes the heads of many people to deflate, and they die.

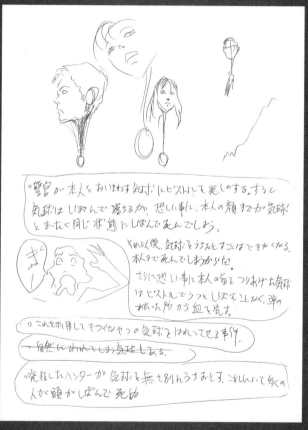

The rotting corpses hanging from the blimps drift through the sky forever. In that sense, you could say they're a kind of zombie. In the story, the younger brother bravely races out of the house to get food, but anyone who says they'll be back soon is guaranteed not to return alive, a staple of the zombie genre.

7. Something that should not exist does: "Tombs"
(First published: *Halloween*, July 1994. Included in *Tombs: Junji Ito Story Collection*)

THIS STORY IS A BIT OF A THRILLER. A brother and sister duo hit the younger sister of a close friend with their car, killing her, and then conspire to keep the body from being discovered. It drew on suspense films like Hitchcock's work or *Purple Noon*, the famous 1960 film starring actor Alain Delon.

Graves are normally in the mountains or outside the city, but I thought it might be interesting if they were in a place where they shouldn't be, like the middle of the road or someone's house. It seemed to me that the images in the manga would have more punch if something you expect to see in a certain place has disappeared. Or, if something suddenly turns up where you don't expect to see it.

The decision to turn dead bodies into stone pillars was heavily influenced by Yasutaka Tsutsui's short story "Standing Woman," about a criminal who is given the death penalty, planted in the ground, and gradually transforms into a tree. The idea that the corpse must remain untouched until it has completely turned into a stone pillar, or else the soul of the dead won't know peace, comes from my own experience with rhinoceros beetle pupae as a child. If you disrupt the pupa, the beetle emerges deformed.

At first, I thought there would be tombs all over the town, and the last scene would have the protagonist looking down on them from atop the mountain and seeing some kind of meaningful signal like crop circles. But I couldn't make the idea work, and I gave up on it.

8. The desire to escape death: "The Long Dream"

(First published: *Nemuki*, Jan. 1997. Included in *Shiver: Junji Ito Selected Stories*)

WHEN I WAS LITTLE, my oldest sister told me a fascinating tale. Even if a dream feels like it's been going on for a long time, it's nothing more than a momentary blip in the real world. In other words, your brain is merely hallucinating that you're spending however many minutes or hours inside of the dream.

Since my sister merely heard this story from someone else, I'm not sure how true it is. But it stayed with me. It fascinated me that real time and subjective time could be different lengths.

Later, when I was writing flash fiction in junior high, I suddenly remembered her telling me this and wrote half of a short story based on this idea, about a person on the verge of death who is put into a special machine and made to dream an eternal dream. I thought that if you could be made to believe you were having a dream that never ended immediately before your death, then it was functionally the same as eternal life.

The story ended up unfinished, but I couldn't quite let go of the idea, so I sat on it for ages, thinking to make it into a manga one day. Then, when I had a relatively free period in my schedule, I spent two months reconstructing it into what turned out to be "The Long Dream." Because a mysterious machine would make the science fiction elements of the story too strong, I changed it so that some unknown substance in the brain is what causes the characters to have endless dreams.

The theme of the work is eternal life, but at the root of this is the fear of death (nothingness). At the start, hospital patient Mami is depicted as being abnormally afraid of death, and during my boyhood, I was also terribly scared of dying. Mami's line "I don't want to become nothing" parallels my thinking exactly. I don't believe in a soul or a world after death.

In order to make the passage of time obvious, I decided to age Mukoda by the number of years he spends in his dreams. In reality, a dream is nothing more than a momentary phenomenon, but if the brain is hallucinating the passing of time, then it seems logical that the body might also be similarly affected.

Personally, though, I don't think our dreams are instantaneous.

→ ★ *It's like living forever in a monotonous, creepy world.*

To show that an astonishing amount of time has passed for Mukoda, I created a future person evolved over some thousands of years from now for his external appearance. In the end, he becomes petrified, weathered away, and crumbles to dust.

160

→ Or he hallucinates that he's dreaming eternally, and even awake, he's in the dream world. What he sees while in the real world is the world of the dream.
"...shimaunda." [incomplete sentence]
"Due to the effect of the medication, you absolutely will not have a dream that comes with anxiety."

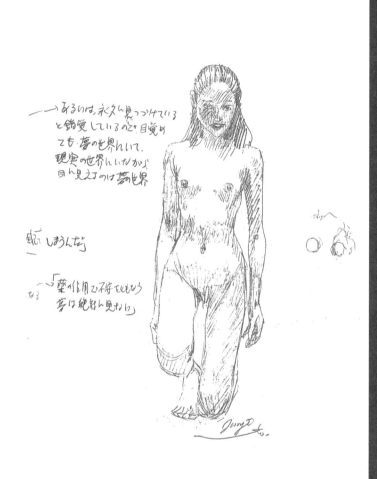

9. Geometric patterns from ancient times: *Uzumaki*

(First published: *Big Comic Spirits*, No. 7, 1998–No. 39, 1999)

UZUMAKI IS THE FIRST long-form manga I attempted. Although it is a longer story, I structured it so that each chapter stands alone. I'd used this format before with *Lovesickness*, but this was the first time I'd drawn a manga where I didn't know how the story would end.

The sequence of events leading up to me drawing *Uzumaki* is a bit complicated. Ever since my debut, I'd published my work in Asahi Sonorama's *Halloween* or *Nemuki*, but in 1995, *Halloween* stopped publishing. So my editor Harada apparently tried to do some PR for me in the final issue, writing something along the lines of "Ito's going to be out of a job here, so please, someone, give him something to do." Seeing this, Ichiro Nakaguma, an editor at Shogakukan's *Big Comic Spirits*, came to me with an offer to do a story for the magazine. (I asked Harada about this later, and he said he had no memory of writing any such thing. I still don't know who was telling the truth.)

To be honest, I had absolutely no idea at the time what sort of magazine *Big Comic Spirits* was. So I bought a copy and read it, only to discover that it was a very big magazine with a number of prominent artists drawing for it. And then, belatedly, I understood the enormity of the offer I'd received.

After a period of indecision, I tried to decline the offer, saying that I very much appreciated the opportunity, but that I thought

I couldn't manage a whole series at my current level of skill. But Nakaguma kept at me and managed to persuade me somehow— he even took me to a hot springs resort. And so, in the end, I accepted the job on the condition that I would only draw a chapter every four weeks.

And so I got to work on drawing *Uzumaki*. But the process was different from the one-shots I'd done up to that point. While the story took on the shape of discrete chapters, it was still a long-form story with all those pieces connected into one larger whole. Which meant I needed to really hammer out the basic themes and overall setting in the early stages.

I decided to make the setting a town where slightly odd things happen, a motif I'd happily used any number of times in the past. The problem was what the odd things were going to be.

I first conceived of an endless row house. It would go on and on in an absurd way like the Great Wall of China. The background for me coming up with this idea was my own experience living in one of a pair of row houses when I was small. If the houses were connected, then the relationship with the neighbors would also be intense, and there would be that much more drama. If I made a succession of row houses the stage, I figured I'd be able to draw all kinds of people and relationships.

But I soon slammed up against a wall. Without a bird's-eye view, readers wouldn't be able to perceive the scale of the Great Wall of China row housing. And the farther away I set the camera to highlight the scale of it all, the finer the line work would be, and the images would lose their punch.

How could I keep the absurd length while still having the images make an impact? The answer I arrived at to balance these two elements was the shape of a spiral.

This might have also been due to the influence of a certain famous gag manga character, but in the beginning, I had this image of a spiral pattern being somehow idiotic and funny. But as I drew all kinds of varied spirals with my pencil, I came to feel that the shape had a particular creepiness to it, and I arrived at the conclusion that it could very well be a subject of horror depending on how I drew it.

The spiral is also a pattern from ancient times, found on Jomon pottery from thousands of years ago, and you can really feel its ubiquity and mystique. What if the spiral pattern held some deeper meaning, like it was connected to some truth of the universe?

I decided to make the theme of this manga "spirals." The editorial department soon sent me all kinds of reference materials on spirals, and these revealed to me objects and events with a spiral shape, such as fingerprints, snails, fish eyes, typhoons, springs, black holes, and more. I took these as motifs for each of the chapters.

As a bit of a digression, while the series was being published, another publisher approached me. They were making a Nostradamus calendar, and they wanted me to do the illustrations. Nostradamus was a European astrologer during the Renaissance, and one of his prophecies was that the king of terror would descend from the sky in July 1999. Because of this, all of Japan was in a panic, worried that the world might end in July.

The calendar job (which I accepted) was filled with this kind of fin de siècle thinking, ending abruptly on the final page of July 1999. So I got a bunch of books on Nostradamus, and while reading them, I stumbled upon an idea called the butterfly effect. Put simply, when a butterfly flaps its wings somewhere on Earth, the breeze generated has an effect on a series of different events. This flapping can even eventually change the future so much that it causes a hurricane on the other side of the world. I took inspiration from this for the hurricane scene in *Uzumaki*. (The calendar project fell apart in the end, but I'm grateful to it nonetheless.)

The thing I struggled with throughout the serialization was the fact that I couldn't kill the protagonist Kirie. I actually wanted to have her as a major supporting character and not chasing danger, but Nakaguma told me that readers wouldn't connect to the protagonist unless she faced some kind of crisis, so I had to come up with some predicament for her every chapter. I remember racking my brain over how to save her in situations where she would normally have died.

Spirits series
• Town that toys with the residents. Various phenomena.
• Creepy siren sounds. Fire, tsunami, landslide.
• Friend wants to get out of this town. Escape. "Bad environment." In contrast, people who say it's a wonderful place. Lots of people moving there. The protagonist loves this town.
x Friend is protagonist? Storyteller is supporting role?
• Front is deep mountains. There is a gloomy sea in the background.
• When the siren sounds, it brings about some kind of change in each of the town residents. Friend's personality changes when they hear the siren.
• Friends slowly disappear. Apparently escaped town.
• Friend has a mean little sister.
• Friend has unfinished business in this town. There's a beautiful girl (girlfriend).
• Abnormally long row house. Ecosystem of strange people living in the row housing. Old building, structure to protect from something?
• Extremely shy person who craves the limelight. Climbs the tower of own house at night and strikes a pose.
• Mysterious machines drop down all over. Machines that use the decomposition of organic matter as an energy source.
• Feels like they're always being watched.
• There's a murderer.
• There are a lot of weird fan groups formed for extracurricular activities.
• There's a strange tunnel, and inside it, there are many holes in the shape of people. There are people in the town who are the exact right shape for those holes.
• Of the clubs, there's one called the pioneer club, and they hate and fear and try to escape this town. This group. But while they find fault with this town, they never seem to make it out.

Graveyard

Crematory

Tunnel

長屋は渦状一列
帆心かけ左巻を
Spiral of row houses
counterclockwise
toward the center

中心に
くすかある.?
What is at
the center?

漁港
Harbor

黒い灯台
Black lamp

隆うつな海
Gloomy sea

While I drew spirals in my notebook, I was on fire with the desire to solve the mystery of the spiral that has bewitched people since ancient days and the fires of ambition. But in the end, I didn't manage to solve anything.

10. Doppelgänger hole: "The Enigma of Amigara Fault"

(First published: *Spirits Comics IKKI*, No. 1, 2000. Included in *Gyo* and *Venus in the Blind Spot*)

IN "HANGING BLIMP," it was a person's face, but this work takes as its motif a person's shape.

One sunny day, I was walking along, and my shadow was projected onto the road. Naturally, the shape of this shadow was uniquely mine, different from anyone else's. So maybe when you're shown your own silhouette, you instinctively know that it's yours.

I feel like my work during my days as a dental technician is also a reason why my eye turned to shapes. To create prostheses (metal fillings and crowns), you pour melted liquid metal into a mold made in the shape of the patient's tooth, and I think that this experience was partially what led me to the idea for this story. The concept of a doppelgänger and the image of a mold came together, giving me the idea of a hole in a mountainside that was a perfect fit for a person's own body shape.

As a reason for people to go into these holes, I first thought of making the hole itself have a narcotic appeal. But I wanted to see something even scarier than that, and I thought it would be more fun to draw someone who went into the hole against their own will. It's maybe along the lines of picking at a scab while knowing that you really shouldn't.

Person-shaped hole. It goes all the way back, still in the person's shape. Looking closely, see holes in all sizes. There's one your size, so you go into it.

Story of human-shaped hole in that tunnel → Prison Gate Tunnel
It's a hole for torture. As you go farther in, you get turned upside down or your body stretches out, but you can't go back. If you can keep going and make it out, you're innocent.

人の形した穴。人型のまま奥の方まで続いている。
よくみると大小さまざまな穴
自分のサイズの穴があるので 入っていく。

例のトンネルの人型の穴の話 → 獄門トンネル
ごうもんのための穴だった。進むにつれて上下逆さんになったり
体がのびていったりする が ひきかえすわけには いかない。進んで外へ出れば 無罪

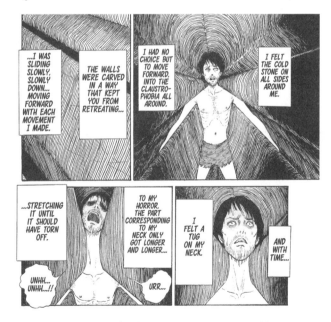

The person-shaped holes were made for torture in ancient times, so I thought up the name "Prison Gate Tunnel." For the structure with the walls of blades facing backward, I took a hint from the tips of green foxtail.

11. Starting with the ending: Gyo

(First published: *Big Comic Spirits*, No. 50, 2001–No. 20, 2002)

THE MOTIF IS THE MOVIE *JAWS*. One thing that I'm scared of is sharks. But no matter how monsterlike a shark is, as long as you don't go into the ocean, you don't have to worry about being eaten. But what would happen if the sharks came up onto land? This story grew out of that thought.

With *Gyo*, right from the beginning, I had an ending that I wanted to draw. The machines get into formation and proceed toward their target. After this picture popped up in my mind, I thought I would give the story the title *The Death-Stench Creeps*. (My editor nixed this, though, so it ended up being *Gyo*.) With this ending in mind, I had to think backward and figure out how the story would get there.

To start with, in order to come onto land, the fish would have to walk on their own somehow. And for that, they would need some kind of mechanism. I decided to attach crab-leg machines to the fish which were slightly reminiscent of a living creature. I also decided that the pistons of these machines would fire because of the pressure of decomposition gases coming from corpses infected with an unknown bacteria, which would give them the dynamic force for walking.

But they wouldn't surprise, much less scare, if all they did was walk. In order to make readers feel fear, the machines needed a will of their own; they needed to go after the main character and other people.

Here, I added an evil will to the decomposition gas itself and made it so that in addition to fish, it would take over the bodies of elephants, lions, and even human beings. Thus, the story of *Gyo* would unfold like a pandemic movie.

When it came to the visuals for the fish walking on land, I was quite strongly influenced by H.R. Giger, a Swiss artist who did the modeling design for the famous movie *Alien*. I think the mechanical life-forms he drew, fusing human beings and machines through wiring, are extremely alluring, boasting a somehow indescribable terror and eroticism.

Of course, I couldn't simply copy Giger's style. I drew with a strong personal interest in the transformation, fusion, division, and destruction of the human body. I'll leave the reason for this to my general remarks later in this chapter, but I do feel that the transformation of the human body is not simply to shock the reader, but rather has roots in a more primitive fear of our own selves as humans.

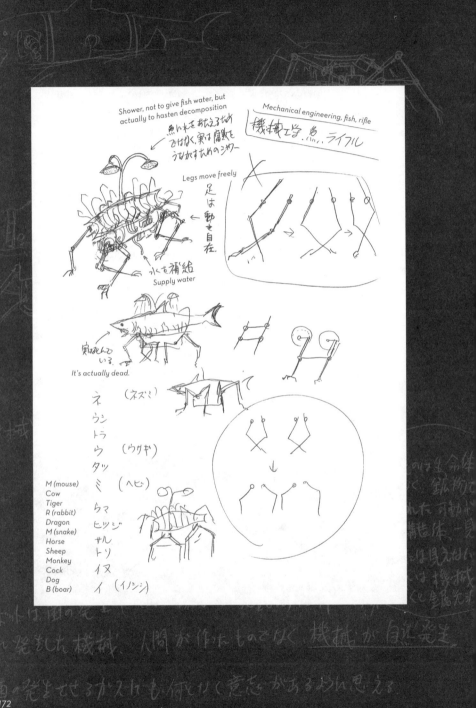

Shower, not to give fish water, but actually to hasten decomposition

魚に水をあたえるため ではなく、実は腐敗を うながすためのシャワー

Mechanical engineering, fish, rifle

機械工学、魚、ライフル

Legs move freely

足は動き自在。

水くを補給
Supply water

実は死んでいる。
It's actually dead.

ネ　（ネズミ）
ウシ
トラ
ウ　（ウサギ）
タツ
ミ　（ヘビ）

M (mouse)
Cow
Tiger　　ウマ
R (rabbit)　ヒツジ
Dragon　サル
M (snake)　トリ
Horse
Sheep　イヌ
Monkey
Cock　イ　（イノシシ）
Dog
B (boar)

172

Demon legs (creepy machines)

· *Find a strange mechanical leg in the mountains. Shower is attached to it.*
Thanks to his invention mania, I (girl) try to understand machines, which I'm not great at...
But she can't put a different machine of the same shape on the body, and it walks around clanging. It is showered from above.
· *Finds a trail of the small legs on small fish walking around, and anxiety starts to spread. Eventually, the sharks come up onto land. But these fish die before too long (failure in water supply). It seems the final objective is not the fish on land. Whales also come up onto the land, but they're too heavy, so the machinery breaks on the shore, and the whales flop over, knocked down by the waves.*
· *A mechanical engineering student is suspected, but he commits suicide.*
· *Mysterious person.*
· *Something attached to mysterious opportunity (several)*
· *When she fiddles with it, the machine needle part digs into her finger, and she screams. The machine is equipped, cradling her finger. (Or her arm, leg, etc.)*
· *Warning goes out that if you find a machine, you shouldn't touch it and instead bring it to the nearest police station right away.*
· *A mysterious tunnel. Mysterious machines come out of it one after the other.*
· *The tunnel's not currently in use. The protagonists explore it.*
· *Mysterious laboratory. Protagonists sneak into the large yard.*
· *At this opportunity, also reacts to sashimi, pork, beef, and other raw meat. When they put raw meat on the machine, it digs in, starts walking, and the little machines, etc., quickly run away somewhere.*

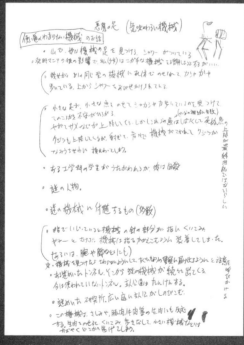

I initially thought of doing a design with a shower attached to hasten the decomposition of the flesh. But then I thought that the machine element would be too strong that way, and I wouldn't be able to mislead the reader (to make them think these were fish that had grown legs), so I scrapped the idea.

12. Embodying the invisible: "Earthbound"

(First published: *Nemuki*, May 2003. Included in *Smashed: Junji Ito Story Collection*)

IN THIS STORY, people become unable to move away from the scene of their crime, bound to the spot by their awareness of that crime (guilt). The theme is just as it seems: crime and punishment. It's a surprisingly socially aware work for me.

When faced with murder, bullying, or abuse, I think all of us are filled with righteous indignation at the horrible senselessness of it. On the other hand, we also assume the perpetrator must be tormented by an awareness of their crime to some degree. I wanted to depict the weight of this guilt in a form that was visible, and the result was "Earthbound."

At the thumbnail stage, however, I realized that like with "Tombs," the details were quite similar to Yasutaka Tsutsui's "Standing Woman." I remember really struggling to try and get away from that, to differentiate my story from "Standing Woman." It also felt a little simplistic to have protagonist Asano's attacker turn out to be her boss, and that never sat quite right with me. I do have some lingering regrets with this one.

→ *Were they caught by ghosts bound to that place?*

The ghost will be bound to the spot, but the person can see it from time to time while they're still alive.
"He's going to be bound in that spot as a spirit."
· *At first, they think he can't move because of his beloved dog, and then a hand comes up from the ground and holds him down.*

· *The boy is steeped in memories of a certain period in the past.*
· *The earthbound do something in that spot. Or something is generated in that spot.*

· *Before long, more and more people are saying they're no longer able to move from a place they have some kind of emotional attachment to.*
· *Some people scream and cry—"Get me out of here!!" But even if someone tries to take them away, they don't budge.*
· *Before long, the earthbound grab on to people who come close and don't let go.*
★ *Some can break free from the attachment, and these people are able to leave the place. (How do they succeed in cutting off the attachment?)*

- その土地の自縛霊んつかまっちゃうんか？

  自縛霊かできる様が、本人が生きているうちが見る事ができる。

  「彼はあの場所で地縛霊んなるのよ。」

- 最初愛犬がいない事かけいっかと思っていたら、地面から手が出ておさえられていた。

  - 彼はふとある時期過去の思い出んひたる。

  - 自縛者は、その場所で何かをする。あるいはその場所に何かが発生する。

- そのうち 自分が何らかの思い入れの ある場所 から 動けなくなるという人々が どんどん 増えていた。

- 人によっては「私をここから 連れだして！！」と泣きさけんでいる人もいる。しかし連れだそうとしても、テコでも動かない。

- そのうち自縛者達は、近寄ってきた人を 捕まえて、はなさなくなる。

★ 中には、思いを断ち切る者もいて、そういう人はその場所から立ち去る事ができる。(彼はどうやって思いを断ち切る事に成功したのか？)

We have the idea of spirits bound to specific places, but I thought it would be interesting if living people ended up like those spirits, and this was the starting point for the story.

13. Developed from a single imagined landscape:
"Billions Alone"

(First published: *Big Comic Spirits*, No. 2, 2004. Included in *Venus in the Blind Spot*)

WHEN I'M WORKING OUT THE STRUCTURE of a story, I often find my way into it through a visual image, as I did with "Billions Alone." I built the story around one mental image—corpses abandoned in a river, literally strung together, a strange object. (As to why this image popped into my head, I can't really explain that myself.)

I also frequently add the theme of the story later, while I'm drawing, as a postscript of sorts. With this work, I decided the theme was connection, as in my initial conception. I also came up with the ironic element that people become so frightened of being killed by some mysterious group and bound by thread hand and foot to strangers, that they actually grow less and less trusting of and compassionate toward other people (weaker emotional connections).

When I put it like this, it perhaps sounds like I predicted the current loneliness of our social media society, but I could never have imagined this back then. The story was published in 2004, a time when users of the internet textboard 2channel (currently 5channel) and social media sites like MIXI were rapidly proliferating. Young *hikikomori* (social recluses) were becoming a societal issue, and the term NEET (not in education, employment, or training) was being taken up with great frequency by the media. I myself started to use the internet during this period, and I included several references along these lines in my work.

Looking back on it now, I wish I had put a little more into developing the story leading up to the conclusion. At the thumbnail stage, I had protagonist Michio get a call from Natsuko, who he has feelings for, so he goes to her house, where he discovers that she and her parents have been murdered and their bodies sewn together. That was the ending, no twists or turns. But my editor asked me to rework it so there's a little more of a surprise, and we landed on the current ending. So really, it was my editor's idea.

I think it's better than the ending I came up with initially, but a small part of me can't help but feel it's unnatural, almost forced, like it was drawn simply as an afterthought. If I'd had the time, I would have liked to have laid down some foreshadowing for this conclusion.

The title I first gave it was "The Case of the Composite Murders."
But my editor was a big no on that, so we settled on "Billions Alone," words I'd scribbled down in the thumbnails.

14. Consideration from a thoroughly scientific perspective: *Remina*

(First published: *Big Comic Spirits Special Edition Casual*, No. 1, 2004–No. 6, 2005)

I DREW THIS BECAUSE OF A SUGGESTION from my editor at *Big Comics Spirits*, Nakaguma. "Ito-san, how about a story about a planet that eats stars?"

I gave the planet the name of a girl, Remina, and decided on a story where this planet brings about a grave crisis for the Earth. However, I thought that the idea of this planet coming to eat Earth alone wouldn't be enough for a series, so I added a witch-hunting element, a group of people who attack Remina because they believe killing the girl with the same name as the planet will allow them to evade its approach. It goes without saying that Go Nagai's *Devilman* was an influence.

The Remina torture scene that appears in the middle of the story also came from a sincere request on the part of Nakaguma. Apparently, he was expecting some kind of extremely erotic and grotesque torture, the fullest manifestation of the perversion of horror manga artist Junji Ito.

But the torture scene I actually drew was received quite poorly. "You always draw such weird manga," he said. "So I figured you were for sure a bit kinky. But you're surprisingly normal, hm?" Which begs the question of what exactly he had been imagining...

The scale of this story is quite large, so I made sure to keep the laws of physics in mind while I worked on it. A planet is basically the same as a ping-pong ball floating in a spaceship without gravity. If an enormous external force is applied, it will without a doubt be easily knocked flying. There's a scene in the story where the planet Remina licks the Earth with an enormous tongue, and I thought that the Earth would spin at high speed, generating a strong centrifugal force, and everything on the surface would be flung up into the air. This led to the development in the second half of tag in midair.

Additionally, because it is set in the future, I tried to imagine and draw my own future cityscape. But later, I read Naoki Urasawa's *Pluto*, and I truly regretted how loose I had been with the details of my future city.

Spirits
Based on space horror idea from Nakaguma

(Nakaguma's sketch)
To Mr. Ito.
Lustily →
Earth
Like it's really licking it...

Planet-eating planet
Planet Mariko
Mariko Oguro   Tsuneo Oguro

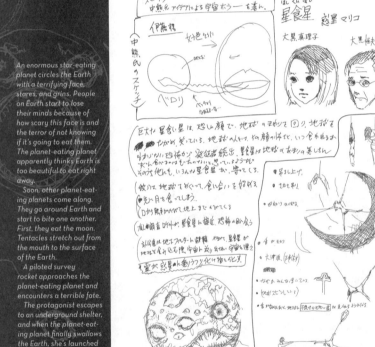

An enormous star-eating planet circles the Earth with a terrifying face, stares, and grins. People on Earth start to lose their minds because of how scary this face is and the terror of not knowing if it's going to eat them. The planet-eating planet apparently thinks Earth is too beautiful to eat right away.

Soon, other planet-eating planets come along. They go around Earth and start to bite one another. First, they eat the moon. Tentacles stretch out from the mouth to the surface of the Earth.

A piloted survey rocket approaches the planet-eating planet and encounters a terrible fate.

The protagonist escapes to an underground shelter, and when the planet-eating planet finally swallows the Earth, she's launched into space and drifts through the universe.

The spirits transfer to the planet and become monsters.

• Hanging
• Hanging upside down, yanked in four directions.

Monument

• Tongue from above
• Large tsunami (doomed)
• Everyone's floating for some reason.
• (Earth is spinning.)
• After the tongue licks it, creepy creatures'? [unreadable] can be seen on Earth.

Idea and story creation

I'D NOW LIKE TO DISCUSS my thoughts on how to generate ideas and create stories in horror manga. To start, I'll say that I've never taken a class on drawing horror manga, and I've never once had this sort of theory in mind while drawing. Please understand that what I'm about to write is at best opinion based on hindsight, nothing more than a summary of my own ideas as I look back on my work and put what I see there into words.

I apologize for not having all the answers, but I don't want to limit reader interpretations of the works or to curb the imagination of any artists with my how-to style notes here. I think both reader and artist should be free.

With this caveat, my hope is that this section could be of assistance in the creative activities of those commendable people who would like to try drawing horror manga and other people who work to make things.

Think from the climax

TO BEGIN, LET'S TAKE A LOOK AT the general flow of a story from start to finish, with the premise that the completed work is a single chapter.

Once I come up the core idea, I jot down a list of related keywords and short sentences in my notebook. (Lately, I often take notes in a Pomera digital notebook to improve my efficiency.) Once I've written a certain amount, I connect the keywords and create the skeleton of the story. This is when I roughly decide on the age, personality, and relationships of the characters.

After I've got the plot together, I type up the script on my computer. I envision the panel breakup and illustrations while I write down specific settings and conversations between characters. I go back and forth with this process, filling out the story, and once all the images are more or less fixed in my head, I start drawing the storyboards (the rough draft of the manga).

This is basically it for my workflow. I think what I'm doing in and of itself isn't so different from how other manga artists work.

When I'm putting together the story, I focus on creating a structure that will make the most interesting use of my initial core idea, which is often a single image. For instance, with "Honored Ancestors" (page 262), the image of several human heads connected to each other came first, an idea I got from a totem pole. "The Long Hair in the Attic" also began with an image, a head tangled up in long hair hanging from the ceiling beams.

Of all the different ways I create manga, using this kind of intense visual for the climax and building the story to get to that place works best for me. But I don't know if the image will hold up as the climax until I actually draw it. So I have to draw something like a piece of concept art at the start of the process and really consider whether or not it's impactful enough to draw the reader's eye.

There are all kinds of methods for story development, including the classic Japanese *kishotenketsu* four-part structure (introduction/ development/turn/conclusion), but I often develop mine so that the climax is the last scene. Revealing the true nature of some spiritual phenomenon or monster in a work of horror is akin to a magician explaining how their tricks work. There is nothing more boring than a magic trick you already know the secret of, and we similarly leave the truth about the bizarre occurrence that befalls the protagonist unknown so that readers can be entertained by and enjoy horror manga. **The anxiety and suspicion raised by the question of what is happening become the propulsive force that allows the reader to advance in the story**, while also heightening tension in the reader as they move toward the climax.

Story is not born from themes (maybe)

ANOTHER FREQUENT PATTERN OF MINE is adding the theme of the work later. "Town of No Roads" and *Uzumaki*—discussed earlier in the individual story section—are good examples of this. Oftentimes, the theme at the root of a work will manifest while I'm in the middle of developing the story from my initial image.

I'm not trying to make excuses for myself here, but apparently, the director Akira Kurosawa had a similar method of creating. In a documentary I watched a while back about the film *Kagemusha*,

Kurosawa talked about how he only had a hint of an image at the start of a project, and how he brought themes and the like to the picture later. I remember nodding along as he spoke, in total agreement.

I can't speak to film since I'm a layperson in that realm, but when it comes to illustration, I have to be thinking of something extremely realistic and concrete before I can begin drawing. For instance, what kinds of images (pictures) pop up in your head when you hear words such as "murderous desire" or "madness"? Concepts like these are hard to immediately visualize, and even if a picture of some sort did come to mind, it's likely be a different picture for everyone. To take this kind of abstract idea and produce a picture that people would look at and find scary is extremely difficult.

On the other hand, every so often, I have a new idea born from a form. With *Gyo*, for example, the idea of sharks walking on land popped up in my head when I was worrying about what I would do if those scary sharks could chase me onto land. From there, I developed the story in a chain: create a walking machine to allow sharks to walk on land → verification of the machine's internal structure → generation of gas to power the machine → zombification of living creatures due to a mysterious bacterial infection.

This method of generating ideas from a quasi–word association game is not guaranteed to succeed. It carries the undeniable risk of ending up with an incoherent mess. On the other hand, it also allows the opportunity to consider ideas you could never have imagined. Sometimes, when you start to dig up a fossil thinking it's a lion's claw, it actually turns out to be a massive *Tyrannosaurus rex* tooth once you get it out of the ground.

The act of deciding on the climax right at the beginning of the creative process can also be seen as imposing a limitation on the work. However, **the stranger the climax of the story is, the more interesting ideas will pop up to make sense of it, which makes it more likely that an unexpected story will develop.**

After all's said and done, the only thing that matters is that it turns out all right in the end. Hip hip hooray!

The origin of ideas is discomfort

NEXT, I WANT TO CONSIDER how to generate the idea that forms the core of a story. Any number of things can bring inspiration, but I find one of them is memories from the past that bother you.

I could list "Bullied" and "Alley" as concrete examples of this, but I want to emphasize that it's not a matter of simply using the past experience or event as is. What's actually important is the **emotion, discomfort, and trauma associated with that experience (memory).** Rather than sitting down and methodically going through your memories, **take as the seed of your idea some fragment of emotion or thought that's been stuck in a corner of your mind for a while.**

For instance, you might get the impression from the character Fuchi in "Fashion Model" (page 214) that a somewhat monstrous model like her in fact existed at some point. But she actually came about when I was flipping through a fashion magazine and stumbled upon a model who was pretty, but struck me as weird somehow. In other words, rather than the creepy model's actual appearance, I wanted to express the discomfort I felt looking at her. Similarly, "Bullied" has its core idea in guilt and "Alley" in claustrophobia.

Many generally scary stories are based on personal experience or the experiences of friends and family, the sort that start with things like, "This happened to my older sister five years ago…" For me, however, city scenes or structures, animal abilities, the human body, laws of nature and the universe, dreams, and other things that are totally divorced from frightening experiences often form the basis of my ideas. (I've never encountered a ghost or any other kind of mysterious spiritual phenomena, so I don't actually have those scary experiences to turn into stories.)

But when you're exploring topics like science fiction or documentary for horror manga, things that at first glance have nothing to do with horror, the power of the illustrations becomes even more important. Because there's no horror element if you draw the scene normally, you really have to think hard from the visual perspective about how to make it look scary. My drawings perhaps tend toward excess because of this.

The moment when the idea jumps up

WHEN I EXPLAIN IT LIKE THIS, you might get the impression that ideas flow from my mind like water from a tap. But unfortunately, that does not happen.

I agonized over "Hanging Blimp" for a long time until I managed to pull together a story I was satisfied with. It was all well and good to take a scene from a dream as the basis for an idea, but no matter how I wrestled with it, I could not make a story happen. I was driving down the expressway, a sour look on my face as I discarded one idea after another, when I suddenly discovered a way in. But another impossible wall immediately jumped up to block the path forward again, and the agony continued. Eventually, when my thoughts had reached a total dead end, I was resting my body in the bath, sick of thinking, when something strange came to me from somewhere unexpected as the solution to all my problems. I go through this cycle with pretty much every story.

There's nothing better than all the pieces of a story falling neatly into place, but you could also say that these hours of agony are necessary to make an idea really sing. Going back to "Hanging Blimp," a balloon floating above a town as an "ominous sign" is not a particularly wild idea. The key is how to start from here and take the concept higher—for example, a blimp with your own face attacking you. I think that how much altitude you can get when you make this leap decides how interesting the final work will be.

To that end, you really do need time to allow the idea to mature. Put another way, you could say that **the power to make a story jump to the next level comes from the tenaciousness to keep at it instead of abandoning a run-of-the-mill idea because you feel like it's not interesting enough the way it is.**

I say all this, but the fact of the matter is that more than a few stories never reach the next level due to the absolute finality of deadlines. But let's leave that for now.

IDEA GENERATION METHOD 1:
Crush the "should"

SO, HOW DO WE THINK UP INTERESTING IDEAS? If anyone has the answer to this question, I'd like to hear it myself. That said, I can perhaps offer up a few hints from past experience. I'll go over one such clue here.

The first method we can consider is overturning assumptions. You could also call it idea reversal. In "Bio House," I took the familiar character of the vampire and reversed its nature to create a character who wants *you* to drink *his* blood. In *Gyo*, I dismantled the idea that fish are creatures that swim in the ocean and developed a story from the hypothesis, "What if they came up onto land?"

This way of generating ideas is not particularly novel, but the fact that it comes up time and time again is proof that it is indeed quite effective. In using it, **it's easier to at first think of something** commonplace and then come up with the converse anomaly. For example, the assertion that children should go to bed early is quite sensible in terms of childhood development, but what happens if you turn this inside out? Wouldn't it be a bit scary if there was a family where the adults went to bed at eight in the evening and the young children stayed up until two in the morning?

Unexpected ideas will come to you once you crush the concept of how things "should" be in this world.

IDEA GENERATION METHOD 2:
Slam together ideas that should absolutely not be slammed together

COMBINING VERY DIFFERENT IDEAS is another method you often hear about. I feel like **the less those ideas are connected, the more they revolt against each other and the easier it is to come up with an unexpected manga.** Putting a tombstone in the middle of the house in the story "Tombs," the last place you would want a tomb, allowed me to draw some fun images. The tombstone is a frequent motif in horror, but we get a new perspective on it when it's combined with something unexpected.

To be honest, luck is a large part of whether or not your combination turns out to be a good one. But there is actually a way of producing chance combinations on purpose. The science fiction author Shinichi Hoshi apparently used something he called "element analysis resonance union" to get story ideas. First, jot down a large number of words or short sentences on individual scraps of paper and put those scraps into a bag. Pull two pieces out at a time like names from a hat to generate word combinations you would never normally think of, like "right-handed/monkey," "inside out/legal constitution," or "hired/monster." As legend has it, Hoshi came up with the concepts for his stories from these curious phrases created through chance.

Naturally, it goes without saying that developing an idea created in such a fashion into a single interesting story demands different abilities and efforts. But there's no harm in keeping it in mind as one practical method for producing surprising ideas.

IDEA GENERATION METHOD 3:
Refer to animal abilities and the structure of the natural world

AS I MENTIONED EARLIER, I took a hint for "Tomie" from a lizard's ability to regenerate its tail, and for "Face Thief" from a chameleon's camouflage abilities. To speak of a more recent work, I came up with the idea for the layered structure of the people in "Kyofu no Juso" (Layers of Terror) (page 278) after seeing growth rings in shells while I was clamming.

Sometimes, you can get new ideas by **applying unusual abilities animals possess to the human body or considering structures in**

the natural world. What's key here is the impact the image has when these attributes are applied to humans. For example, if you were to draw a girl with a dog's sense of smell, she wouldn't look any different from a normal person, so there's nothing interesting about it. This factor is extremely important because the creepiness or novelty of the illustrated idea will affect the later development of the story.

You also want to carefully examine the necessity or logic of the animal ability or shape transplanted to the person. Gaining this special ability should result in the fulfillment of a universal appetite or desire that people already have, like the immortality and eternal beauty in *Tomie* or the desire to transform into someone else in "Face Thief."

This kind of trick gives what first seems to be a preposterous setting a persuasiveness and sincerity, and also strengthens the framework of the story.

Tell only one lie

WHEN APPLYING IDEAS YOU COME UP WITH to a story, there is one thing you have to be careful of, and that is not to lie. To be exact, I allow myself one big lie per story. It could be that a blimp with your face has arrived to string you up, or perhaps a planet-eating planet has come from sixteen light-years away to eat the Earth.

What I'm trying to say is that usually the core idea for a manga itself is utter nonsense. And to make this nonsense make sense, you cannot overlook the details of the story. I decided the material for the face balloons in "Hanging Blimp" was nylon because a terrifying monster being made of the most everyday and ordinary material lends an unexpected reality to the story. In *Remina*, I hypothesized that if the Earth were rotating faster than it is now, the centrifugal force would exceed gravity and the mass of objects would become essentially zero, which led me to the developments of the latter half of the story.

Of course, I'm not a scientist, so I'm sure I made some mistakes. But in order to make my preposterous fictional world have a persuasive power, it was very important for me to consider the science and make the necessary assumptions from there. I think **an accumulation of small facts and plausible supplementary details is necessary to pull readers into the world of the big lie of the story.**

When I was a kid, I enthusiastically believed in ghosts and UFOs and all of that. Even when I was in high school and the story about *kuchisake-onna* (the slit-mouthed woman) was sweeping through Japan, I would walk to school thinking about how if she really did exist, I wanted to catch at least a glimpse of her. A lingering trace of my youthful belief is the contradictory desire to experience some kind of unnatural event even though I no longer believe in that sort of thing.

It's because I can't experience this kind of supernatural phenomenon in reality that I want to have a pseudo-experience of it in the world of manga, which is a big reason why I insist on reality in my work. **The delusional desire** to have something mysterious happen to me in real life might just be the driving force for me to produce new stories.

Jaws is packed with the grammar of horror

SO FAR, I'VE GONE OVER MY OWN WAYS of building story and generating ideas. But a picture is indeed worth a thousand words. If you want to learn how to create horror manga, the fastest thing is to look at great works from the past. In fact, I've absorbed the grammar of horror by doing exactly that myself.

Naturally, a great way to do this is to read the work of Kazuo Umezz, Shinichi Koga, and the other artists I've mentioned. And if you want to experience the real thrill of horror in a film, I recommend the movie *Jaws*. I watched it on TV when I was in grade six, and I ended up with a phobia of sharks.

Maybe there's no need to explain at this point, but for those who don't know, *Jaws* is a 1975 American film directed by Steven Spielberg. The basic story is of three men fighting a giant man-eating shark, but this plain and simple plot comes together into a panic-horror film that leaves the viewer breathless thanks to the clever storytelling. *Jaws* truly excels in how stingy it is with the man-eating shark.

In the film, the chief of police, a marine biologist, and a fisherman get on a boat and go out to sea to exterminate a giant shark that is slaughtering beachgoers. But that shark refuses to show itself. Before long, night falls, the men start drinking, and the fisherman recounts his tragic past. When he was young, he was in the navy during the war, and his ship was sunk by an enemy torpedo. A large group of sharks closed in on the wreck, and his comrades were eaten one after another.

As he tells them how shark eyes roll back in their heads when sharks eat people, the fisherman shows them the scar from where he himself was bitten, and the other two men recoil. Even though the viewer has barely caught a glimpse of the man-eating shark, this scene succeeds in planting a seed of dread in them—"This thing's gotta be some kind of murder machine…"

On top of that, the film is filled with stories like urban legends—"a huge tooth stabbed through the bottom of the fishing boat," "the shadow on the surface of the water was about eight meters long," "it dragged the whole wharf into the water with the bait"—and these tales make viewers build the terror of the shark all on their own.

This sort of thing is extremely effective in the horror genre, where the true nature of the monster is carefully guarded, and I think this film is a model example.

The scariest thing is yourself

SHARKS ARE DEFINITELY SCARY, but human beings and especially myself are the scariest. I've had this horror of the self for a long, long time. I remember feeling something indescribably strange when I heard my own voice on a tape when I was little. And after the proliferation of home video, I was so uncomfortable seeing my recorded self I could hardly stand it. I was right there, and yet there was another me on the TV. I felt an intense discomfort at the fact that another person was recognized as me in a place separate from where I actually was.

Many of my works have as their motif a doppelgänger (avatar) which stems from this instinctive fear of myself. In *Tomie* the biggest threat comes from the self, though her self-replication, and my stories featuring Oshikiri depict another self who comes from a parallel world to kill him. Similarly, you could say that "Hanging Blimp" and "Lovesickness" instill in readers the fear of a doppelgänger. In my more recent work, *No Longer Human*, I added a scene where Yozo Oba, a stand-in for author Osamu Dazai, meets Osamu Dazai himself in a mental hospital.

There is no doubt that the self is a motif from which I can't break free, but I think that maybe everyone feels something along these lines, more or less. There is **the fear that comes from not knowing exactly how other people see you**, and **the fear of not understanding the point of your own existence**. Similarly, there are as many ways of perceiving the self as there are people, and you could say that this terror of the self exists in proportion to that. In that sense, perhaps **the self is a primal fear shared among human beings**.

The boundary between life and death is ambiguous

I DON'T KNOW IF THIS IS RELATED to the idea of fear of the self, but when I was little, I was truly terrified of death. My teacher aunt would tell me stories about the misery of the war years, and when she told me how all the men were taken as soldiers and died, I assumed that when I grew up I would become a soldier and die, and I cried and cried. She told me that we were at peace now, so that wouldn't happen, but I nevertheless had dream after dream about war. When I played with my friends at the park, I would sometimes think it was strange that they could all be so happy.

My young mind was ruled by something like an obsession with death. (The photograph in our house of my uncle who died in the war might have also contributed to my fear of death.) This excessive fear of death had subsided somewhat by the time I was in fifth or sixth grade, however. You could say it was just that I'd grown and learned to separate things, and that was that. But when I really think hard about it, I feel like the possibility of death still spills over into every aspect of my daily life.

If you were told that today you would fall down the stairs and die, you would no doubt laugh it off as ridiculous, like the majority of people. But you have no guarantee you won't die today. Every day, somewhere in this world, people lose their lives after being hit by a car or having a heart attack or drowning in the ocean. This kind of catastrophe could easily befall you any second.

The fact that I was abnormally frightened of death as a child, and the fact that children can enjoy getting lost in scary stories is perhaps because **children grasp that being alive and being dead are equally probable.** There's meaning in making this possibility of death that lurks in the everyday visible in horror manga. ◎

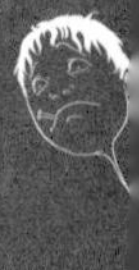

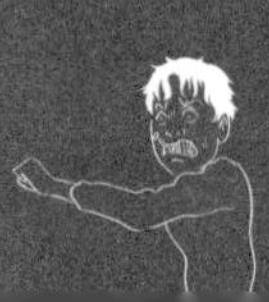

4

Creation: When a lovable character is born

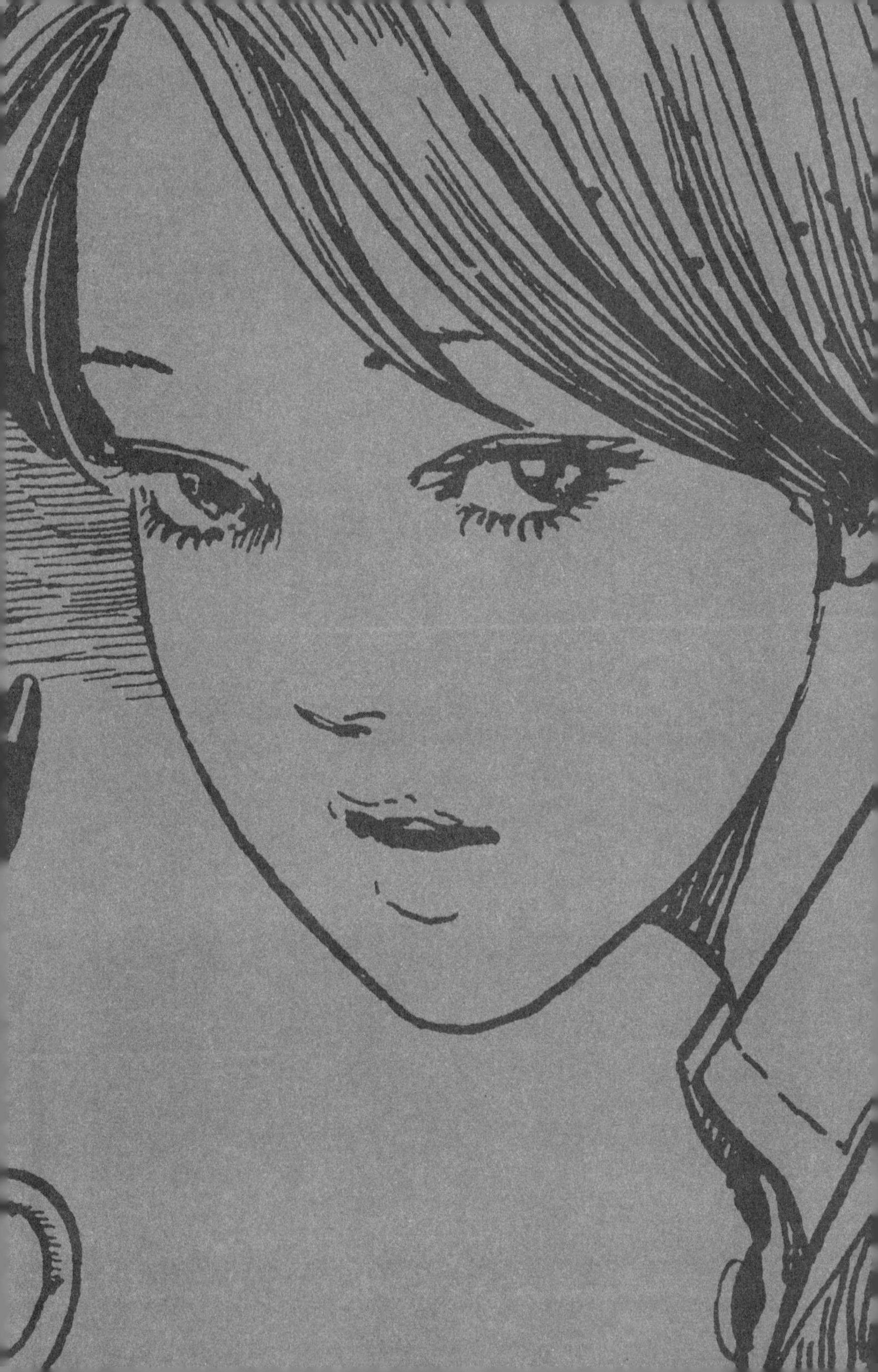

MANY FAMOUS HORROR FILMS TURN THEIR FOCUS ON MURDEROUS MONSTERS AND PSYCHO KILLERS, characters like Leatherface in *The Texas Chainsaw Massacre*, Jason Voorhees in *Friday the 13th*, and Freddy Krueger in *A Nightmare on Elm Street*.

About characters

I'VE SEEN MY FAIR SHARE of horror movies and, of all of them, the character Teraoka from Shochiku's 1968 film *Goké, Body Snatcher from Hell* made the deepest impression on me.

After killing a foreign ambassador, the terrorist Teraoka hijacks a small passenger aircraft to escape. But the plane encounters a mysterious ball of fire in the sky and is forced to make an emergency landing in the mountains. There, Teraoka discovers a glowing flying saucer and is almost compelled to enter it. When he does, **his forehead splits open, and the mysterious alien Gokemido enters him**. Taken over in both body and mind, Teraoka turns into a vampire and attacks the other passengers from the stranded plane.

The scene where Gokemido slithers into Teraoka's body through the opening on his forehead was particularly frightening to me. My manga frequently depicts the human body being destroyed or transformed, and I really do feel that it's scarier when **a regular person changes into an abnormal creature** rather than having a monster on the scene right from the start. Not to mention, the actor playing Teraoka, chanson singer Hideo Kou, has a strong presence on-screen, with cold eyes and a bewitching air that really are perfect for the role of the vampire.

Speaking from the position of a creator, however, I have to say I'm not very good at character-driven works. Often, I start with a particular setup, and my characters simply follow along. "Slug

Girl," for instance, came about when I noticed that the shape and movement of my tongue in the mirror were pretty sluglike, which led to the question, **"What if a tongue was really a slug?"** Fuchi in "Fashion Model" was also born from a personal fear, the idea that **a shark woman would be really scary.**

When I make manga, I don't start out trying to dream up some scary monster. In fact, once the monster does show up, I sometimes have trouble figuring out what happens next, and eventually I turn to my usual bag of tricks. (This is also partly why I'm not so great at long-form stories…)

The starting point for the majority of the many different characters I've drawn is usually born from my distrust of others. I consider how I would react to a situation I was put in, or to other people coming into my life. **Enigmatic human beings** are far more terrifying to me than spirits, *yokai*, demons, monsters, or any other supernatural phenomenon.

JUNJI ITO CHARACTERS

1 *Toru Oshikiri*
Page 208

2 *Soichi*
Page 211

3 *Fuchi*
Page 214

4 *Ryo Tsukano*
Page 216

5 *Frankenstein's monster*
Page 218

6 *Hikizuri siblings*
Page 220

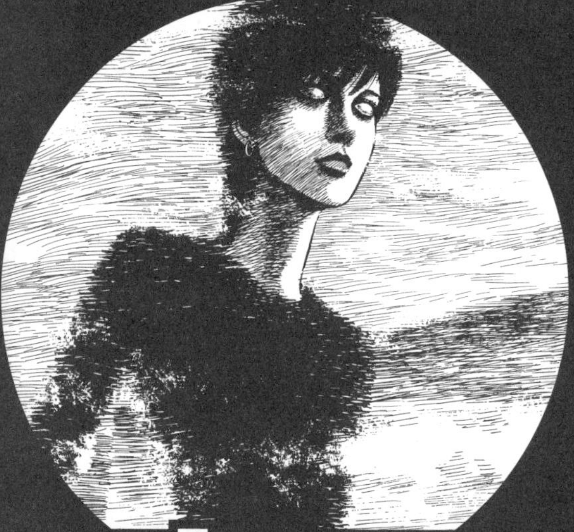

7 The beautiful boy at the crossroads

Page 222

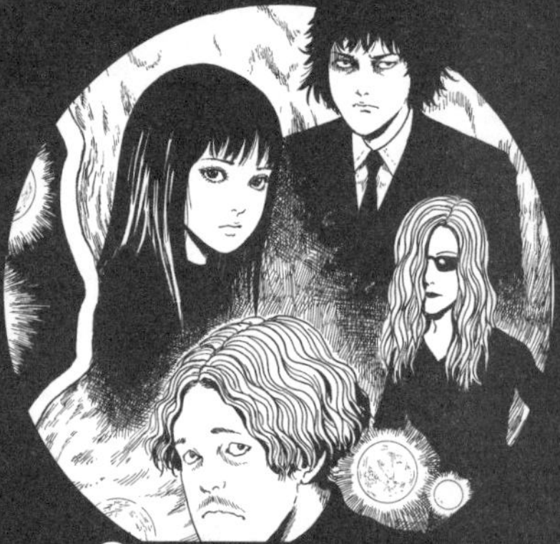

8 Taburo, Pii-tan, Baracchi, and Maruso

Page 226

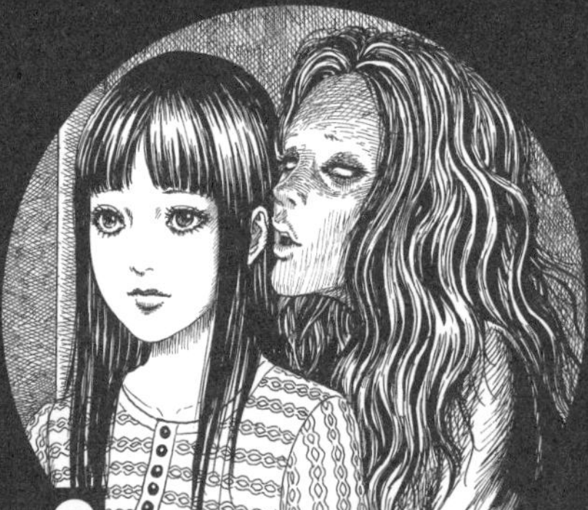

9 Mayumi Santo, Mitsu Uchida

Page 228

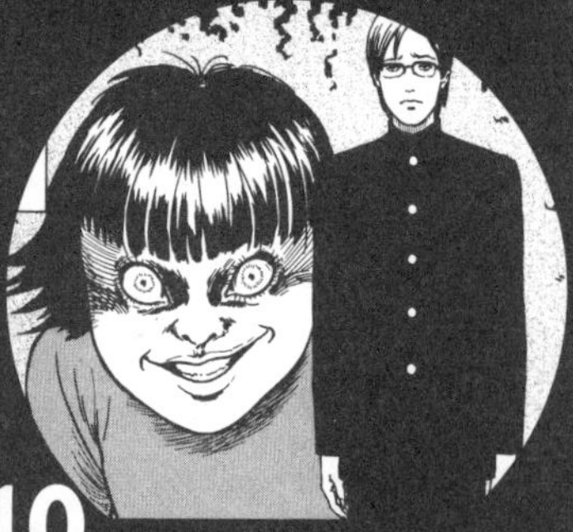

10 Yuuma and Chizumi Azawa

Page 230

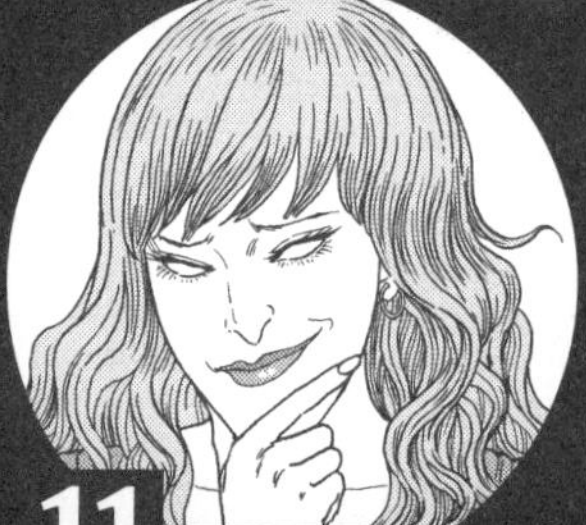

11 Magami Nanakuse

Page 232

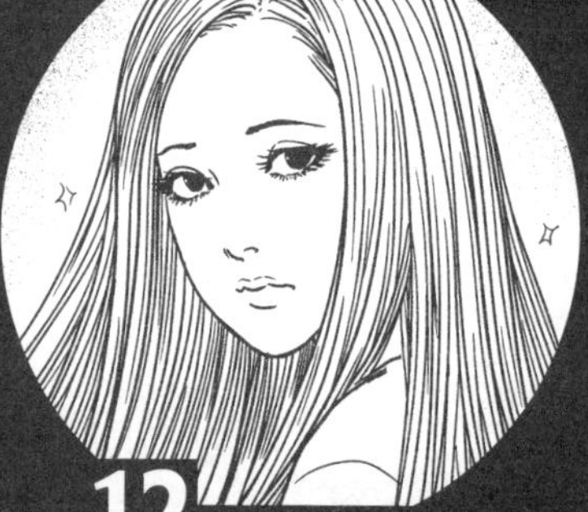

12 Kyoko Byakuya

Page 234

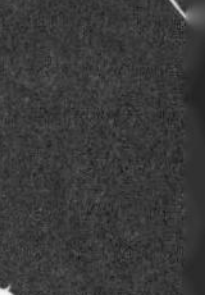

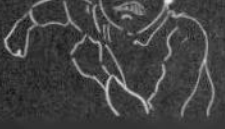

1. A beautiful boy reflecting a boyhood complex
"Neck Specter"
Toru Oshikiri

(First published: *Halloween*, Mar. 1989. Included in *Frankenstein: Junji Ito Story Collection*)

TORU OSHIKIRI, the protagonist of "Neck Specter," is a character I drew for my first series after *Tomie*. To tell the truth, turning this Oshikiri story into a series was the furthest thing from my mind when I wrote it, which is why it begins with him abruptly murdering his friend and burying him in his backyard, a cruel act unbefitting of a protagonist. On top of that, I also made him fairly psychopathic—the reason he killed his friend was because his friend was taller than he was.

Although I drew "Bog of Living Spirits" as the second story in the series, the idea was originally entirely unconnected to Oshikiri. The inspiration was a dream I'd had. My high school classmates were hanging out on top of a cliff when one of them slipped and fell into the bog below. I watched from the bottom of the cliff as he slammed into the water and died. It was a particularly vivid dream, so I figured I could turn it into a story.

But when I tried to draw it, the story felt aimless; it wasn't interesting at all. Out of desperation, I jumped at the idea of bringing back a character I'd previously drawn, and I settled on Oshikiri as the last-minute protagonist. This is how the series came to be.

About Oshikiri's parents   Oshikiri profile

Oshikiri is half Japanese. One of his parents is a foreigner.
His father is half Japanese. (Maybe British or Dutch and Japanese) Fairly tall.
Parents work overseas. When he was in grade six, his father went overseas, and then a
year later, his mother joined him. Toru Oshikiri was also urged by his parents to come
abroad, but he stubbornly remained in Japan.

The dad maybe isn't very affectionate with him? A little cold? About 45 years old.
Hideo Oshikiri

The mom is young. Around 35. Beautiful. Yuka Oshikiri

Toru

Draw with
left hand

Toru hates his dad?

Great-grandfather Vincent Lawrence
(or Netherlander. Japanese name is Gohei Oshikiri)
Great-grandmother Saki Oshikiri
Father Hideo Oshikiri
Mother Rika Koizumi (maiden name)
Toru Oshikiri
Uncle Shozo Koizumi
        Masako Koizumi (married name)
Takayuki Koizumi (cousin)

If I'd been planning from the outset to make a series with Oshikiri as the protagonist, I could never have made him kill his friend. (Although this would have still been an option if he were a villain like Tomie.) And it's totally unnatural how he commits murder in the first story and yet goes to school in the second as though nothing had happened. In order to make the overall plot make sense, I decided the Oshikiri house is connected with a parallel world, and the actual murderer was an Oshikiri from a different universe. Looking at it now, it's clear to me that I put this series together pretty haphazardly.

Meanwhile, for the world of the story, I wanted to draw something with a gothic horror style, the kind set in a Western rather than a Japanese building. With that in mind, I also referenced the boy Damien from the horror movie *Damien: Omen II* for Oshikiri's appearance and gave him the face of a blond Western boy, a bit removed from the face of a Japanese boy.

Oshikiri's glum, shy personality is a projection of myself as a boy. After I started junior high and began to grow taller, my father would always tell me, "You gotta get taller than that." He was a small man himself, so most likely he was projecting his own complex onto me. But I took his words to heart because I wasn't particularly tall, and I developed a bit of an unwarranted inferiority complex. You can see this kind of slightly warped boyhood emotion reflected in Oshikiri.

2. A troublemaker who brings nothing but annoyance
"A Happy Summer Vacation"
Soichi

(First published: *Halloween*, Aug. 1991. Included in *Soichi: Junji Ito Story Collection*)

THE *SOICHI* SERIES ORIGINATED from an idea I had to draw something based on my happy childhood memories of playing in the countryside, while giving the characters a slightly odd experience in every chapter. So I sat down to consider who could drag the protagonists into mysterious incidents over and over again, and I ended up with Soichi.

I did intend to make this one a series right from the start. What I didn't expect was that Soichi would be the protagonist. At first, I was certain he would be a side character, but readers liked him more than I expected, and before I knew it, he had become the main character.

His creation was influenced by the American science fiction program *Lost in Space*. The show starts when the Robinson family, selected to be humanity's first space colonizers, departs Earth for the star Alpha Centauri. However, Dr. Smith, a spy from an enemy nation, has snuck on board. With the unplanned extra weight, the spaceship is knocked off course and they end up lost, wandering through space.

The Robinsons visit one planet after another, and on each one, Dr. Smith causes the family no end of trouble. So what begins as a hard science fiction show turns into more of a slapstick comedy centered on Dr. Smith. I personally like Dr. Smith, and I secretly harbored the desire to feature a troublemaker like him in my own work.

There are scenes in the *Soichi* series where he uses dubious mental powers and black magic, but this wasn't part of my initial plan. I originally envisioned him as a malicious but normal boy who says ominous things and acts suspiciously, but doesn't have any actual powers. While I was drawing the series, however, my editor Harada suggested that it was about time I show off what Soichi could really do. So, in the middle of the series, he "awakens" and acquires magical power, uses cloth dolls, brings his dead grandfather back to life with a curse, and more.

Personally, I wanted to make the supernatural phenomena that happened around Soichi be the result of a series of coincidences rather than any power he had. But I had a lot of trouble building out the story in that direction, so I do have some regret about how this series turned out.

But it is a fact that making Soichi's character somewhere between human and yokai was what made him so popular with readers, so I think things turned out all right, after all.

- Goes to the countryside (Yusuke remembers coming when he was little)
- Met by Koichi and his mom
- Sayuri comes out to welcome them when they get to the house.
- There are two extra bowls of shaved ice. Supposed to be for Soichi (who is shy). Mom takes them to him.
- Told that they have to go through an underground passage to the washroom.
- They go swimming at the pool. Reaction of Koichi and Sayuri's friends. Yusuke doesn't swim, so he sunbathes poolside. Michina urges him to swim.
- Go home and have watermelon. Mother goes to bring Soichi some. Yusuke says he'll bring it so he can say hi at the same time, and after a moment of confusion, the mom says okay and gives the plate to him. When Yusuke and Michina go to his room, they hear voices muttering in conversation. They peek in and see Soichi talking with a doll. Sensing their presence, he calls out, "Who's there!" A nail comes flying at them and stabs into the pillar. And then he grins, so the nails are like fangs. Surprised, the siblings run away.
- When they tell the others what happened, they're told he tends to be anemic, so he sucks on nails (for the iron). After Koichi hears about the nail flying at the siblings, he goes to Soichi's room and yells at him.
- Soichi holds a grudge. "I'll get you for this... I'll show you true horror!"
- In the evening, the four of them are playing cards, and Soichi peers at them from behind the sliding doors. Michina whirls her head away, ignoring him, and "Heh heh heh. Ignoring me... I'll show you true horror."

The idea was actually that Soichi was the older of a pair of twins. I thought about alternating the chapters between Soichi and Soji, who looked and acted just like Soichi, and at the end of the series, I'd reveal they were twins. But I gave up on that in the end.

3. A young lady who is a hybrid of uncomfortable and terrifying

"Fashion Model"
Fuchi

(First published: *Halloween*, July 1992. Included in *Shiver: Junji Ito Selected Stories*)

AS I MENTIONED BRIEFLY in the last chapter, the core idea for "Fashion Model" came to me when I was casually flipping through a women's fashion magazine. But the visuals for Fuchi are nothing like the model who made me so uncomfortable; her look is modeled after something entirely different.

Her facial structure was based on a character I came up with when I was still in school named "Biemzo," a play on "zombie." He had the face of a macho sort of man, like a masked pro wrestler. This may seem like nonsense to you, but he was another big hit with my friends. For some reason, Biemzo popped into my head out of the blue, so I used his long face as the base for Fuchi's. Additionally, to intensify the horror feel of her look, I added elements from a shark, like the countless teeth you see when she opens her mouth, because I think sharks are scary.

Given this design, I was originally planning to draw a story with the concept of a shark woman. But not long before I started working on it, a fisherman was attacked by a shark in the Seto Inland Sea, so I decided to not move forward with that idea.

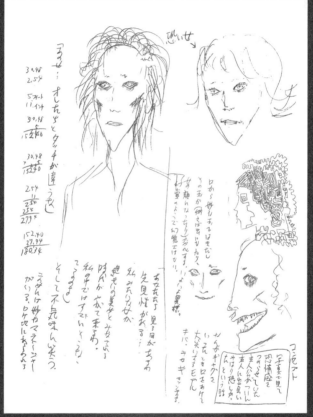

"That woman. She's got a different style."

"You all have eyes that can see. You have real vision. The time when a woman like me is deemed an unequaled beauty is finally here. It's already the truth in my heart." And then she laughs creepily.

The woman has a weird manager. He shows up at the shoot location.

Spits out strange spheres from her mouth, and these transform (ex., into insects, a woman's face). Increasingly bizarre. Like a hallucination, except it's not.

Concept
After seeing her photo, the protagonist's fear only increases, and then he happens to meet her, and she really is scary.

Model laughs loud and hard when someone tells a joke. Fangs. Everyone is shocked.

When I'm drawing a character, I'm generally not the type to come up with an overly detailed design, but I did draw several versions of Fuchi's face to nail it down. Flipping through my notebook from that time, I notice that her hairstyle and eye shape are different from the final version.

4. Skeptical realist with supernatural powers
"Supernatural Transfer Student"
Ryo Tsukano
(First published: *Halloween*, July 1993)

THIS IS A STRANGE STORY of supernatural phenomena happening in the various places transfer student Ryo Tsukano turns up. Unusually for me in developing the story, I gave the side characters individual quirks, like the psychic abilities Shibayama claims to possess and the spirit powers Kitagawa says he has. Originally, I wasn't thinking about this as a one-off story, but a series that would allow me to draw all kinds of supernatural phenomena by having Tsukano visit a variety of towns. But in the end, I couldn't think of any good plot points, so that initial concept went nowhere.

I know I've mentioned this several times, but I'm essentially a skeptic when it comes to supernatural abilities and phenomena. I did believe in the spoon-bending phenomenon popularized by the psychic Uri Geller when I was in elementary school, but once I got to junior high, I began to think the majority of these things were really just magic tricks. In fact, I tried spoon bending myself—which takes advantage of metal fatigue and which Tsukano actually does in the story—and found that it's quite easy to do.

With "Supernatural Transfer Student," I reworked this realist side of myself into a story with a bit of a sarcastic edge. (This is also something I've said before, but I honestly would like to witness some supernatural power or phenomenon, and I definitely don't look down on people who believe in the paranormal. It's simply that the supposedly supernatural things I've encountered have generally seemed fake to me. Maybe my skepticism is a defense mechanism because I've been disappointed so many times.)

Supernatural Club members

Ryo Tsukano   Mai Hosoya   Leader: Hikaru Shibayama

Kiyoshi Kitagawa   Miyoko Watanabe   Katsuko Iwai

- *Transfer student causes abnormal things to happen, allowing people to experience weirdness in a boring (not socially, but in terms of nature) world.*
- *Protagonist is an unlikable girl (cute, though) who takes a philosophical view of things even though she's only in elementary school. She thinks that's just the way the world works, and has a tendency to look down on her classmates a little. (Girl with a large physique) (Used to believe way back when)* → *Started a new religion by herself when she was little, and made all the neighbor kids believers?*
- *Believes in the supernatural and seeks it out in daily life. Trouble between group and protagonist girl. Annoyed by this, the protagonist persistently comes at them. "Ghosts exist." "UFOs exist." "ESP exists."*
- *Protagonist makes fun of shows on TV about UFOs, spiritual stuff, etc. Especially makes fun of ones with psychics. "So you can see a spirit over there?"*
- *There's a self-professed spiritualist in the group, who tells her, "I can see a spirit behind you, too, you know."*
- *And she's all, "Well, I can't so I don't care."*

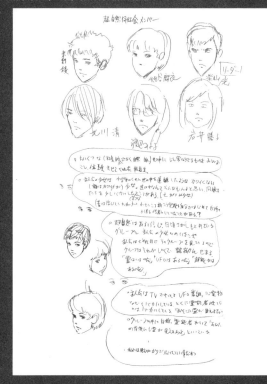

In the beginning, I thought of making the protagonist a girl who totally doesn't believe in spirits or supernatural powers, and then she experiences a real paranormal event because of Tsukano. Part of this story stemmed from my own desire to join a supernatural club; if only there had been one when I was at school.

5. Reinterpreting a classic

Frankenstein
Frankenstein's monster

(First published: *Halloween*, Sept. 1994. Included in *Frankenstein: Junji Ito Story Collection*)

I DREW THIS TO COINCIDE WITH the release of the Kenneth Branagh film *Mary Shelley's Frankenstein*. The *Halloween* editorial department caught wind of the film production and came up with a plan to make a manga version to go along with the film's release, which led to my editor coming to me.

In turning the story into a manga, I wanted to be as faithful as possible to the original novel. *Frankenstein* is a classic work released in the UK in 1818, but the visual from the 1931 film (the monster with the square head and bolts sticking out of its neck) is stronger in our minds now, I think. So rather than simply taking my cues from that adaptation, I spent a lot of time struggling to create the look of the story from the details in the novel.

That said, however, there are parts that I decided to do differently in order to enhance the horror elements of the story. For instance, in the novel, the monster demands that the scientist Victor Frankenstein make him a bride, but this project ends in an unfinished attempt. In the manga, though, I changed it so that Frankenstein does actually create the monster's mate.

I saw the Kenneth Branagh film after I'd already drawn the manga, and I was surprised to see that he chose to make the mate in the same way in the movie. Which maybe begs the question for many of us as to why Frankenstein didn't create the mate in this way (with this material) in the original novel.

Monster
8 feet

1 foot
  30.48 cm
8 feet = 243.84 cm
2 m 44 cm

Robert Walton
Ocean explorer.

Very rich
person.
P100

Monster's mate.
Big woman.
Justine's face

Professor Waldman,
around 50
(Chemistry)
Salt-and-pepper
hair. Likable. Short.

Professor Krempe
(Natural philosophy)
Uncouth. Little squat
man. Conceited.

William

Caroline
(Frankenstein's
mother)

I hunted down reference materials to draw the laboratory equipment
that scientists used back then, as well as for the last scene set at the
North Pole, but I recall having quite a hard time with all of it. I would've
also liked to have spent more time tweaking the form of the monster
itself, if I could have.

6. Bizarre codependency inspired by a family situation
"The Strange Hikizuri Siblings: Narumi's Boyfriend"
The Hikizuri Siblings

(First published: *Halloween*, Nov. 1995. Included in *Lovesickness: Junji Ito Story Collection*)

WHEN I'M CONSIDERING THE STRUCTURE of a story, I almost never start by thinking about the characters. (I'll go over the reason for this later.) But this story was unusual in that it grew out of the character design—codependent siblings who live together and sabotage each other.

My father's family gave me the idea for the Hikizuris. Let me say right from the start, however, that this doesn't mean my father and his siblings were sabotaging each other under the same roof. Their parents passed away soon after the end of the war, so my father and his three siblings (excluding his oldest brother, who died in the war) got through the lean postwar years by relying on each other. Once I learned about this, I felt like it might make for an interesting drama if I drew the siblings fighting and working together and living their lives.

Their personalities and behavior are depicted extremely negatively in the story, but that's simply because this is horror and it's more entertaining that way. My father's family wasn't actually like that (just to be clear).

I got quite detailed in creating the sibling characters, as you can see on the next page. I dug deep into their appearances, personalities, likes and dislikes, behavior patterns, pasts, and more.

Codependent siblings, the strange Hikizuri siblings.
They fight with each other but can't be apart.

Shigoro
Second son
Age: 16
Clingy, creepy
Flair for modeling/sculpting.

• Despises his older brother from the bottom of his heart.
• Still holds a grudge over the time Kazuya took a manju bun from him. Also holds a grudge becauce Kazuya stepped on his pet cockroach, camel cricket, etc. Says bad things about his brother behind his back. Kazuya doesn't know this yet.
• Absolutely does not believe in supernatural phenomena, but pretends he does to keep his brother in good humor.
• Knows Kazuya is afraid of their father Gozo and occasionally pretends to be possessed by him.
• Very good mimic.

Kinako
Oldest daughter
Age: 18
Very jealous
Ugly, but stylish

• Held back by memories of the boys who dumped her.
• She once killed a boy who dumped her.

Kazuya Hikizuri
Oldest son
Age: 19
Acts like an upstanding citizen.
Respected by his siblings, sort of.
Considers himself to be one of the elite.

• He's done all kinds of things he could never tell anyone about.
• He thinks about ways to make money, but they're unrealistic.
• He tells people he gave up on going to university to take care of everyone, but he doesn't have any real academic ability.
• Finds an old report card.
• Believes in supernatural phenomena.
• No match for their father.

Narumi
Second daughter
Age: 14
Narcissist
Beautiful
So-called fashion victim. Does nothing. Only dresses up.

• Extremely passive. (Regular suicide attempts? But she doesn't want to die.)
• Pretends to commit suicide, upsets men.
• She's normally quiet and calm, but she'll suddenly burst into tears and attempt suicide.
• Has a habit of running away from home.
• Doesn't go to school. Truant.

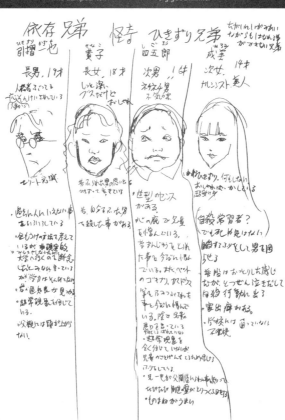

THIS STORY ORIGINATED WITH me reading about crossroads fortune-telling in a book I happened across, *Kangaeru Gijutsu, Kaku Gijutsu* (Thinking Techniques, Writing Techniques) Published by Kodansha. I found it interesting, so I looked it up in an encyclopedia to learn more.

I had assumed that crossroads fortune-telling was a fortune teller working at a crossroads. But that is apparently not the case. To find out where this tradition started, we have to go back to ancient times, given that crossroads fortune-telling is mentioned in the poetry anthology *Manyoshu* from the Nara period.

The practice was apparently devised to hear the divine messages of Sae, the god of roads and journeys. Those who wanted their fortunes told would stand at the crossroads either in the morning or in the evening, at times of day when passersby couldn't be seen very clearly. They would then listen to the words (conversations) of the people walking through the crossroads and divine their fortune from the meaning of those words. The belief was that the will of the gods lay in these coincidentally overheard snippets of conversation.

After learning all this, I immediately came up with a story and a character for a long-form manga with crossroads fortune-telling as the starting point. *Lovesickness* has two protagonists: the mysterious beautiful boy at the crossroads and a boy with a dark past, Ryusuke Fukada. The point-of-view character in the main story is more or less Ryusuke, but in my initial idea, it was the beautiful boy. I actually thought him up for an extremely commercial reason—the story was to be serialized in a shojo manga magazine, so a handsome boy character seemed like a good idea.

At first, the story was about this beautiful boy working underground as a fortune teller. He would listen to people who were struggling and resolve their issues. I myself was once a boy with a lot of problems, and at the time, I was religiously listening to the radio program *Telefon Jinsei Sodan* (Telephone Life Advice) hosted by sociologist Taizo Kato and other specialists. I always felt like it would have been so reassuring if I'd had someone like them to give me advice.

I assumed Ryusuke would simply be there to advance the story. But in the end, I made him a character that incorporated the doppelgänger motif I often use. In contrast with the beautiful boy of the crossroads who plunges people into despair, Ryusuke saves the people who struggle with their crossroads fortunes. The two seem like polar opposites at first glance, but the fact is, I created them with the idea that they were two sides of the same person, like the black and white of an Othello piece, and added an episode where Ryusuke commits the same crime as the beautiful boy at the crossroads in the past.

• Couple who doesn't get along. Constantly complaining, denigrating.
Cold and rude to each other.
Time doesn't matter for crossroads fortunes in this town.
Name → Tsuchiiro

★ First chapter
Protagonist high school student getting advice (serious person). Intersection in town called "crossroads fortune intersection."
At dusk, people with secret problems share those troubles with the first person who happens to pass by and ask their opinion on what to do. For some reason, the protagonist often ends up giving advice to people standing at the crossroads.
When he was a child, an adult woman (with romantic troubles) got a crossroads fortune from him, and because he gave her some unserious, childish advice, the woman ended up dying. Boy with this kind of trauma in his past. His guilty conscience leads him to be abnormally enthusiastic about undertaking crossroads fortunes.

★ In chapter four, separate from Ryusuke, a group of girls chases after the beautiful boy. Whenever they hear he's shown up somewhere, they race over as a group. It's a bit weird. Eventually, they commit group suicide. Girl corpses in heaps at the crossroads.

★ Version with crossroads fortune telling near the end after a bunch of different incidents

• *Crossroads fortune telling trend (don't make main idea of story)*
Crossroads fortunes popular with junior high and high school students.
• *A strange girl doing crossroads fortune telling calls out to a boy who is sick of the world.*
Asks for guidance on what she should do
Lots of people show up giving weird advice.
• *Girl says she doesn't like this part of her face and talks about her anxiety with her boyfriend. He tells her she should just get plastic surgery. She does, but it's a disaster.*
Tells the boyfriend who recommended surgery about this anxiety and her anger.
Troubled, he comes for advice.
Girlfriend wants to break up. Even if he doesn't. She can only see his bad points.

★ *Chapter 4*
Protagonist is totally absorbed in giving advice (lots of danger, too), and, growing dissatisfied with this, the girlfriend kills herself after they have a fight. (Protagonist doesn't realize his girlfriend is struggling.) She stands at the crossroads to try and get him to talk to her when he's doing his rounds, but he can't see how she's feeling. Another girl is always coming to the protagonist, who he met at a crossroads, with all her problems and constantly hanging out with him. When the girlfriend notices, she gets jealous. Plus, the protagonist says the ghost of the woman he pushed to her death as a child has started standing at the crossroads, and as atonement for his past, he begins to seriously involve himself in her troubles.

★ *Chapter 2*
Beautiful girl with many problems. The protagonist's friend passes by the crossroads as a joke, and the beautiful girl with a lot of problems begins to haunt him. And then destroy him.

★ *In chapter four, to meet the beautiful boy, the protagonist goes around to stand near the intersection and wait (troubled by the woman's ghost, too) instead of passing through the crossroads. Eventually, the beautiful boy comes! And then the showdown! The tall beautiful boy...*

◎ 辻占の流行. （ストーリーの一構 メインアイデアにはせず）
　中高生の間で辻占がはやる.

・◎ 世の中がいやになった少年が、辻占をやっている少女が声をかけられる
　　少女は何かいう物をあるいんだとうていたのだ.

・ 少女 アドバイスをするやつが ゾクゾク 現れる

◎ 彼女が、顔のこの部分が気に入らないっていい、彼氏に悩みとして 話してる.
　彼氏は整形したらいいかもしれし、いいよ. 彼女は整形するが 失敗.
　整形を すすめた彼氏に その悩みと 怒りをいう.
　それに悩んだ彼氏が、相談にやってくる.

・別れたいと思ってる彼女、彼氏が いやで、もう別れない. 彼氏の いやな面が 目につく.

悩み 相談をやりこむ 私公（危険も多い）にくの カールといっには しだいに 不満を
もつようにり つけた ものごとをおこして 自殺してしまう. （私公は 自らのガール
の悩みには気ばないなかった. 彼女の 姿態を 書く 私公に相談にやっていると
矛盾点が生まっているか 私公は なくくな処理せ与かない.） ある少女が せら気意に:
やをく 私公に しつこく. あ物に絡みもつかせ. まとわりついついるのを見しかい
しらつ しらは 嫌妬をしてる. また, 私公は 子供の頃へ死へ追いやってしまった女性の
幽霊が 辻占に立つようられだと, いいなし. その悩みに, 罪ほろぼしとして
真剣にとりくみはじめた.

悩みの多い 美少女, 私公の 友人が, いやかしで 辻 と通り 始め, みを 美少せんつせつ
わけにはじめる. そして, けぬつ 与る.

☆第4話 美少女に会うために 私公 はじと通りとやへや, じけい立つ 倒れ らに 近く待つ.
　やがて 美少年が 通りなぐって くる！ そして 対決！ 背の高い 美少年

8. Concept: Rock band

Black Paradox
Taburo, Pii-tan, Baracchi, and Maruso

(First published: *Big Comic Spirits Special Edition Casual*, No. 16, 2007)

I GOT THE IDEA FOR THIS STORY from a documentary on space development, which discussed a number of incidents in the space race between the US and the USSR. I found the thought of dying to achieve spaceflight very frightening. At the same time, I wondered if I couldn't express this terror in some other form. As a result, I decided to dig into "the other side" and draw a story featuring all kinds of accidents.

My protagonists are generally loners, so this work is unusual for me in that it is a group piece with the four characters of Taburo, Pii-tan, Baracchi, and Maruso. The concept behind the character design was "rock band." Originally, entirely separate from this, I was working on a story where a mysterious band performs in hell and drives people insane, and I adapted several of the ideas for the characters in that to *Black Paradox*. The collarless suit and the black jacket came from the fashion of the Beatles (I'm a fan).

For Spirits
Black Paradox
Each chapter, members try to take down the other members.

Protagonists with problems
Tell the story of some kind of issue in each chapter
Girl band dressed all in black? One man (two?)
Two men, two women (?)
(Ignored by the media)

Maruso   (Keiichi Hashimoto)   Taburo   Baracchi
          Pii-tan

9. Wishing for control, wishing to be controlled
"Whispering Woman"
Mayumi Santo and Mitsu Uchida

(First published: *Shinkan*, 2009. Included in *Fragments of Horror*)

SOMETIMES, WHEN A PERSON isn't confident in themselves, they leave all their decisions to other people. Some people are constantly on edge until someone else approves of even the smallest of their everyday acts. When I imagined what would happen if you took this behavior to the extreme, I got the story "Whispering Woman."

I first came up with Mayumi Santo, the ultimate passive person who can't decide what she should do of her own free will. But when I pushed this idea to its logical end, I realized that Mayumi would literally not be able to do anything unless someone was by her side giving her instructions throughout the day. That's when I created Mitsu Uchida in the role of Mayumi's support.

In the beginning, Mayumi is the one who seems ill, but once she has Mitsu to help her, she blossoms into health, while Mitsu grows ill. And, if I do say so myself, I think this contrasting structure is quite good. But given how effortlessly Mitsu slipped into the role of being Mayumi's decision maker, perhaps there was always something off about her psychological makeup. Together with the Hikizuri siblings stories, this is one of the rare cases when I created the story based on the characters.

TOP: Storyboard
BOTTOM: Final page (printed in *Fragments of Horror*)

10. Generating twisted characters from everyday stressors

Dissolving Classroom
Yuuma and Chizumi Azawa
(First published: *Motto!*, vol. 2, 2013)

THE BIZARRE CONCEPT of older brother Yuuma Azawa melting people's brains with his apologies came from personal experience. When I wrote this story, we had just moved to our apartment in Chiba. I woke up one morning to find our cat had peed on the blankets. So I took them to the bathroom and scrubbed them clean, but then they were dripping wet. I couldn't leave them like that, so I carried them out to the balcony to hang them to dry. But due to my own carelessness, they fell with the laundry pole from our fourth-floor apartment. Fortunately, the whole mess landed without incident in the empty yard, but I raced down the stairs right away to go and apologize to the residents on the ground floor.

This was a period when I did a lot of apologizing. For instance, I also drilled some holes in the wall so we could fix the dresser in place, and we got complaints from the people downstairs about the noise. All of the issues were indeed my fault, but even so, the constant apologizing was stressful for me. Thus, in my manga, I melted the brains of the people receiving apologies, and in this way, expressed all of my annoyance.

Attractive brother and sister. They live alone, just the two of them, no parents. Despite her beautiful countenance, the little sister is a malicious troublemaker. The brother is always cleaning up after her, going around and apologizing for things. But he gets pleasure from apologizing (a narcotic high). And the people he apologizes to meet unfortunate ends. Hizumi always makes trouble that's just barely not a crime.

美しい 兄と妹の 兄妹. 親はおらず, 2人で暮らしている

妹はその ~~髪姫~~ 美貌にも かかわらず トラブルメーカーである

兄はいつも その あとしまつで, 謝罪に回る ことが しばしば.

しかし, 兄は 謝罪に 快感 をおぼえている. (麻薬的な快感)

そして, 謝罪を受けた方は 不幸な 結末をたどる.

ヒズミは いつも 犯罪 スレスレの トラブルを引き起こす

常にイライラしている

ひずみちゃん

主人公の少女 町. 美しい少年は いつも 主人公に 謝ってくる. (理由 はいろいろある).

少年には 邪悪な ~~◯◯◯~~ 妹がいる.

少年が 謝るたびに, 主人公は 苦しむ.

実は, 少年が 妹に 悪さをするように しむけている.

Always annoyed.

Hizumi

Protagonist girl Cute boy always comes to apologize to her on some pretext or another. (He has all kinds of reasons.) The boy has a mean little sister. Every time the boy apologizes, the protagonist suffers.

The truth is, the boy makes it so that his sister does bad things.

In the beginning, I thought about making the little sister Chizumi cuter. But because my editor requested a character more like Soichi, I made her a little younger and changed her personality to be more contrary.

"Magami Nanakuse"
Magami Nanakuse

(First published: *Nemuki+*, May 2014. Included in *Fragments of Horror*)

FOR THIS MANGA, I took up the motif of a tic disorder, a condition in which the sufferer repeatedly and unconsciously performs a specific action or makes a particular sound, such as clearing their throat, blinking, or shaking their head. When I was younger, I actually suffered from a tic disorder myself, and so you could say that this work was born from my own past experience.

While tic disorder is in fact a type of illness, I was nonetheless interested in the question of what would happen if individual quirks were taken to the extreme. So, as I did with *Uzumaki*, I gathered all kinds of information on habits and compulsive acts, including tics.

This idea led to the name of the character Magami Nanakuse, as she was a person with a great number of quirks. The name Nanakuse itself comes from a Japanese saying about how every person has their own little ways of doing things, with the word *nanakuse* meaning "seven quirks."

"Magami Nanakuse" is the second of my stories after "Tomie" where a character's name is the title. The story itself, however, is quite different from "Tomie," and the tone is very much a joking one. Because of this, I think the characters have a fairly human way of speaking and expressing emotion compared with my other works.

12. A woman who grows more mysterious as the story progresses

Sensor
Kyoko Byakuya
(First published: *Nemuki+*, Sept. 2018)

UNUSUALLY FOR ME, this character raced ahead on her own—and in a bad direction, to boot—so I really struggled with this story, as I noted in the afterword of the book. I had originally planned to use Kyoko Byakuya as the main point-of-view character, traveling around the country and encountering bizarre phenomena. But in the first chapter, she somehow ended up holding the key to a mystery of the universe, which meant I couldn't actually let her say much of anything, after all.

So for chapter two, I brought in the journalist Wataru Tsuchiyado as the new protagonist. But once again, contrary to my wishes, he turned into an ordinary middle-aged guy in love, chasing after Kyoko instead of the bizarre phenomena I wanted him to go after. It might be more accurate to say that rather than the characters selfishly doing whatever they wanted, I simply wasn't able to control them because my initial setup wasn't strong enough.

The story was first serialized under the title *Travelogue of the Succubus* because I initially intended to do a travelogue like the works of manga artist Daijiro Morohoshi. But I'm a homebody, and when I finished drawing chapter one, I realized it lacked any travel elements, so I gave up on that.

At the plotting stage, I included the idea of Kyoko wetting the bed in the shape of a map. I thought she could perhaps use this map to chase after the mysteries of the bizarre phenomena in different regions. But my editor put a halt to that. He said to please at least make it night sweats, and I eventually scrapped the idea entirely. (I also didn't want to draw any details alluding to bed-wetting.) When I think about it now, I think I'm happy that I decided not to make it a travelogue.

I changed the title to *Sensor* for the release of the book to connect with the theme of the work: the mystery of the existence of the universe and human beings. For some time, I'd wanted to draw something asking the question of why human beings exist, and it was in this book that I took on that challenge. Human beings could not exist if there was no universe, but doesn't this also mean that the universe couldn't exist without something to experience it? In other words, I took as my main topic the sensory organs of a human being (sensors) based on the concept that perhaps existence isn't independent, but instead comes into being because we are aware of each other.

Unfortunately, however, due to my own lack of ability, I wasn't able to completely fully explore these ideas. I'd like to come back to this theme one of these days.

Town where angel hair is always in the air.

The female protagonist Kyoko Byakuya comes to this town.

Kyoko Byakuya   Beautiful, serene woman with angel hair.

- Beautiful, blond an-
gel hair turns jet-black
in the blink of an eye.
- Side character →
Bed-wetting
- Angel's slaughtered
body (Angel is her?)
- Appearance of angel
(her)
- Angel hair attached
to scalp
Angel corpse
- Angel hair is always
in the air in this village.
Kyoko Byakuya comes
along.
- Villagers admire her
golden hair, but at
some point, it changes
color to black.
- Hair jets out from
vents all over the
place.
- Abnormally long
angel hair

エンゼルヘアー が日常的に舞う町。

そこに主人公の女、白夜京子がやって来る。　　　　　クールな
　　　　　　　　　びゃくや きょうこ　　　　　　　エンゼルヘアーを持つ美女。

白夜 京子
びゃくや きょうこ

　　　　　　　　　　　　　　　　　　　漆黒の
・美しい金髪のエンゼルヘアー が いつの間にか、黒髪に変わった。

・サブキャラっおねしょ

・エンゼルの惨殺死体　（エンゼルは大人？）
　エンゼル型場（大人）　　　　　　　　UFOとの関連

・頭皮のついたエンゼルヘアー

　エンゼルの死散

・ど一村でのエンゼルヘアーが日常的に舞う。そこに白夜京子が現われる。
　村人は、金色の髪をめでているが、あるとき 漆黒の遺髪に変わる。
　ついた所々ある噴出孔らしが小ヘアーが吹き出る。
　異常に長いエンゼルヘアー

A character's first cry

I'D LIKE TO NOW DISCUSS methods of character creation. That said, I don't actually have any hard and fast rules when it comes to generating characters—it might be more accurate to say that having no rules is my rule.

In crafting a story, my priority is the **creation of a worldview**, an idea which I also touch upon a bit in chapters three and five. Rather than scaring readers with a parade of creepy monsters, I sincerely hope to entertain them by drawing bizarre events and phenomena unthinkable in the everyday world of the story. While it's true that my work features numerous depictions of various abnormalities, I draw these in a scary fashion to make the story more compelling; the depictions themselves are not the point. You might shudder at first glance when you come across some grotesque image I've drawn, but as you read, you grow accustomed to such portrayals.

Similarly, I have almost no interest in drawing the idiosyncrasies of my characters. I'll outline my reasons for that over the next few pages, but for now, I'll say that given the fact that I'm putting other worlds on the page, I think it's preferable for characters to have little to no personality. By pushing aside elements like individual personalities and relationships, I hope to be able to depict insanity, narcissism, social approval, self-esteem, and other **universal desires and inclinations.** (That's my hope, at least…)

At any rate, before we begin, I want to note that for me, characters are not the center of the world (not even the protagonist). They're nothing more than one of many elements in constructing the world.

How to design characters

IN MY CASE, I almost always do the character design at the same time as I work out out the structure of the story. As I noted in chapter three, I first get the seed of an idea for the plot, and I then consider how to nurture that seed to effectively communicate what's interesting about it. I think about the protagonist (the main point-of-view character), side characters, monsters (villains), and other characters necessary to advance the story, along with the following design elements, which are the bare minimum necessary for the story development:

- ◆ Name
- ◆ Gender
- ◆ Age (student, working adult, senior, etc.)
- ◆ Appearance (beautiful, weak, fresh, etc.)
- ◆ Nature (cheerful, determined, gloomy, etc.)

If the story needs it, I also add in things like family structure and social standing—"second daughter in a family of four" or "second-year at XX high school"—and relationships between the protagonist and the people in their lives—"know each other from

XX group," or "friends since elementary school." This is more or less my character design process.

People often say that creating appealing characters is important for longer serializations. You hear stories about how if the characters are fully fleshed out from the outset, they'll move on their own and the story will write itself, but I personally have never encountered this kind of supernatural phenomenon. I'm not being sarcastic when I say that I think it's truly amazing to be able to breathe this kind of life into characters.

I'm honestly terrible at constructing that sort of character-focused manga. I know I'm repeating myself here, but what I want to draw is not the people or the monsters, but the world itself. I want to depict a microcosm of various bizarre worlds and explore what would happen if flesh-and-blood human beings were thrown into them. I'm unable to draw the sort of story where the characters are central and change the world around them.

Thus, the protagonists I draw are often sensible and passive because I think **the less personality a character has and the more neutral they are, the more fitting they are as a guide to lead the reader into a fantastical world**. In my opinion, if the characters were forever showing off what made them unique, the reader would conversely not be able to immerse themselves in the bizarre world.

Science fiction writer Shinichi Hoshi simply called his characters things like "Mr. N" rather than giving them names, and similarly, the characters in my manga could be said to fundamentally be nothing more than symbolic presences.

The difference between long- and short-form stories

TO FURTHER ELABORATE, I think the difference in construction between long- and short-form stories is a major factor in the necessity for characters to become symbols. For instance, in a longer manga, the principal focus is often the relationships between the protagonist and others in the story. At the center, we have the protagonist and their overall objective, and they're surrounded by supportive friends, someone who has romantic feelings for them, rival organizations, and all of that. The story essentially develops by going round and round inside of this circle.

With shorter stories, even if you take the trouble to build up the characters, they basically get to stand onstage one time and then that's the end of them. The more complicated you make their personalities and relationships, the more limited page space you have to spend explaining them, and this can turn into shackles that hinder your story's development. Because of this, we might actually prefer **characters who are as easy to understand as possible, almost stereotypes.**

Even with a one-shot structure, however, you could follow in the footsteps of series like *Chibi Maruko-chan*, *Sazae-san*, and *Case Closed* and use the same protagonist in each story, changing only the scene. This is a method that I applied in my own work with the *Tomie* and *Soichi* series, and *Uzumaki*. I think it makes the characters more relatable and the work easier for the reader to follow, but I'm not very comfortable with this format.

The emphasis in my work really is on the world-building, so changing the character designs each time allows me to do what I want without restraint, and I feel it increases the purity of the work. Plus, another issue in the case of horror manga is the **lack of reality if the protagonist is the same every time**. It's one thing if they have supernatural powers, but it's a bit harder to swallow an average high schooler getting dragged into bizarre phenomena everywhere they go. (Although depending on how you think about it, a person in your life dying every week without fail could be said to be the most horrific of horror stories.)

My final point here does depend on the individual plot, but with long-form work, you're usually faced with the necessity of keeping the protagonist alive the whole time, which can be quite difficult. In *Uzumaki*, for instance, I agonized over every chapter to make sure I didn't kill the heroine Kirie Goshima when she faced some new danger, and because of this, the story occasionally developed in unplanned directions for the sake of expedience.

I'm not saying that horror simply can't work as a long-form story. This is a matter of individual skill and preference, rather than a structural issue. Naturally, there are high-quality horror stories out there that are complete in and of themselves while still depicting real relationships quite well. Now that my own ideas have dried up, I'm always thinking I need to read more Stephen King and other horror writers to learn a few new tricks.

The role of the horror manga protagonist

IF I WERE TO MAKE ONE MORE COMMENT about the characters in my work, it would be that **the protagonist does not grow.** Normally, the protagonist's growth is an essential element in a compelling story. They go on an adventure with their friends, learn to care for others in deeper ways, slam up against walls and barriers, and while they sometimes fail or run away, they eventually meet with success. The reader feels a real catharsis at the end of this series of dramas.

I have absolutely no objection to any of this. But—maybe because I'm lazy—pretty much all of my work comes to an end without me depicting this kind of human conflict or growth. My usual pattern is that **once the protagonist leaves for the adventure, they are never coming back.**

The reason why I have trouble making the protagonist grow or manifest special talents is probably in part due to the special nature of the horror genre. One of the more basic templates for horror is that one day, the helpless protagonist encounters an incomprehensible situation. Whether it's being attacked by a monster or entering a bizarre new world, **the protagonist has to encounter the strange phenomenon with an extremely "normal" outlook.** Otherwise, the reader won't be surprised by or afraid of the irrational incident.

Wouldn't you feel a bit deflated as a reader if the protagonist were excessively courageous and didn't even flinch when the

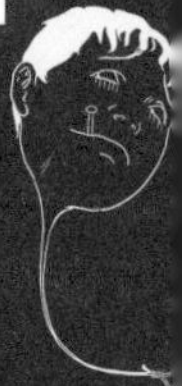

monster appeared? Or how about if the monster or paranormal phenomenon could be defeated by science or scared off by the protagonist simply bulking up? These stories might be interesting in and of themselves, but they are perhaps outside the realm of the horror genre.

A horror manga protagonist must experience unusual worlds and be an anchor to explain to the reader what's so scary about the situation. In other words, **they must not overcome the terror**.

Contrast in horror is key

IF WE CONTINUE to think along these lines, we could also say that clarifying a contrasting structure is important in horror manga.

Tatsuhiko Yamagami's gag manga *Gaki Deka* (Bratty Cop) was very popular when I was in middle school, and like everyone else, I was obsessed with this manga. It had a serious influence on me. Komawari, a boy police officer, comes up with one surreal, novel, and nonsensical line after another, and the people in his life offer up punch lines and witty repartee to flesh out the story. The contrast between this particularly weird boy and the regular people in the world with him creates the laughter and the drama, while the fact that he is surrounded by regular people is precisely what highlights the excellence of the eccentric Komawari. (Now that I'm thinking about it, Soichi from my *Soichi* series was absolutely influenced by *Gaki Deka*. Like Komawari, Soichi is an abnormal boy, and the people around him are normal.)

My example of *Gaki Deka* is a gag manga, but I think contrast is key in horror manga as well.

Normality and abnormality.

Beauty and ugliness.

The clearer the contrast between these, the darker the shadow of terror becomes. So to highlight the bizarre world or abnormal presence, it's best if the people facing it are colorless and transparent.

The subject of terror is inside you

SO FAR, I've discussed ways of thinking about character design that prioritize the story world, but to conclude, I want to list an exception—the creation of abnormal people, like Tomie, Soichi, Fuchi, and the beautiful boy at the crossroads.

Just as I mentioned when going over each of their creations, if I were to list one point they all have in common, it's that **they originate in my own self.** Characters with their own particular personalities are generally created through reflection on some aspect or memory inside of yourself. For example, Magami Nanakuse is based on the tic disorder that troubled me in my boyhood, and *Dissolving Classroom*'s Yuuma Azawa on my history of apologies during that time of my life. Perhaps we can say that **you interpret your emotions and memories in an extremely broad way** and attach these to the characters as personalities.

There are two big reasons why abnormal characters should be drawn from yourself. One is that the character is easier to create if there's a part that resembles you. The other is the fact that **of all the characters I've drawn, the one thought to be the scariest is abnormally obsessed with herself.**

I also talked about how the self is scary in chapter three (page 196), and the theme of the self is apparently hard for me to get away from in my work. The fear of those with narcissistic personality disorder—narcissists—has been a throughline in my work since my debut with "Tomie." (Tomie is the ultimate narcissist in my mind.) Whenever I go to draw the thing that's really scary to me, the thing I honestly never want to encounter, I always arrive at narcissism.

Perhaps I find narcissists frightening because, beyond my hatred of being manipulated and hurt by someone like that, I'm aware of elements of narcissism in myself. During my time at the technical school in Nagoya, I was sometimes caught up in the delusion that everyone passing me on the road was staring at me. Maybe it was scopophobia. Whenever I went anywhere where there were a lot of people, I was trapped in the self-conscious thought of "they're all watching me," and I'd get so scared I would almost cry.

Fortunately, this phobia was only temporary, and reading books by psychologists and so forth gradually took the edge off my symptoms and allowed me to feel more at ease. I myself don't know if this is narcissism or not. At the very least, however, I do seem to have inside of me an excessive concern about how I look to other people.

Deformations beyond
repair produce monsters

ANY NARCISSISM INSIDE OF ME springs from the difference
between my world and those of the people I encounter. Whenever
I come up against this difference, I feel an indescribable terror, almost like I'm peering into a gaping, bottomless pit. This is a bit of
a leap, but you could perhaps say that **narcissism is a distortion
of the recognition of individual worlds**.

The difference between the world that you perceive and the
one others perceive; the difference between the person you think
you are and the person that others think you are. The stronger
the narcissism, the more intense this distortion becomes. It grows
broader and deeper to the point where the gulf will always remain
no matter how you try to talk to each other and bridge the gap.

Everyone has this distortion of recognition of the world and
the self, more or less. To be more precise, it's impossible for one
version of the world to be common to all people. Despite this, for
some reason, we talk as though we live in the same world and have
some understanding of each other. When you think about it, this
is extremely strange.

This contradiction may well be the basis of the abnormal presence I fear: **a being that clearly demonstrates our despair that
we can never understand each other.** ◎

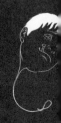

CHAPTER

5

Production: Creating an instantly traumatizing picture

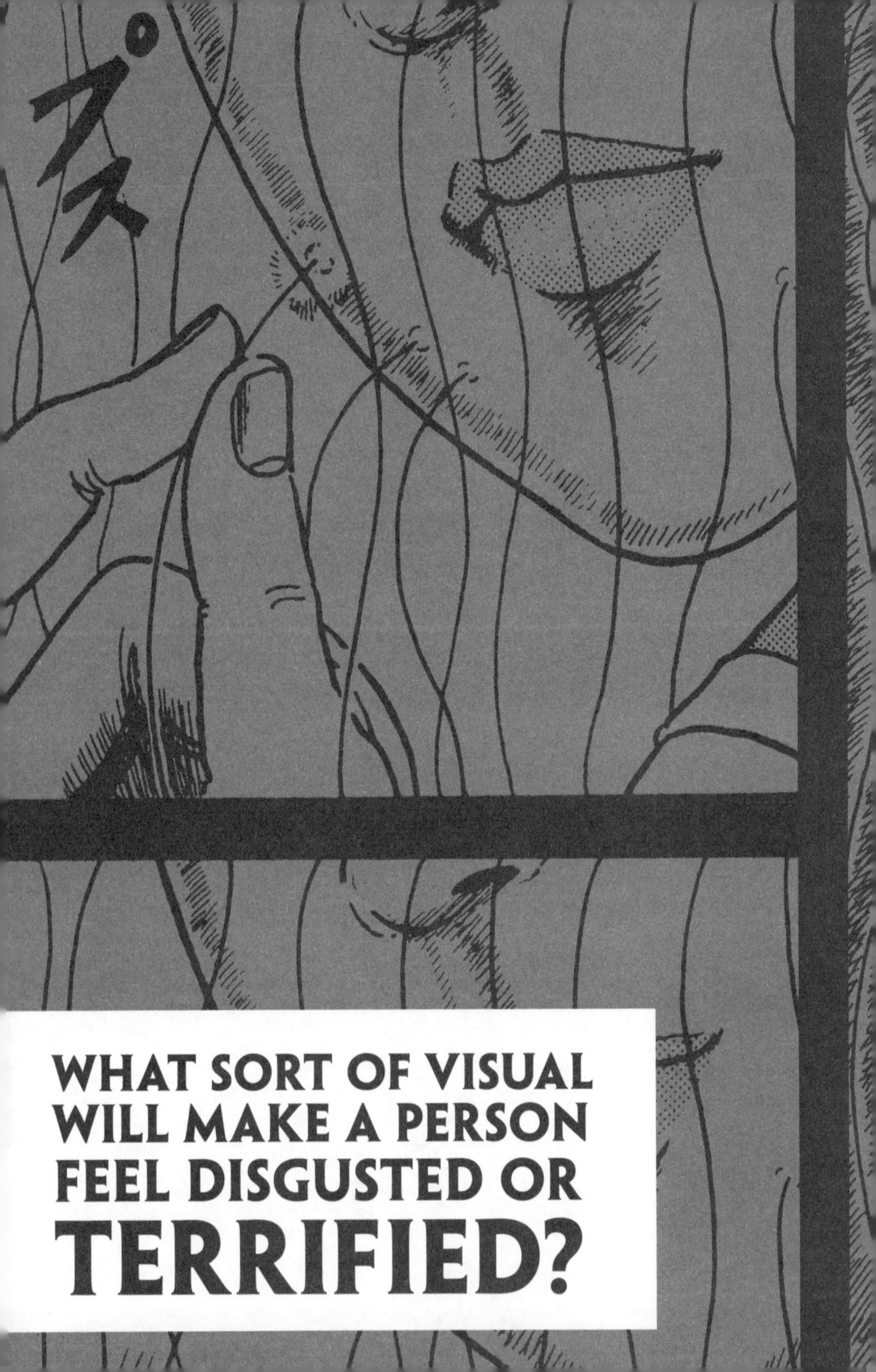
プス

WHAT SORT OF VISUAL WILL MAKE A PERSON FEEL DISGUSTED OR
TERRIFIED?

THIS OBVIOUSLY DIFFERS FOR EACH INDIVIDUAL, but one thing I feel a visceral revulsion toward is a radial shape. Things like a spider with its legs outstretched, or fungi multiplying, are especially disturbing.

About art

IN THIS FINAL CHAPTER, I want to discuss my own process and techniques for creating the art.

My work frequently **portrays the human body being destroyed or transformed**, such as in "Shiver," "The Moaning Drainpipe," "Honored Ancestors," *Uzumaki*, and "Smashed." These depictions call to mind injury, illness, and death. Strangely enough (for me, anyway), the broken body of an animal isn't particularly scary. It really does have to be a human being.

I think the difference comes from the spirit and mind contained within the body; what some might call a soul. **I'm afraid of a body equipped with human thoughts and emotions.** And when you deform that body, it gets even scarier. In other words, what terrifies me is a human being, with a mind I can't really understand, becoming even more baffling and incomprehensible through the process of transformation.

When I draw the destruction and mutation of the human body, I focus on doing so as accurately as possible. In the story "Flesh-Colored Mystery," for instance, I referenced an anatomy book used by medical students to draw the **scene where the mother peels her skin off and tosses it away.** Personally, I think the best transformation I've ever drawn is **the father spiraled up dead in the tub** (see page 271). I don't think a corpse would actually end up looking like that, but nevertheless, I took care to ensure that there were no contradictions in the proportions and placement of the limbs and torso, as compared with a normal body.

Perhaps there's no such thing as accuracy when drawing an atypical being that couldn't exist in reality. But I think terror comes from those moments that stir up anxiety and imagination, the feeling that **maybe this could happen to me.**

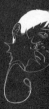

1. A myriad of holes all over

"Shiver"

(First published: *Halloween*, Nov. 1991. Included in *Shiver: Junji Ito Selected Stories*)

MY MANGA OFTEN TAKES UP THE SUBJECT of body horror (a technique using the transformation/destruction of the body to make the viewer feel terror), but this story might be the prime example of that.

The motif here was inspired by insect spiracles (openings to allow air into the body; respiratory holes). I was looking at pictures of rhinoceros beetle larvae in a field manual, and I started to wonder what it would be like if people had spiracles. When I sketched it out, the concept was unexpectedly interesting and surreal.

I came up with the idea for "Shiver" in 1991, but in the early 2000s, images collaging lotus seed pods onto faces and bodies suddenly started trending online. Apparently, the sight of a collection of countless small holes or tiny protrusions arouses an instinctive horror and revulsion in us. In the world of psychology, this is called trypophobia (fear of collections), and the cause of the fear is hypothesized to be that the little holes or bumps are reminiscent of parasites or infectious disease.

Either way, we can safely say that the deformation and destruction of the human body is the ultimate in horror manga techniques.

GRANDPA.
HE'S GONE.
GRANDPA'S BODY WAS RIDDLED WITH HOLES.

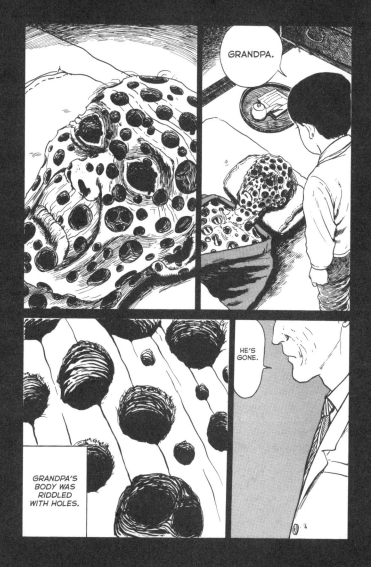

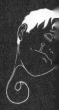

THE IDEA FOR THIS STORY came from the tale of a stalker that one of my colleagues told me during my dental technician days. This man dislocated his own shoulders to sneak into the house of the woman he was in love with through the ventilation fan. I couldn't get the image out of my head, and I eventually landed on the thought that it would be even scarier if someone came into your house through an even smaller hole—through the bathroom drain, for instance—like a snake.

In the last part of "The Moaning Drainpipe," the younger daughter Mari is pulled into the drain by the male stalker, and I really wrestled with whether to leave her upper or lower body remaining at the end of it all. Eventually, I decided to have just her legs sticking out of the drain, because I felt that the drawings of her bones smashed and her being silently swallowed up by the hole would have a creepier effect than leaving her upper body and allowing her to plead for help with words and the expression on her face.

But her face twisted up in fear as she was dragged into the hole would also have been powerful in its own way, so I still go back and forth on which is best to this day.

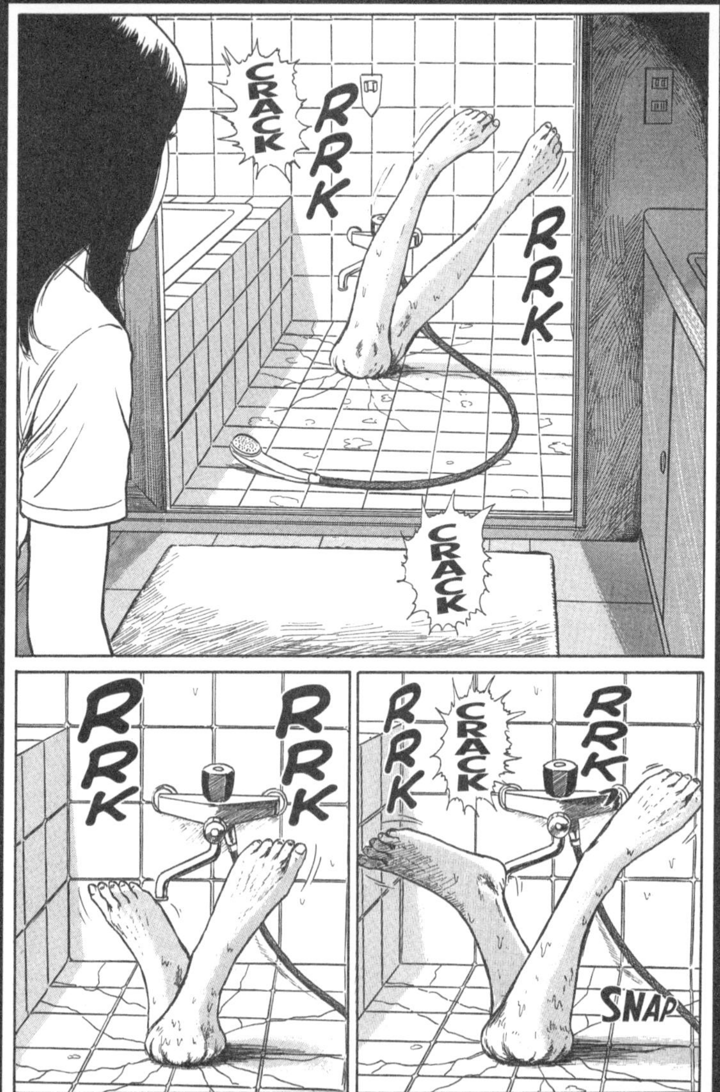

CRACK
RRK
RRK
CRACK
RRK
CRACK
RRK
SNAP
RRK
RRK

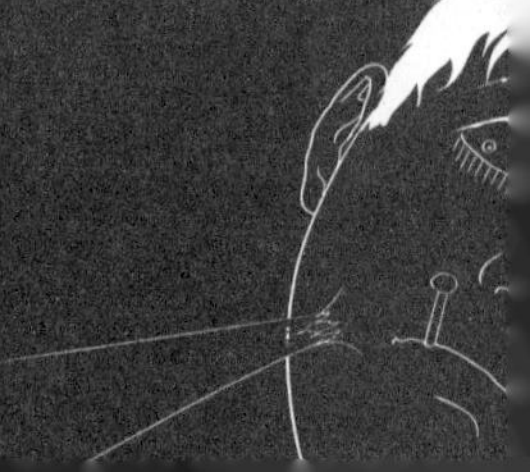

3. Blood fruit cultivated from human seeds
"Blood Orb Grove"

(First published: *Halloween* Nov. 1993 issue. Included in *Moan: Junji Ito Story Collection*)

PLANTS GROWING FROM BODIES, and vampires eating the blood fruit these plants produce: this concept came to me from mosquito ecology. When mosquitoes have a blood meal, their stomachs swell up and grow firm like a red jewel. At first, I was going to turn it into a story where some fictional mosquito-like creature drinks large amounts of human blood, which is then used for transfusions. However, this idea went absolutely nowhere at the plotting stage, so I was forced to give up on the mosquito and shift my focus to plants.

We naturally think of vampires when we think of bloodsucking monsters, but the ones in "Blood Orb Grove" are not the sort that bite necks to drink blood. These vampires grow blood fruit in human beings for their food source. In other words, they're vampire farmers, not hunters.

It took a long time to draw the spread featuring hundreds of blood fruit orbs. I think I probably spent about ten hours on those two pages alone. But although it took a long time, it wasn't that taxing mentally. I can draw these kinds of curves freehand, so I don't have to fuss about too much. What actually gives me trouble is when I have to use a ruler; I've always hated doing backgrounds with buildings.

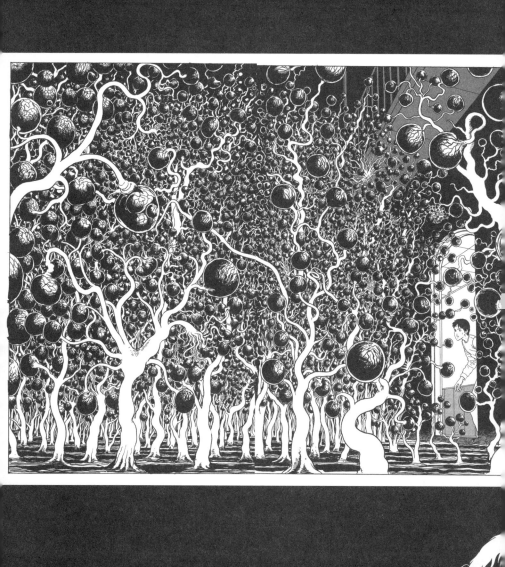

4. Body parts becoming different creatures
"Slug Girl"

(First published: *Nemurenu Yoru no Kimyona Hanashi: Nemuki*,
vol. 21, 1994. Included in *Tombs: Junji Ito Story Collection*)

"A HUMAN TONGUE RESEMBLES A MOLLUSK in both its appearance and movement," I said to myself out of the blue when I was looking at my own tongue in the mirror. "Slug Girl" bubbled up from the wild follow-up question: "What if my tongue turned into an actual slug one day?"

Toward the end of the story, Yuko gets into a bathtub filled with salt and her body dissolves. I thought it'd be interesting if her tongue was a slug and only her head remained, so then she would end up as something like a snail. I made up some plausible reason to get rid of her bothersome body. But when I think about it now, there's no way her body would disappear just because it was salted, and I wonder with a little regret if there wasn't a slightly better way of handling it. I took the gag a little too far.

I gave the story the title "Snail" at first, but the editorial side pointed out that a slug and a snail were completely different creatures, biologically speaking. In the end, I settled on the current title after a suggestion from my editor, but then I learned that there was already a manga with that very title, and I got pretty panicked about that. (I did check what that manga was about later on, and the story is totally different, which was definitely a relief.)

YUKO ...
LRRM
NGEH!

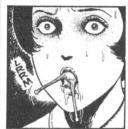

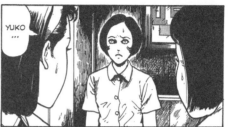

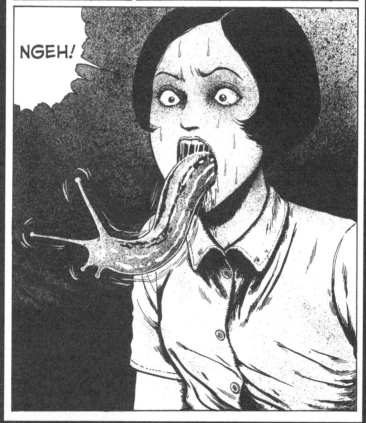

5. Inescapable chain of terror
"Honored Ancestors"

(First published: *Nemurenu Yoru no Kimyona Hanashi: Nemuki*, vol. 29, 1996. Included in *Shiver: Junji Ito Selected Stories*)

THE LIST OF THINGS THAT INDUCE FEAR in the human heart is actually long and varied, the trypophobia I discussed in "Shiver" (page 254) being only one example. Some of the major ones are heights, enclosed spaces, pointed ends, eyes, spiders, and snakes. There are even people who are terrified of sleeping or hair.

The cause of these fears is apparently not only personal experience. One theory I've heard is that the memories of the dangers faced by humanity's ancestors (natural predators, illness, disaster, etc.) are etched into our DNA, and we all are instinctively afraid of these things. From this starting point, my imagination drifted off to the question of what it would be like if a single individual could inherit all the memories of their ancestors, and that led to this manga.

Incidentally, I took a cue for the visual of the ancestors' skulls piled up on top of the character's head from the totem poles carved by the First Nations peoples of Canada.

The story ends with the heroine Risa passing out, but to be honest, she was going to make it out alive in my first draft. In that version, Risa flies out of the house, and the monster chases after her, only to be hit by a truck and die. But as always happens with me, I ran out of pages while I was drawing it, and I was forced to leave Risa in there, unconscious.

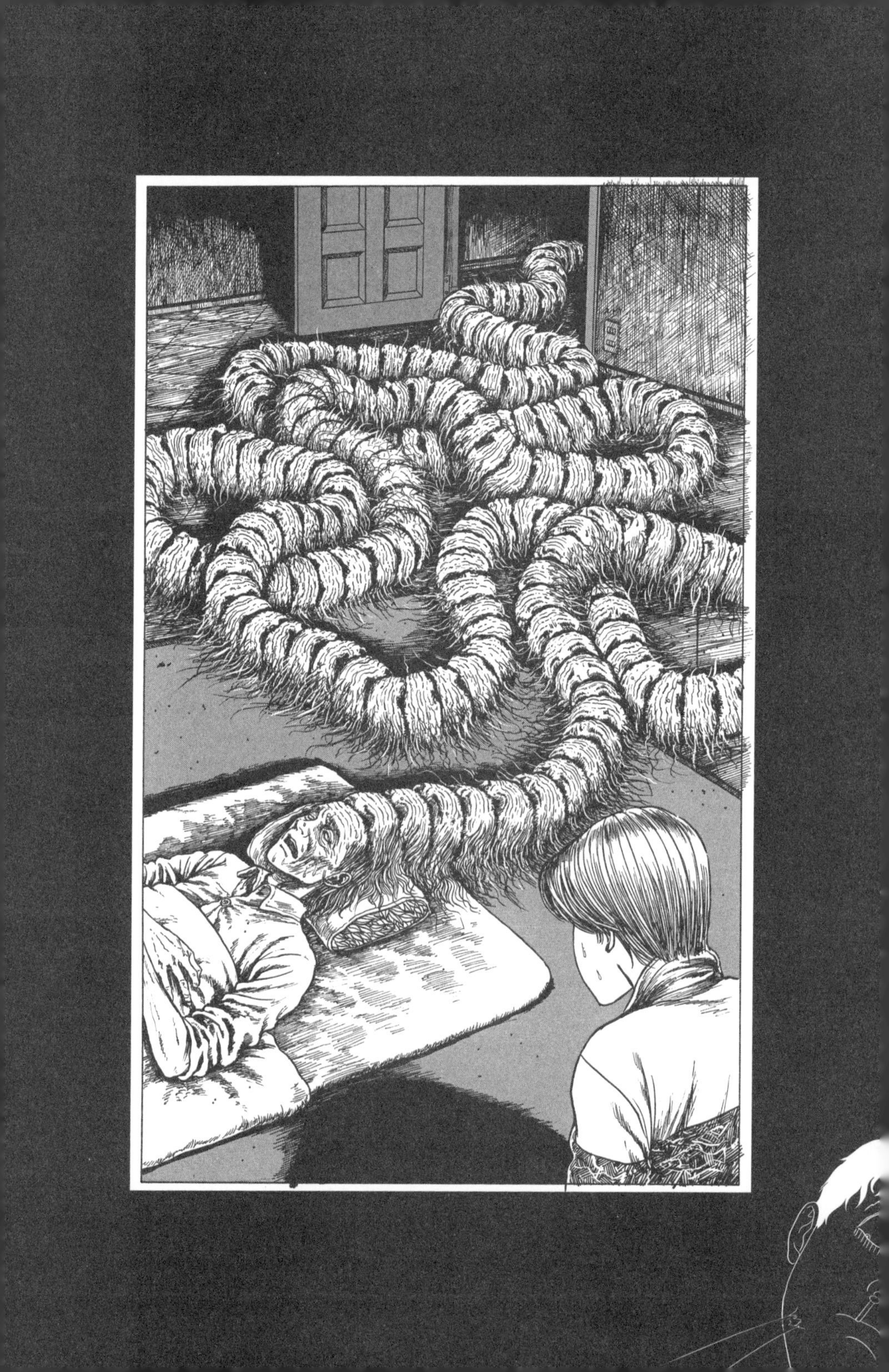

THE SETTING FOR THIS STORY is a foggy town, so I added depictions of fog to nearly every panel to really bring out the otherworldly feel of the place. Normally, screentone might be better to accurately depict a thin fog, but I drew it all in pen one line at a time. I wasn't aiming for a particular effect, it was simply easier to do it that way.

I am very bad at pasting screentone, and I tend to finish even the shadows of buildings and the color of hair in pen or ink as much as possible. This is, in fact, the reason why some of my early-to mid-career work has too strong a contrast between light and dark, or an excessive amount of drawn information on the page. Because I've shifted to an entirely digital process now, pasting tone has become an incredibly easy job. But it's so easy that I'm now forced to consider the possibility that I use too much tone and my images have lost the impact they once had.

But I digress. In addition to the depiction of the fog, I also took great care with people's shadows. Many of the characters I draw have plain features overall and rather flat faces. In this story, however, it's as though the town itself is struggling—it's a town of shadows, so I wanted to make the facial contrasts quite stark. I made a doll out of white modeling clay to be my model, and I referenced the shadows created by light hitting the doll to draw the characters.

While it's a little embarrassing to note this myself, I feel my artwork was at its most dense and complete during the period of *Lovesickness* and "The Long Dream." I'm actually impressed that I managed to draw the scene at the end of the story, where the ghosts gather around the protagonist Ryusuke in such detail. At any rate, I was overly serious back then and wouldn't tolerate blank space on the page. And I had the physical endurance to fill it in!

For a long time after my debut, I drew for *Halloween*, and I was able to carry a monthly series by myself when I was younger without many issues. But now I hit a wall in terms of stamina. As I approach the latter half of a story, my hand starts aching, my pen slows, and just when I'm thinking I'd like to fill in a little more of the detail, the deadline arrives. The older I get, the more my stories tend to end like this, and I often do revisions later when the stories are collected into books. (I learned after the fact that these additions incur extra printing fees, and I felt quite bad about that.)

This is steadily devolving into me grumbling and complaining, so I will simply say that I wish I could actually take an extra month or so and properly finish each of my stories.

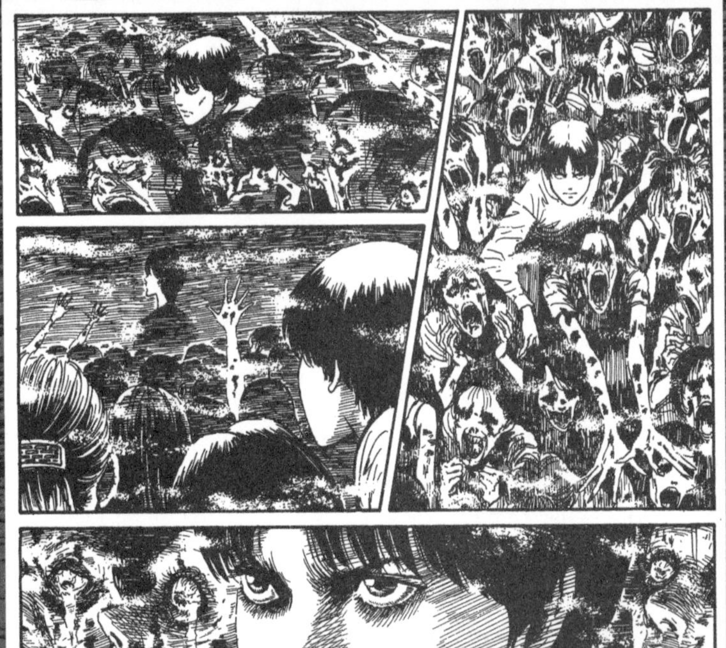
CHK CHK CHK

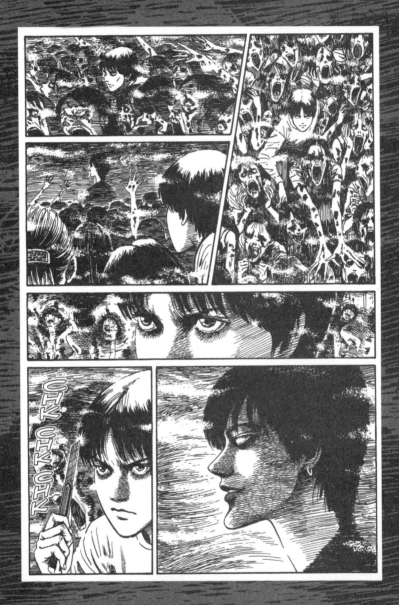

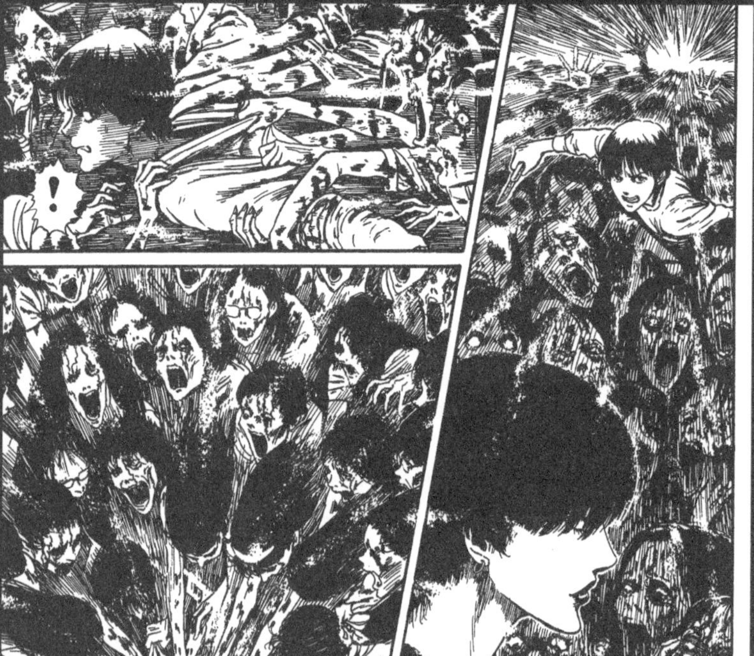
!

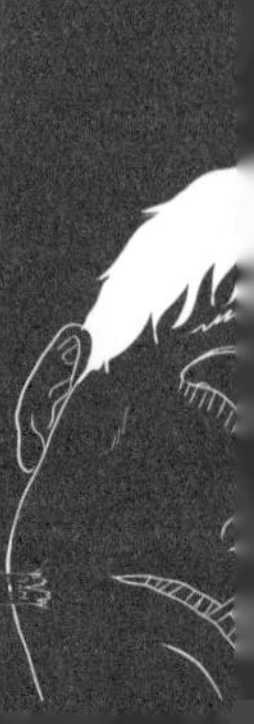

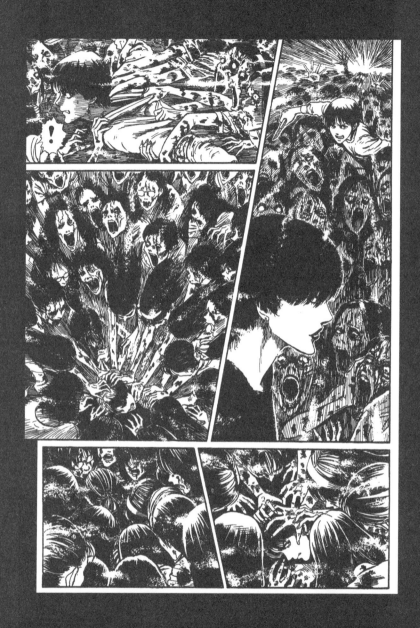

7. Devilish design bewitching people

Uzumaki

(First published: *Big Comic Spirits*, No. 7, 1998–No. 39, 1999)

I WROTE ABOUT THE HISTORY of how *Uzumaki* came to be on page 162, and the truth of it is, I had a great deal of trouble finding the spiral motifs. The story was in an omnibus format, with something related to spirals in every chapter (black holes, typhoons, curly hair, snail shells, etc.). But when it came down to actually selecting these spirals, I couldn't find anything that really spoke to me. So before serialization began, I got my editor to send me anything about spirals that he could find.

Among the materials he sent was a fairly specialized book called *Kodai no Jomondoki ni Kakareta Uzumaki ni Kansuru Kosatsu* (Investigation of Spirals Drawn on Ancient Jomon Pottery). The author's name was like something from a research institute. I figured it was most likely a university professor summarizing the results of their research.

While reading, I happened upon a section that caught my interest. According to the text, a rope is formed with two strings in a spiral shape, with one string spiraling clockwise and the other carving out a counterclockwise spiral, so that the two strings come together to make a single rope. However, I wondered if this description was indeed correct. While it's true the two strands wind together in a spiral, they should have been turning in the same direction. Otherwise, the strings would push back against each other instead of coming together to form a neat unit.

I mentioned this to my editor in an offhand kind of way, and he said, "Let's go ask the author!" And so it turned out that we suddenly went off to meet the author of the book, A-san.

On the day of our visit, I was a little anxious as I waited with my editor behind Nagoya Station for the author A-san. He was a university professor, after all. I worried he might get angry if a lay-person were to make some misguided comments about his work.

Before too long, a silver Mercedes-Benz pulled up, and an older man with silver hair stepped out; the author, apparently. He was well dressed and had an intellectual air. Increasingly anxious, I followed my editor into his car.

During the drive to A-san's home, I told him that I was a manga artist and I was working on a project that took up the subject of spirals. I explained that I had read his book while I was doing research on the topic.

A-san was quite delighted. "I wrote it out of simple interest. I can't believe you read it," he told me, sounding thrilled. He must have really been into spirals to have written a book on them for fun. Impressed, I asked what kind of research he was currently doing. He shook his head, humbly. "Research, oh no," he said. "I run a video rental shop. This is just a hobby."

A half an hour or so later, we were gazing absently at the beautiful flowers blooming in the garden of the home of video

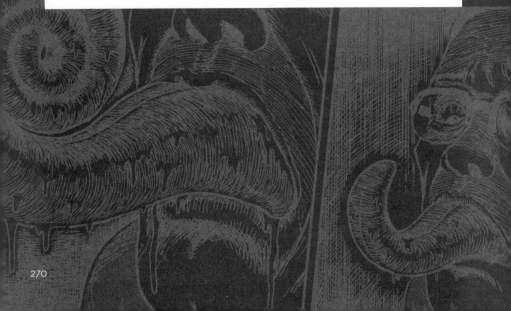

rental shop manager A-san. With a bright smile, he explained, "These flowers, you see, their leaves unfurl in a twist from the base of the stem to the tip. Spirals, in other words."

Since we were there, my editor also asked about the rope description that was our initial reason for contacting him, but that prompted an explanation from A-san that I'm not sure I entirely understood. We simply nodded and made some vague remarks in response without pushing it any further before we took our leave.

Looking back on it now, I think A-san was perhaps obsessed with the magic of the spiral. He wrote an entire book on the spiral pattern, so there really must be some kind of irresistible charm to it.

Later, my editor told me that after the series was finished, he got a message from A-san saying he'd made a new discovery about spirals.

What on earth could he have discovered…?

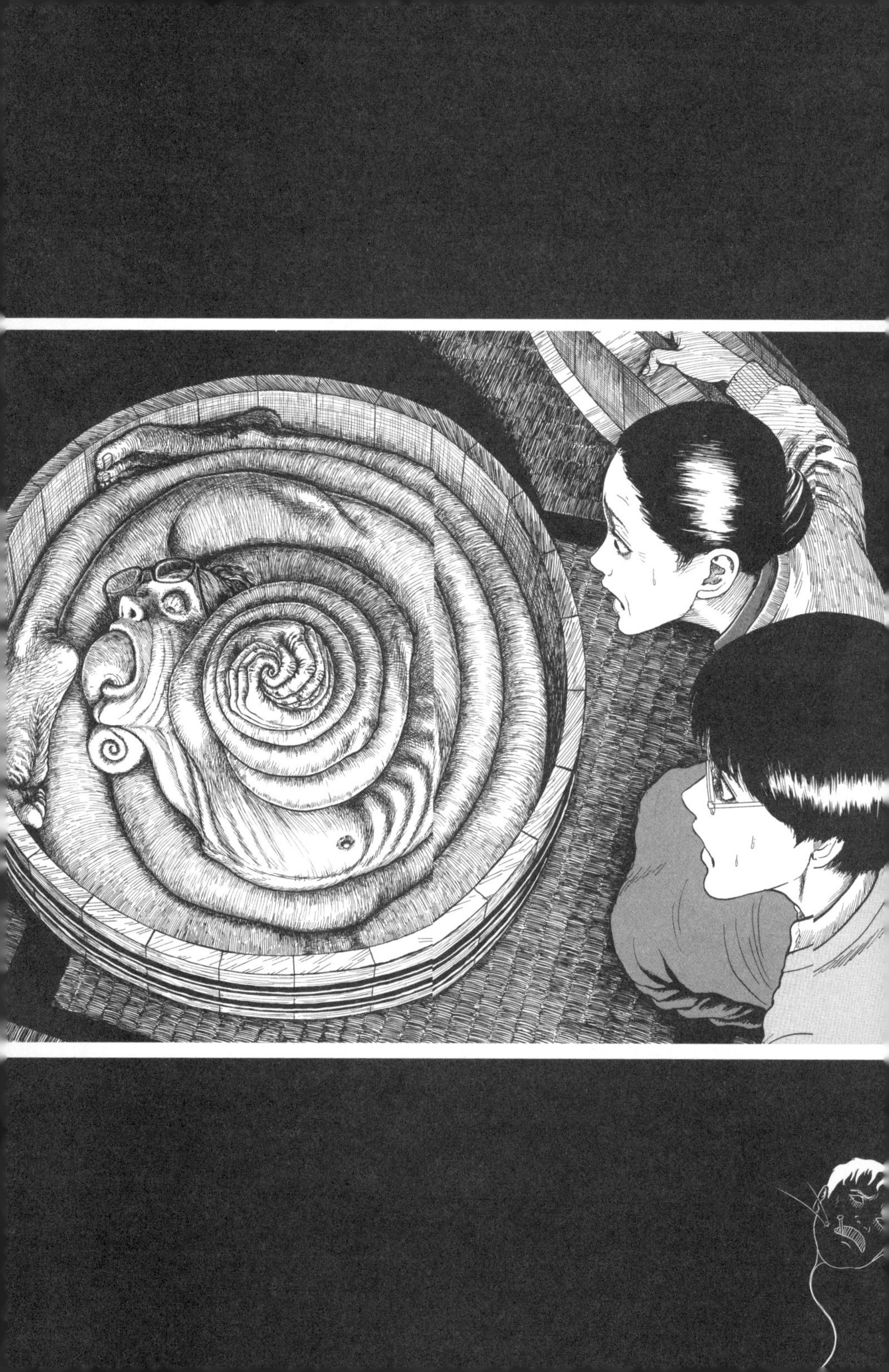

8. Fading memories of tragedy

"Roar"

(First published: *Nemuki*, Nov. 2002. Included in *Smashed: Junji Ito Story Collection*)

I FORGET WHAT STARTED ME ON IT NOW, but I wanted to take up the theme of floods in my work. With *Lovesickness*, it was the fog, and in "Roar," I worked hard to express everything about the flow and speed of water with nothing but pen lines.

A man who survived the flood that plowed through his village thirty years earlier watches as that same flood reappears as a phantom time and time again. Originally, I'd conceived of a story about a submerged village where infectious disease was rampant. But as always, I got stuck when I tried to flesh it out. I just happened to have an existing idea about cassette tapes in mind, so I combined the two to get the story as it currently exists.

I'm sure this will be hard for younger people to imagine, but way back in the day, we recorded music on things called cassette tapes, and every time you played the tape back, the sound quality deteriorated. I had the idea of an illusion that was something similar, a vision that played back inside the brain, and thus it might also deteriorate with the passage of time. I combined this concept with my original flooding motif, and the result was that the outlines of the people and buildings washed away in the original flood gradually grew hazier each time the phantom flood charged past.

ROAAAARR

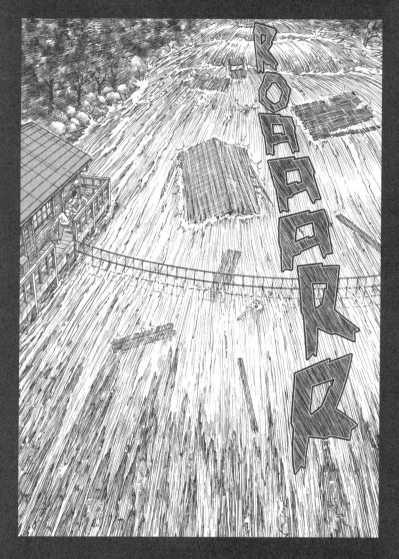

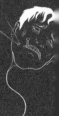

9. The ultimate in disgusting
"Greased"

(First published: *Nemuki*, Mar. 2003. Included in *Shiver: Junji Ito Selected Stories*)

THE HEAD OF THE DENTAL TECHNICIAN SCHOOL that I attended in Nagoya was a strange person, being both a dentist and the chief priest of a Buddhist temple. Perhaps because of that, the school had what amounted to Buddhist training. Every year, the first-years would go and stay at the temple for several days, do cross-legged zazen meditation, and chant prayers.

Of all of the things we underwent there, the hardest was trying to sleep at night. The futons the temple set out for us were absolutely filthy. They looked as though they had been shoved into a closet and not washed once in who knows how many years, and they were sticky with the oil and sweat of all the people who had studied there before.

"Greased" is a work that expresses my intense discomfort at being placed in this situation. I depicted the oil that stains the clothing and walls by dabbing the page with a handkerchief damp with ink, like a stamp. This technique is often done with gauze, but I used a handkerchief with finer lines. This, too, is something you could normally do with screentone, but I really do hate working with it. When I was first starting out, I even made a roller stamp–style tool so that I wouldn't have to use screentone. I do feel this style suits me best, even if it means that people tell me I'm too slow or I have to draw each and every line in pen.

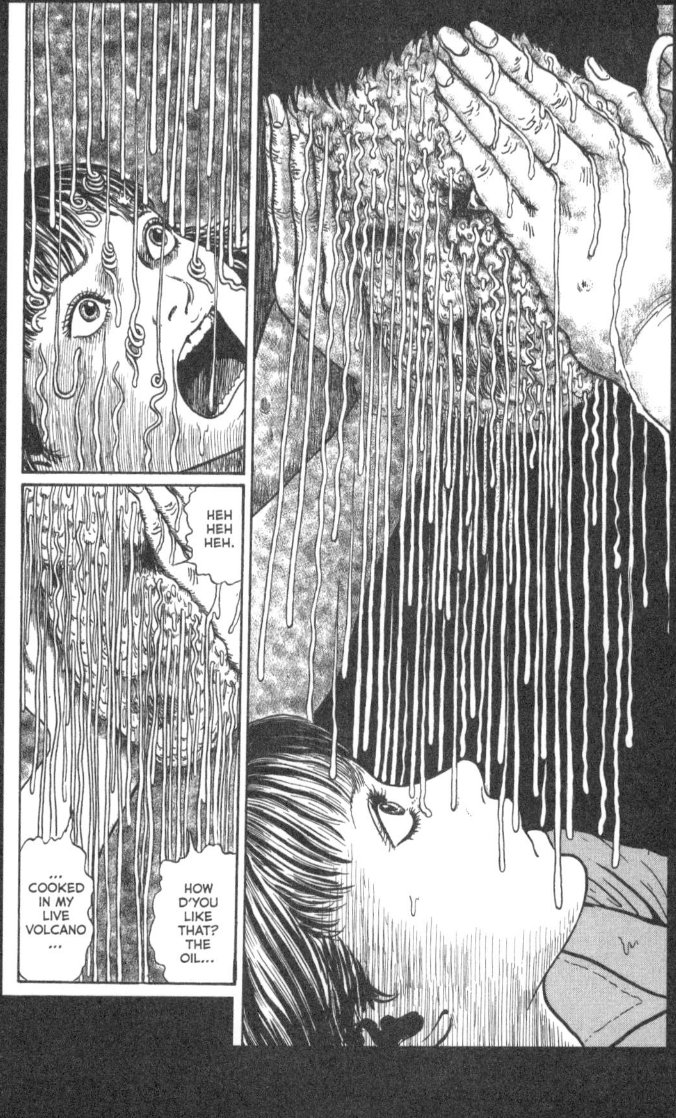
HEH HEH HEH.
HOW D'YOU LIKE THAT? THE OIL...
...COOKED IN MY LIVE VOLCANO...

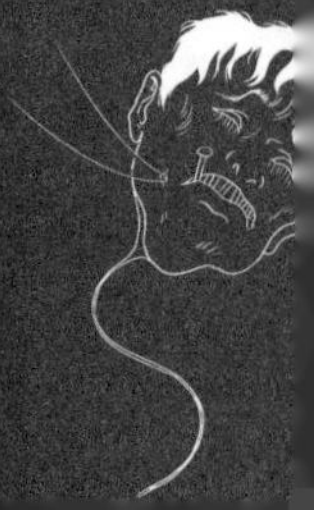

10. Body flattened in an instant

"Smashed"

(First published: *Nemuki*, May 2006. Included in *Smashed: Junji Ito Story Collection*)

THIS STORY DEPICTS the battle between humans who try to lick a mysterious nectar from plants, and the plants that try to defensively crush those humans. This hostile relationship is modeled on the interaction between humans and mosquitoes. Mosquitoes are unpleasant to us, so we try to slap them down whenever we see one. Meanwhile, human blood is an essential source of nutrition for the female mosquito in laying eggs, so she has to do whatever it takes to suck our blood without being noticed. Taking a cue from this one-sided connection, I turned the human beings slapping down mosquitoes into plants and the mosquitoes drinking blood into human beings licking their nectar to end up with this story.

The scenes where someone gets smashed by a plant are the highlight, but since it's not possible to actually die this way, I drew them completely from my imagination. I worked hard to ensure features from when they were alive were still visible in their corpses, making them crushed in the same pose as when they were licking the nectar or leaving the girl's hair clip behind on her smashed body. But to be honest, I don't quite like any of those scenes, especially the corpse glued to the plaster wall in the beginning. I should have made that wall concrete. (An impact like that would have made a hole in a plaster wall.)

As for the hot topic of conversation in this story—how to drink nectar without being noticed by the plant—just as we human beings will smash mosquitoes without a second thought, there is absolutely no way to safely lick the nectar.

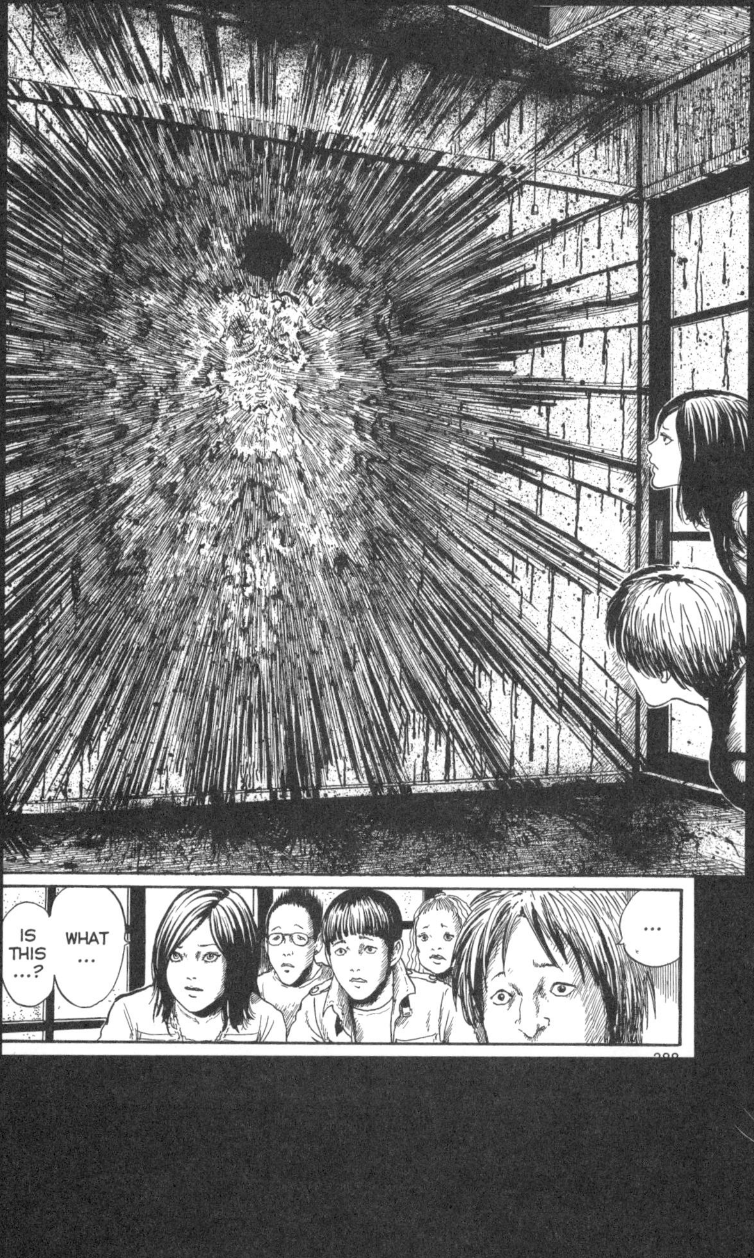
...
WHAT ...
IS THIS ...?

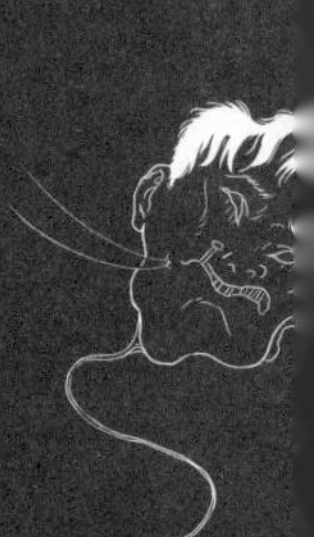

11. Past self imprisoned in the body
"Kyofu no Juso" (Layers of Terror)
(First published: *Nemuki+*, Mar. 2017)

THE IDEA OF A PERSON'S BODY having a layered construction came from a memory of a shell I saw while clamming. The two parts of the shell have growth lines like the rings in a tree. The bigger the shell gets, the more lines there are—in other words, several layers pile up on top of each other. I thought that it might be fun to apply this to human beings.

I was working out the details of the plot when I came up with the scene in the latter half of the story where they peel away the layers of the girl cursed with a layered construction to find the girl from her infancy. But then I thought about it a little more and realized that not all parts of the human body grow to equal lengths. So the infant girl inside couldn't be as she was at the time; her limbs would have been stretched out as the outer girl grew.

At first, I figured that was the end of that, but fortunately, I managed to tie it all together in a scene with real impact, as shown on the right. This is another instance where I've realized some contradiction in my setup at the detailed drawing stage and added new elements to eliminate that contradiction. But one of the strengths of horror is how you can always make things work out somehow.

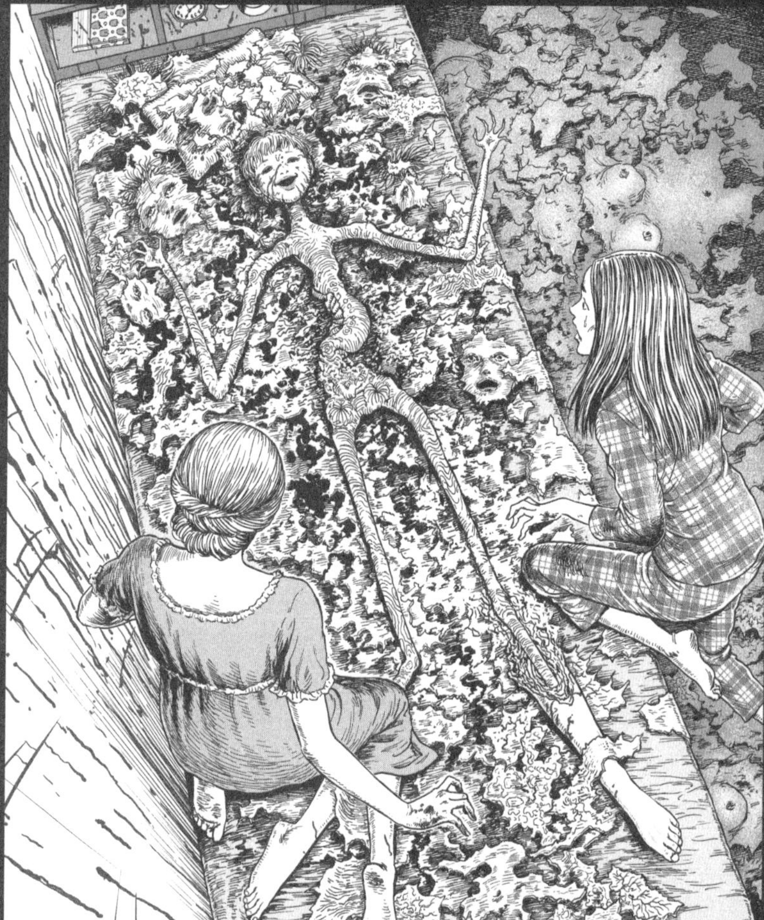
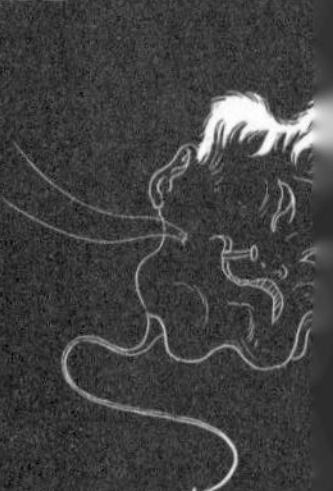

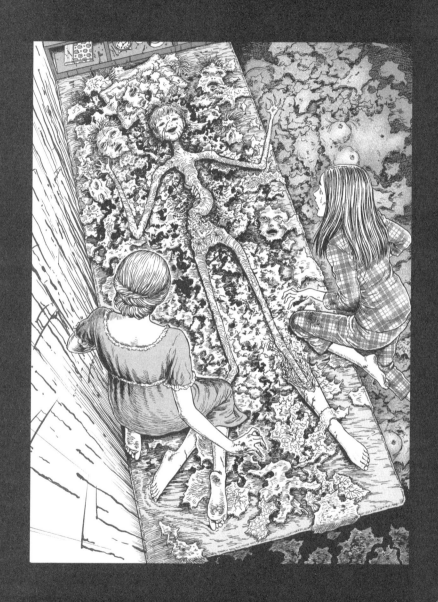

CHAPTER 5 GENERAL REMARKS

How to burn terror onto the page

HERE, IN THE LAST CHAPTER OF THE BOOK, I want to talk about the performance element of horror manga, and how to come up with pictures that people will find scary and fix those images to the page.

The pictures I draw are often kindly assessed as being very detailed. Setting aside the question of whether or not my my art is denser than that of other manga artists, it is true that I will scribble away to fill up the white space until time runs out. When I appeared on the NHK E program *Manben: Behind the Scenes of Manga with Urasawa Naoki,* Naoki Urasawa offered me the compliment (?), "The speed of your pen is the slowest of any manga artist who's appeared on the show so far." This surprised me because, to me, the speed of my pen is simply normal.

He also noted, "When you're drawing horror, I guess you really have to draw every last detail or it doesn't work." I personally hadn't been conscious of this, but it just might be that **short strokes caressing the page generate an eerier atmosphere than long, smooth lines.**

But while I might be the type to fill in the blank spaces, I still have nothing on Kazuo Umezz. When I read his *Kowai Hon* (Scary Book) series, I was astonished at how he drew everything from the roof of a mansion to the walls and furnishings in such subtle detail. I devote a fair amount of time to drawing my characters, but when it comes to backgrounds, I can be fairly haphazard. Looking at this aspect of Umezz's work was a reminder to apply myself and not take the easy way out.

The art takes a minimum of two weeks

THERE IS ONE SERIOUS BARRIER to drawing creepy and powerful images that we must first overcome, and that is the deadline.

I touched on this a little at the end of chapter two, but because I work alone and my pen moves slowly, the art inevitably takes me a long time. Given a monthly series and assuming that a single chapter has 32 pages, I need a minimum of fifteen days for the art. I can't do it any faster than that.

Naturally, this means that I have to complete the work of thinking of a story proposal, typing out the script, and drawing the thumbnails in the other two weeks left in the month, but it's a constant struggle these days. I can't quickly come up with a plot. (On top of that, I have less stamina the older I get, so it takes me even longer to do the art.)

I make sure to jot down any ideas that come to me, and I keep a list of them in my notebook, but turning these ideas into a detailed story still requires a fair bit of time. Once I find my footing, I can write all the way through to the last scene. But the six or seven—or even ten—days until I get to that point are spent in anguish. And the longer this process takes, the less time I have for the art, so that more often than not the chapter will be printed in the magazine before I've drawn in all the details to my satisfaction.

I fight this battle against time with each and every chapter.

For a manga artist, the first half is mental labor, the second physical

BECAUSE I ALREADY TOUCHED ON STORY in chapter three, I'd like to focus here on the process of creating the art. I say "art," but there are roughly three steps from concept to finished manga: storyboards, rough sketches, and final drawing. Of these, the storyboards are what becomes the framework for the manga.

To put it simply, storyboards are the blueprint, the process of imagining the scene (panel) from the script (text) and actually drawing the pictures. At this stage, you decide the number of panels per page and their placement and size, allocate the dialogue to the different panels, and lay out the script so that the story fills the pages in a balanced way. You also add in specific details of panel composition, along with the general expressions and movements of the characters that appear in the story.

In my case, assuming I have 32 pages for one chapter, it takes me about two days if I'm fast and five if I'm slow to draw the storyboards (although it's started to take me more time lately). Once the storyboards are complete, I sketch the manga out in pencil, and finally, I go over the rough sketches in pen (the actual drawing) to complete the chapter.

When I take this bird's-eye view of the process, it becomes clear to me that the work of drawing manga is mental labor in the first half, and physical labor in the second.

The sad part is that working hard on the first half, the story production and storyboard process, doesn't mean that the drawing of the latter half will be any easier. In fact, I've sometimes spent too much time figuring out the story and then been forced to pull all-nighters to get the art done in time. As I draw, I reject one idea after the other, struggling to make sense of things on the page until the bigger picture becomes clear. I do this over and over again.

Control the tempo with paneling

WHEN I'M WORKING ON THE STORYBOARDS, I'm most careful about the paneling. In the course of actually dividing up the script into panels (pictures), I'll often discover discrepancies and contradictions I didn't notice in the text. And sometimes, the story turns out to not be very interesting if I draw it exactly as outlined. The grammar of prose and manga are different and, because of this, I have changed the script at the paneling stage to match the pictures more than a few times.

Something I'm particularly conscious of when paneling is the tempo. While there are no hard and fast rules, in general, the more

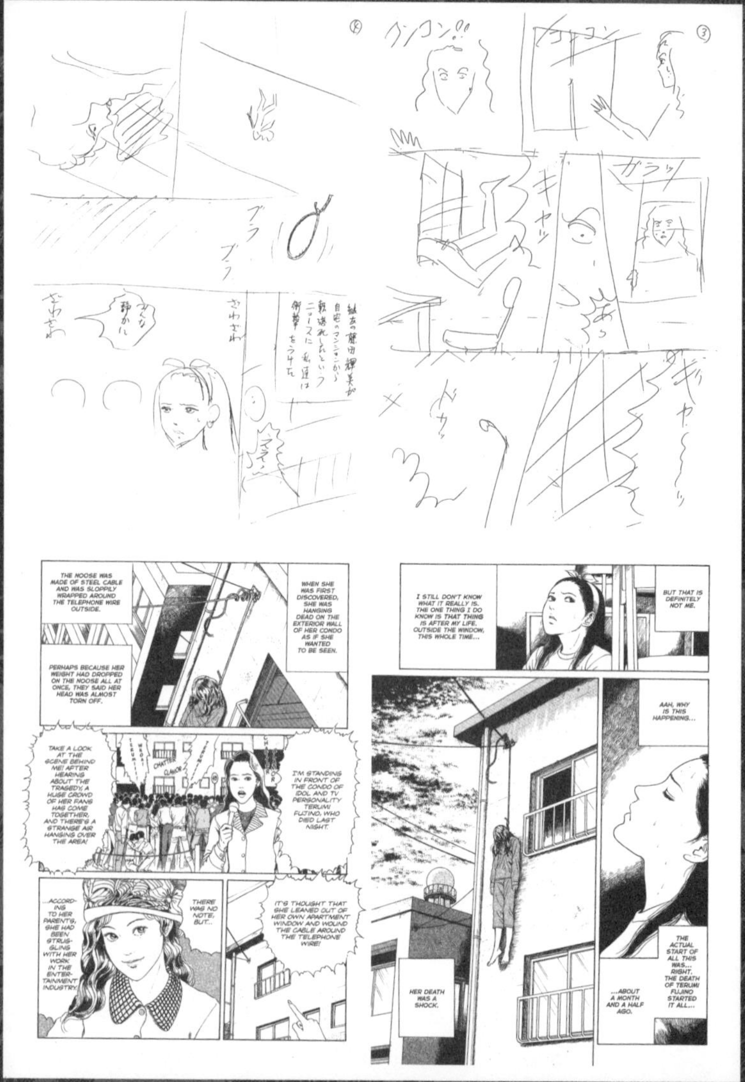
BUT THAT IS DEFINITELY NOT ME.
I STILL DON'T KNOW WHAT IT REALLY IS. THE ONE THING I DO KNOW IS THAT THING IS AFTER MY LIFE. OUTSIDE THE WINDOW, THIS WHOLE TIME...
AAH, WHY IS THIS HAPPENING...
THE ACTUAL START OF ALL THIS WAS... RIGHT, THE DEATH OF TERUMI FUJINO STARTED IT ALL...
...ABOUT A MONTH AND A HALF AGO.
HER DEATH WAS A SHOCK.
WHEN SHE WAS FIRST DISCOVERED, SHE WAS HANGING DEAD ON THE EXTERIOR WALL OF HER CONDO AS IF SHE WANTED TO BE SEEN.
THE NOOSE WAS MADE OF STEEL CABLE AND WAS SLOPPILY WRAPPED AROUND THE TELEPHONE WIRE OUTSIDE.
PERHAPS BECAUSE HER WEIGHT HAD DROPPED ON THE NOOSE ALL AT ONCE, THEY SAID HER HEAD WAS ALMOST TORN OFF.
I'M STANDING IN FRONT OF THE CONDO OF IDOL AND TV PERSONALITY TERUMI FUJINO, WHO DIED LAST NIGHT.
CHATTER
CLAMOR
TAKE A LOOK AT THE SCENE BEHIND ME! AFTER HEARING ABOUT THE TRAGEDY, A HUGE CROWD OF HER FANS HAS COME TOGETHER, AND THERE'S A STRANGE AIR HANGING OVER THE AREA!
IT'S THOUGHT THAT SHE LEANED OUT OF HER OWN APARTMENT WINDOW AND WOUND THE CABLE AROUND THE TELEPHONE WIRE!
THERE WAS NO NOTE, BUT...
...ACCORDING TO HER PARENTS, SHE HAD BEEN STRUGGLING WITH HER WORK IN THE ENTERTAINMENT INDUSTRY.

Initially, I thought about making Terumi Fujino, the person who triggers the action in "Hanging Blimp," an average student. But then I thought that if I made her an idol, I could add in commentary on how her death impacted society, including copycat suicides, so I changed the plot significantly at the storyboard stage.

detailed and numerous the panels, the slower time advances in the story; conversely, the fewer panels the page is divided into, the quicker things move. Take, for instance, a scene where a friend is waving and approaching the main character. You could depict this in two panels—"Friend notices character, says 'hey,' waves" → "(Friend running over omitted.) Character starts talking with friend"— Using four panels for this scene—"Friend notices you" → "Calls out 'hey' and waves" → "Runs over" → "Starts talking with friend"— will make the flow of time feel much slower.

For a manga, a good tempo is determined by your decisions about which panels to include or omit. Naturally, this depends on the story you're telling, but readers will no doubt be bored by a scene that's nothing but friends chatting for twenty panels.

This is not to say that the fewer panels there are, the better the tempo. If a character is in the classroom talking with friends in one panel and then suddenly outside playing soccer in the next without any preamble, the reader won't be able to follow what's going on. The key is to speed up or slow down the progress of story in line with reader comprehension.

Silent time to amplify fear

LINING UP THE SPEEDS of reality and physical sensation are also important in paneling. Consider the opening of a fridge door. In reality, this happens in a mere instant, so if you spend five panels on this in a manga, the reader will realize it's not natural and intuit that the scene has been put together that way for a particular purpose.

To say it another way, **you can use unnatural paneling to communicate fear and tension to the reader more effectively.** In fact, this is where paneling in horror manga shines.

What if we drew our opening the fridge scene as follows?

"*Thud* from inside the fridge" → **"Man looks toward the fridge, surprised"** → **"Fridge motor makes a creepy *vwwwn* sound"** → **"Man very timidly places a finger on the fridge door"** → **"The moment he yanks the door open, a woman's head tumbles out."**

What do you think? Parts of this might be a bit hard to understand with text alone, but I think you can see how the unease and tension are amplified by deliberately extending time as the man opens the fridge.

So what if we took this example and drew it in the two panels of **"*Thud* from inside the fridge"** → **"The moment he yanks the door open, a woman's head tumbles out"**? Most likely, the reader will be more surprised than scared and turn their attention to understanding the situation—"Wait, what just happened?"

If you play with the paneling like this, you can suggest the presence of the unfathomable or allow the character to sense that danger is coming for them without having to explain it in the text or dialogue. This could be said to be an effective method of expression for horror manga in particular, given how it develops fear and anxiety in the reader.

KREEEE
ZZM
ZZSH
ZZSH
ZZSH

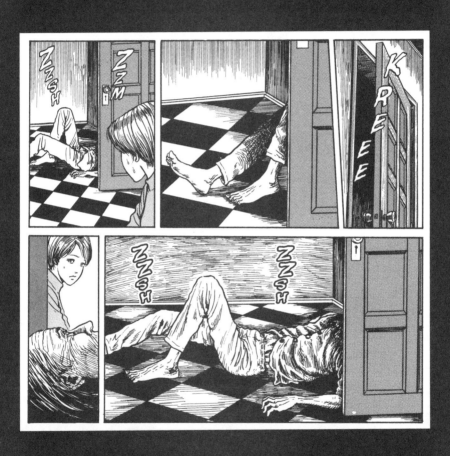

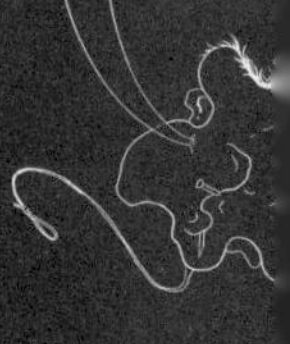

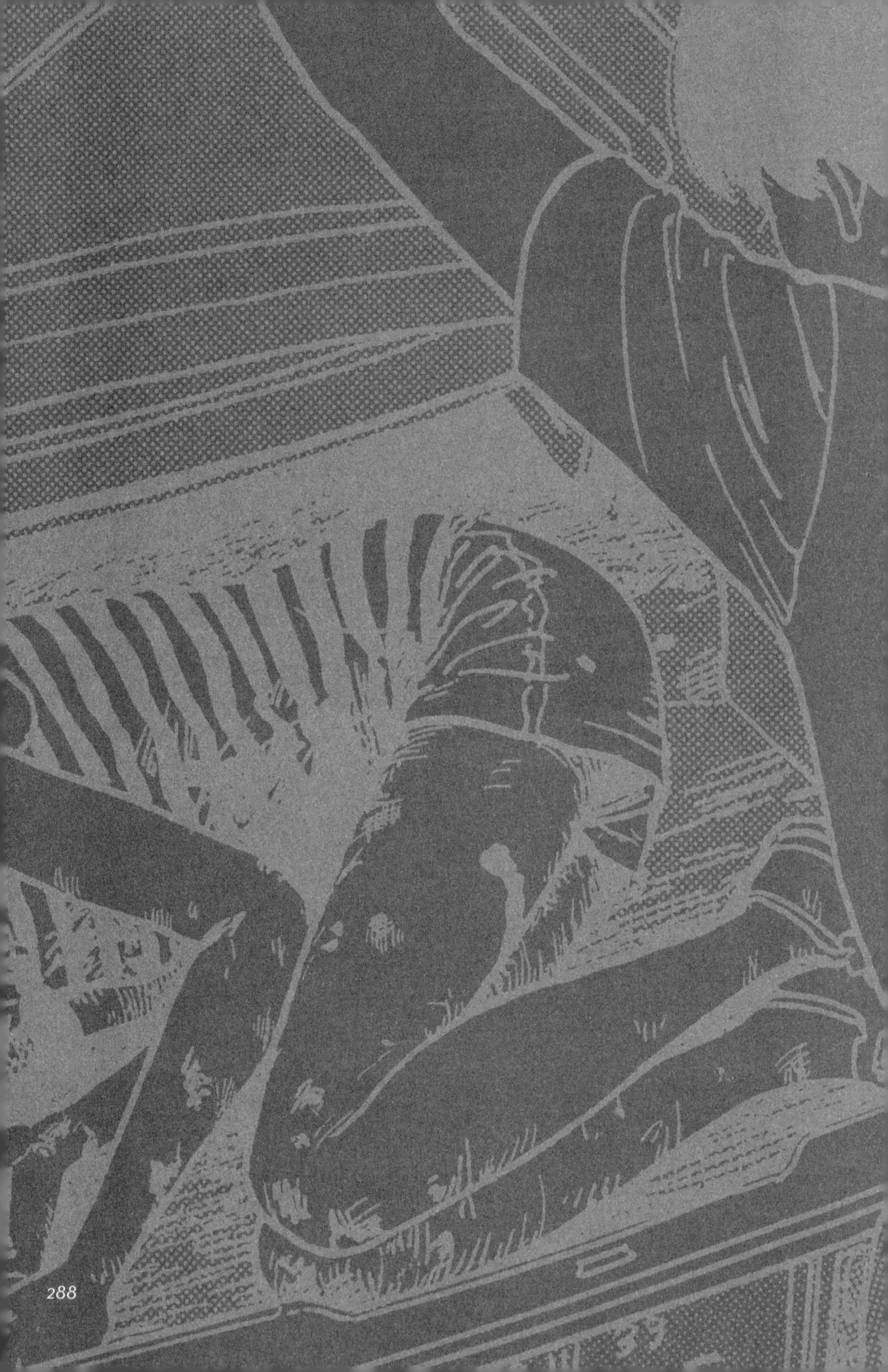

Shadows and eyes create expressions of horror

ANOTHER METHOD OF DEPICTING FEAR is to draw distinctive shadows and eyes. Maybe you also shone a flashlight underneath your face to surprise people when you were a child. You can **amplify creepiness by making the light hit from an angle that would normally be impossible**, a classic means of expression in horror manga. Drawing the eyes so they're blacked out by shadow, having darkness fall on only one half of the face, or leaving the facial expression unclear because it's backlit are all techniques seen in a variety of manga that produce an ominous atmosphere.

Additionally, I often **draw the eyes differently depending on the emotion**. For example, adding shadow around the eyes gives the impression of someone in emotional pain, while making the brow furrowed and minimizing the colored part of the eye creates an expression of terror. When drawing people who are hallucinating with fear or who have lost all reason, I often express the irises with horizontal lines instead of making them circular so that they're a bit hazy, something I picked up from Hino. Simply changing up the way you draw eyes will drastically change how the reader views the character.

These expressions of terror are very much traditional techniques passed down over the generations in the world of horror manga.

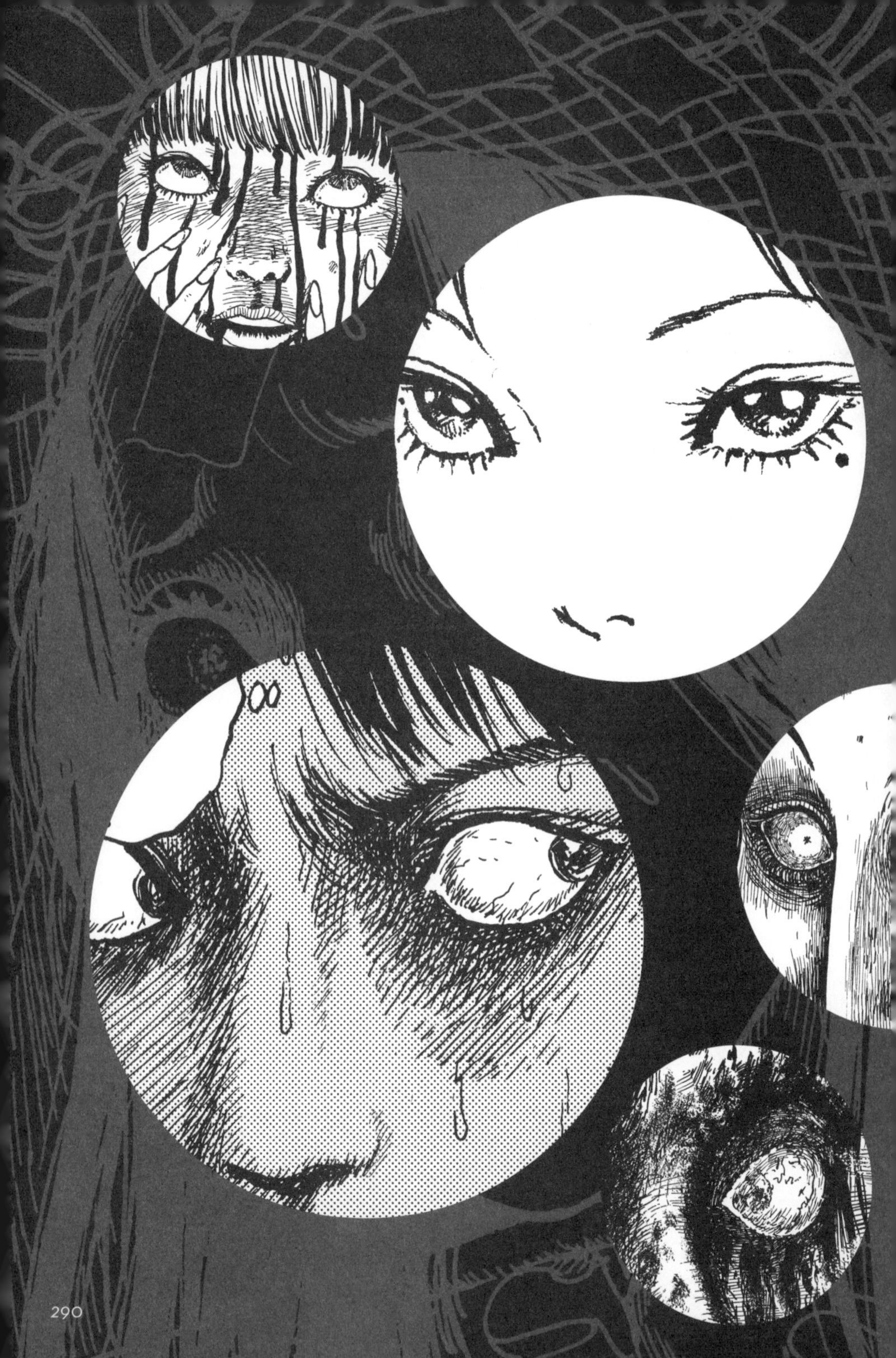

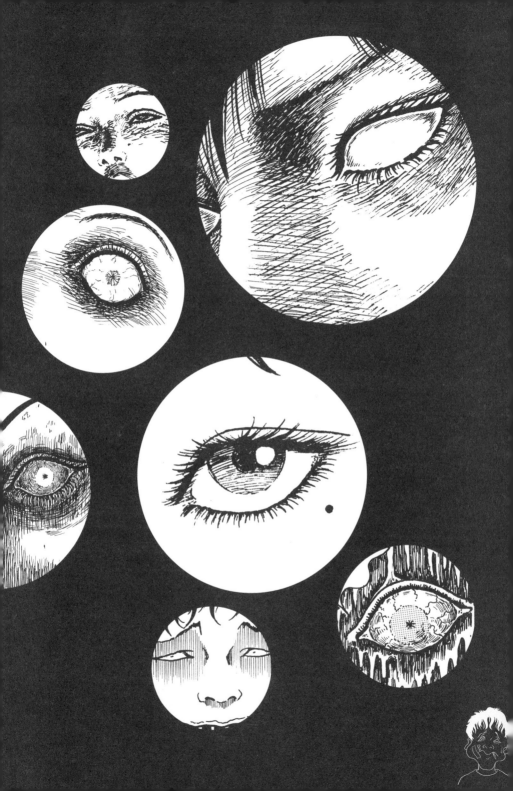

Smash safety with impossible combinations

UP TO NOW, I've mainly discussed how to draw scary pictures, but now I'd like to briefly touch on how to visualize those scary pictures.

When drawing monsters or abnormal human beings, I generally focus on creating an **impossible combination**. In "Hanging Blimp," for instance, the combination was "face + balloon." It was "human being + insect spiracles" in "Shiver," "old people + totem pole" in "Honored Ancestors," "model + shark" with "Fashion Model" and Fuchi, and "girl + shell growth lines" in "Layers of Terror."

I'm a fan of Swiss artist H.R. Giger, and apparently he took a cue for the design of his masterwork *Alien* from the penis. Maybe it is because the frenzied and sinister elements of the penis are so wonderfully reflected in the modeling that people who see the alien instinctively feel the danger of it.

I'm not speaking only about my own work when I say that the monsters and supernatural phenomena in horror manga do not exist in the real world. But it is extremely difficult to draw something you've never actually seen, something that doesn't even exist. It's a bit of a Zen dialogue, and it's basically equivalent to drawing nothing, an act replete with contradictions. But we are in fact capable of creating from zero something that doesn't exist, and **by combining something that does exist with something else that exists, you can create a new thing you've never seen before.**

But even supposing you can produce an absolutely foreign being, there's still the question of whether people will be afraid of it. People feel fear when their safety is threatened. When we look at it that way, the deformation and destruction of the human body is an obvious collapse of safety—a body like yours, something you've thought inviolable up until that point, suddenly transforms into a hideous and aberrant being. It might be this difference and instability that causes us to feel fear.

Conversely, wouldn't we sense danger if something with absolutely no humanity to it, something we've never seen or touched before, were to appear before us? The reason that so many of the monsters generated with the impossible combinations I listed earlier are based on human beings might be because we intuitively understand this.

As a horror manga artist, I sincerely want to create thoroughly unfamiliar creatures that don't fit into any previous monster mold. I can think of no greater joy as an artist than being able to scare readers with such novel creations. My sincere wish is to draw a work like this at least once in my life.

Reality is what makes horror convincing

ON THE OTHER HAND, I strongly believe I should pursue realism to the extent possible in my drawing of creatures that can't actually exist. To draw the scene of Shuichi's father distorted into a spiral shape in *Uzumaki*, I calculated in my own way the balance between the lengths and placement of the limbs so that the overall effect wouldn't be unnatural. I also made sure to use shadow to bring out the three-dimensionality of the image, and drew the details of the skin, wood, steel, and other textures.

The reason I place such emphasis on adding realistic details to the art is for the sole purpose of bringing about a sense of reality. A person dying in a spiral shape is unnatural, regardless of how realistic the image is. But if you make light of the depiction of the body because of that fact, your story will start and end as something preposterous in a world removed from reality.

To look at an extreme example, the eyeballs popping out in surprise that you see in old-timey gag manga are a good demonstration of this principle. Those scenes are funny because the human face and physique are deformed, and their depictions are unrealistic or merely symbolic of reality. But if you were to draw those same scenes in a hyper-realistic style, they instantly change into horror.

In other words, in order for the reader to look at the pictures and feel fear, we need enough of **a sense of reality to allow the reader to believe that the characters in the manga are living in the same space and with the same rules as those of us in the real world.**

But to take a step back from the demands of structure and expression, I have sincere desire to have scary experiences myself. Reality is so tiresome. I would love it if the Loch Ness Monster and UFOs were out there somewhere in the world, and yet I will never get to see them in real life. So part of the reason why I tell stories in worlds as realistic as I can make them is to allow myself to at least experience these things vicariously through manga.

Better if they don't resemble anybody

I'VE BEEN RATHER FREE IN MY DISCUSSION about how to draw, but naturally, I didn't start out drawing with all of these ideas weighing my pen down. In fact, these theoretical ideas are more of a postscript to my actual practice. It would be more accurate to say that my current style came about very naturally as a result of being obsessed with and reading the works of my favorites, such as Kazuo Umezz, Shinichi Koga, and Hideshi Hino, and always drawing myself.

The truth is, other artists continued to be an influence on me even after I started drawing manga as a career, which has led me to tweak my writing and drawing styles. When I was being published in *Halloween*, there was also an artist who drew the kind of emotional manga that tugged on the heartstrings, and after reading their work, I thought about a change of course and grew interested in drawing something a little weepy myself.

My illustrations have changed a lot from the early days. In my initial publications, I drew with a Rotring drafting pen, and the lines overall were thicker, which meant that my story was always darker and blacker than any of the other stories in the magazine, and I felt a bit awkward and out of place when I saw it alongside the others. So I gradually changed my line to be thinner and landed on the weight I currently use. (Along the way, it actually got too thin, so there was some back-and-forth there.)

Thinking about it now, however, I feel like it might actually be a good thing for my work to be totally different from that of other artists.

In the end, the scariest thing of all is people

I HAVEN'T ONLY been influenced by manga artists, though. Novelists have also played a huge role in the development of my work. One of my favorite science fiction authors is J.G. Ballard. He wrote a rather surreal short story called "The Drowned Giant" that I particularly like. In it, the body of a giant washes up on the beach and begins to rot until, finally, only the bones remain, and these become a playground for children. It's almost a rule that if something's going to be washed up on shore, it's going to be a ship or a whale, so the fact that it's a giant's corpse in this story fascinates me. I've consistently drawn abnormal human bodies since my debut with "Tomie," and this might be more than a little due to Ballard's influence.

Additionally, at some deep, fundamental level I'm terrified of human beings in a way that's hard to dismiss. If I saw the ghost of an animal pop up, I don't think it would be that frightening. It's really the complex thoughts and emotions human beings have that scare me—**hatred, jealousy, narcissism, bloodlust, despair**. The domain in this world where human understanding fails completely is perhaps in the **unfathomability of desire and a volatility that can't be checked with reason or logic**.

The fact that I often choose the human body as my motif might be rooted in this fear of human beings, and I'm simply expressing it over and over in a variety of forms.

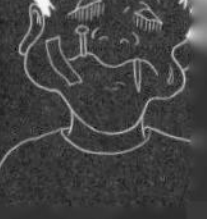

AFTERWORD

I BELIEVE IT WAS AROUND 2017 when I was first approached about a book with the provisional title of *Inside the Head of Junji Ito...* But things happened, the COVID-19 pandemic perhaps first among them, and the book kept getting pushed back and put off. But here it is at last with the title *Uncanny: The Origins of Fear* (or, in the original Japanese, *Bukimi no Ana: Kyofu ga Umare Izuru Tokoro.*) I know some of you have been looking forward to its release for some time now, and I'm terribly sorry to have made you wait for so long.

My editor Takahashi, the reason this project came about in the first place, landed on the Japanese title after thinking long and

hard. Maybe the words *"bukimi no ana"* give you a clue, but the concept was *bukimi no tani* (uncanny valley), a place where creepy things crawl up to the surface. I think it's a pretty good title myself.

This book digs deep into the creation of my manga while also posing as something along the lines of an autobiography, discussing everything from my upbringing to my present life as a manga artist. I don't consider methodology while I'm drawing my manga—I'm not systematically analyzing terror and then creating art based on that. Most of the time, I'm drawing intuitively.

But I'm frequently asked about my motivation in drawing a particular story, and so I am faced with the need to put the process of creation into words and explain it in some way or another. You could say that this book is those spoken explanations put into text form. Thus, in laying down those origins, it might be

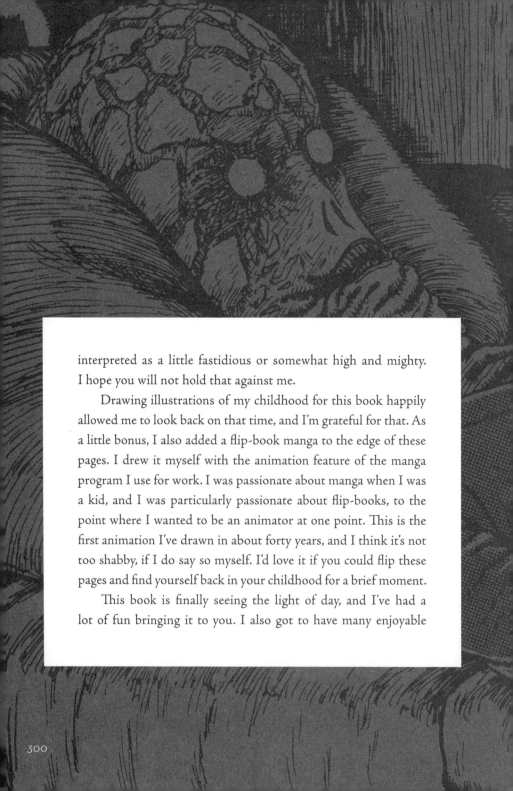

interpreted as a little fastidious or somewhat high and mighty. I hope you will not hold that against me.

Drawing illustrations of my childhood for this book happily allowed me to look back on that time, and I'm grateful for that. As a little bonus, I also added a flip-book manga to the edge of these pages. I drew it myself with the animation feature of the manga program I use for work. I was passionate about manga when I was a kid, and I was particularly passionate about flip-books, to the point where I wanted to be an animator at one point. This is the first animation I've drawn in about forty years, and I think it's not too shabby, if I do say so myself. I'd love it if you could flip these pages and find yourself back in your childhood for a brief moment.

This book is finally seeing the light of day, and I've had a lot of fun bringing it to you. I also got to have many enjoyable

conversations about my past and my childhood during numerous production meetings.

I owe a number of people an enormous debt of gratitude, starting with the aforementioned Kazuki Takahashi, who kicked this whole thing off, freelance editor Ken Sawada, and my manga editor Makiko Hara. I also want to extend my sincere gratitude to September Cowboy, a.k.a. Hidenori Yoshioka, who did the wonderful book design. Thank you so much.

—JUNJI ITO
January 1, 2023

JUNJI ITO BOOKS FROM VIZ MEDIA

LONG FORM

- BLACK PARADOX
- GYO
- NO LONGER HUMAN
- REMINA
- SENSOR
- TOMIE
- UZUMAKI

SHORT STORY COLLECTIONS

ALLEY:
JUNJI ITO STORY COLLECTION
- Alley
- Descent
- The Ward
- The Inn
- Blessing
- Smokers' Club
- Mold
- Town of No Roads
- Memory
- Ice Cream Bus

DESERTER:
JUNJI ITO STORY COLLECTION
- Bio House
- Face Thief
- Where the Sandman Lives
- The Devil's Logic
- The Long Hair in the Attic
- Scripted Love
- The Reanimator's Sword
- A Father's Love
- Unendurable Labyrinth
- Village of the Siren
- Bullied
- Deserter

FRANKENSTEIN:
JUNJI ITO STORY COLLECTION
- Frankenstein
- Oshikiri Series
- Neck Specter
- Bog of Living Spirits
- Pen Pal
- Intruder
- The Strange Tale of Oshikiri
- The Strange Tale of Oshikiri:
  The Walls
- The Hell of the Doll Funeral
- Face Firmly in Place
- Boss Nonnon
- Hide and Seek with Boss Nonnon

LOVESICKNESS:
JUNJI ITO STORY COLLECTION
- Lovesickness
- The Beautiful Boy
  at the Crossroads
- A Woman in Distress
- Shadow
- Screams in the Night
- The Beautiful Boy in White
- The Strange Hikizuri Siblings
- Narumi's Boyfriend
- The Séance
- The Mansion of Phantom Pain
- The Rib Woman
- Memories of Real Poop

MOAN:
JUNJI ITO STORY COLLECTION
(upcoming in 2025)
- Supernatural Transfer Student
- Moan
- Blood Orb Grove
- Flesh-Colored Mystery
- Near-miss
- Under the Ground

SHIVER:
JUNJI ITO SELECTED STORIES
- Used Records
- Shiver
- Fashion Model
- Necklace Blimp
- Marionette Mansion
- Painter (from Tomie)
- The Long Dream
- Honored Ancestors
- Greased
- Fashion Model: Cursed Framing

SMASHED:
JUNJI ITO STORY COLLECTION
- Blood-Sucking Darkness
- Ghosts of Prime Time
- Roar
- Earthbound
- Death Row Doorbell
- The Mystery of the
  Haunted House
- The Mystery of the Haunted
  House: Soichi's Version
- Soichi's Beloved Pet
- In Mirror Valley
- I Don't Want to Be a Ghost
- Library Vision
- Splendid Shadow Song
- Smashed

SOICHI:
JUNJI ITO STORY COLLECTION
- A Happy Summer Vacation
- A Happy Winter Vacation
- Soichi's Happy Diary
- Soichi's Home Visit
- Teacher of Cloth
- Soichi's Birthday
- Soichi's Petty Curses
- Four-Layered Room
- Coffin
- Rumors

TOMBS:
JUNJI ITO STORY COLLECTION
- Tombs
- Clubhouse
- Slug Girl
- The Window Next Door
- Washed Ashore
- The Strange Tale of the Tunnel
- Bronze Statue
- Floaters
- The Bloody Story of Shirosuna

FRAGMENTS OF HORROR
- Futon
- Wooden Spirit
- Tomio Red Turtleneck
- Gentle Goodbye
- Dissection-chan
- Blackbird
- Magami Nanakuse
- Whispering Woman

THE LIMINAL ZONE, VOL. 1
- Weeping Woman Way
- Madonna
- The Spirit Flow of Aokigahara
- Slumber

THE LIMINAL ZONE, VOL. 2
(upcoming in 2025)
- Demon King of Dust
- Village of Ether
- The Strange Hikizuri Siblings
  Chapter 3: Uncle Ketanosuke
- The Shell of Manjunuma

MIMI'S TALES OF TERROR
• On the Utility Pole
• The Woman Next Door
• Rustling in the Grass
• Grave Placement
• The Shore
• Just the Two of Us
• Scarlet Circle
• Sign in the Field
• Mimi's Tales of Terror Afterword
• Monster Prop

VENUS IN THE BLIND SPOT
• Billions Alone
• The Human Chair
• An Unearthly Love
• Venus in the Blind Spot
• The Licking Woman
• Master Umezzu and Me
• How Love Came
  to Professor Kirida
• The Enigma of Amigara Fault
• The Sad Tale of
  the Principal Post
• Keepsake

OTHERS

• THE ART OF JUNJI ITO:
  TWISTED VISIONS
• STITCHES

ABOUT JUNJI ITO

JUNJI ITO made his professional manga debut in 1987 and since then has gone on to be recognized as one of the greatest contemporary artists working in the horror genre. His titles include *Tomie* and *Uzumaki*, which have been adapted into live-action films; *Gyo*, which was adapted into an animated film; and his books *Alley, Black Paradox, Deserter, Fragments of Horror, Frankenstein, Lovesickness, No Longer Human, Remina, Sensor, Shiver, Smashed, Soichi, The Liminal Zone, Tombs,* and *Venus in the Blind Spot,* all of which are available from VIZ Media.

He is a four-time Eisner Award winner. In 2019 his collection *Frankenstein* won in the "Best Adaptation from Another Medium" category, and in 2021 he was awarded "Best Writer/Artist," while *Remina* received the award for "Best U.S. Edition of International Material (Asia)." *Lovesickness* won "Best U.S. Edition" in 2022.

UNCANNY: THE ORIGINS OF FEAR
BY JUNJI ITO

Bukimi no Ana: Kyofu Ga Umare Izurutokoro
© JI Inc. 2023
Originally published in Japan in 2023 by Asahi Shimbun Publications Inc.,Tokyo.
English translation rights arranged with Asahi Shimbun Publications Inc.,Tokyo
through TOHAN CORPORATION, Tokyo.

TRANSLATION: Jocelyne Allen
COVER & GRAPHIC DESIGN: Adam Grano
COPY EDITOR: Justin Hoeger
EDITOR: Masumi Washington

Printed in the U.S.A.

Published by VIZ Media, LLC
P.O. Box 77010
San Francisco, CA 94107

10 9 8 7 6 5 4 3 2 1
First printing, October 2024

PARENTAL ADVISORY
UNCANNY: THE ORIGINS OF FEAR is rated T+
for Older Teen and is recommended for ages
16 and up. This volume contains horror images.

VIZ SIGNATURE
vizsignature.com

VIZ MEDIA
viz.com

A SPECIAL BONUS ILLUSTRATION!
What Junji Ito's brain looks like.

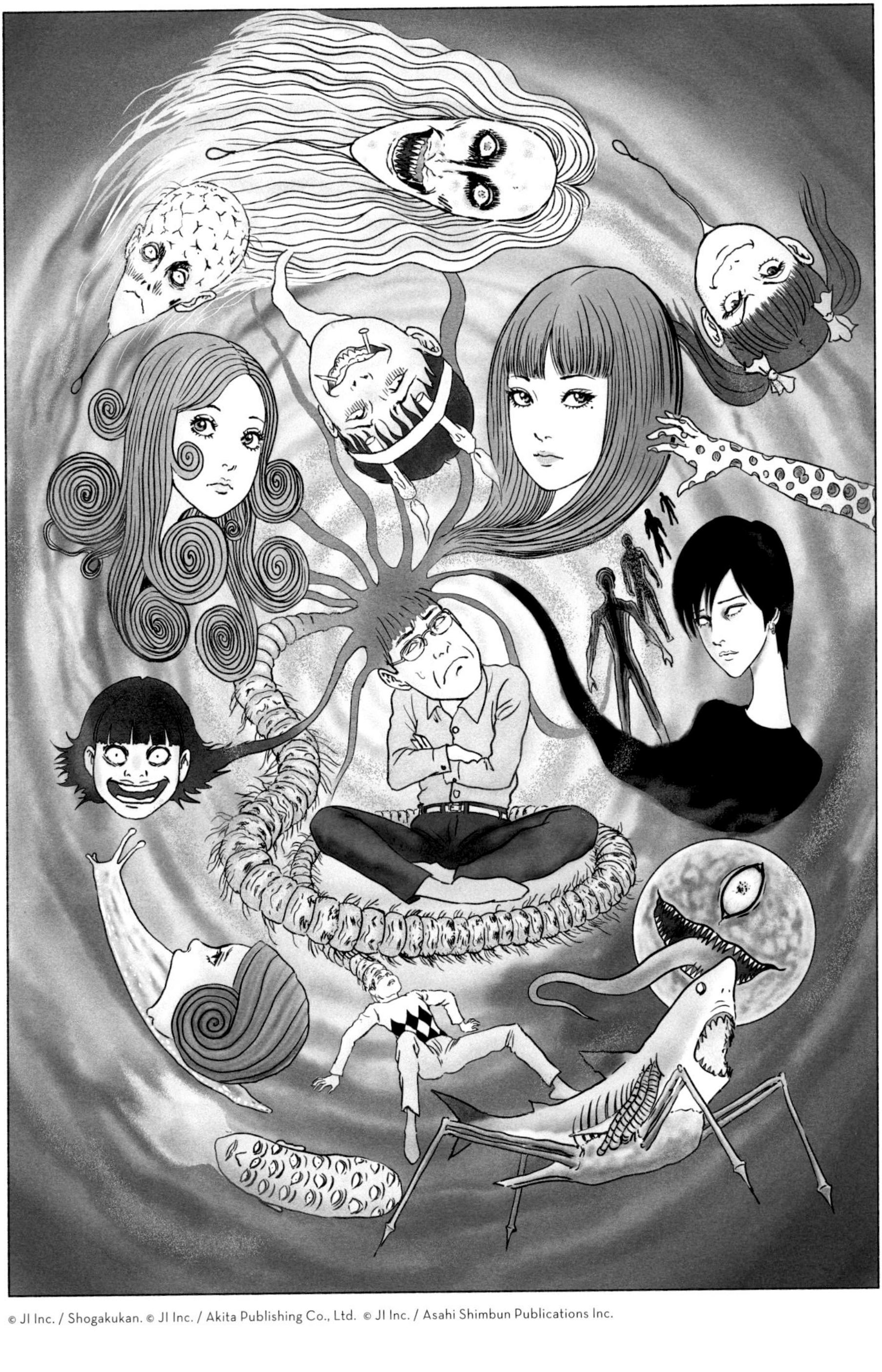